ASE Guide to
Secondary Science Education

Edited by Mary Ratcliffe

STANLEY THORNES (PUBLISHERS) LTD

Acknowledgements

Thanks go to the ASE Publications Committee for their support and comments and to the authors who all contributed so willingly.

Kind permission has been granted for the use of the following extracts in this book: Fig 2.3A KS3 continuity map for plants (from the Learners' Co-operative Ltd); Fig 2.3B A burr and a 'burr of burrs' for the concept of variation at KS4 (from Deirdre Lucas); Fig 2.3C (from the original Learning Map by Jeff Rothwell); Fig 2.3D KS4 rates of reaction memory map (from the Learners' Co-operative Ltd); Fig 2.3E Separation of mixtures (from the Learners' Co-operative Ltd and Bedfordshire Science Team); Fig 3.5A (from Keogh, B. and Naylor, S.(1997) Starting Points for Science, Millgate House Publishers).

ASE has made efforts to contact any copyright holders and would be happy to hear from anyone whose rights they have unwittingly infringed.

The views expressed in this book are those of the authors and not necessarily those of their employers.

Published in 1998 by:
The Association for Science Education
College Lane
HATFIELD
AL10 9AA

Produced in 1998 for The Association for Science Education by:
Stanley Thornes (Publishers) Ltd
Delta Place
27 Bath Road
CHELTENHAM
GL53 7TH

A catalogue record for this book is available from the British Library.

ISBN 0 86357 291 X

00 01 02 / 10 9 8 7 6 5 4 3 2

Typeset by Action Typesetting Ltd
Front cover designed by DHH Printing & Design
Printed and bound in Great Britain by TJ International Ltd, Padstow, Cornwall

Contents

Introduction   v

Section 1 Setting the Scene   **1**

1.1   The Purposes of Science Education   *Mary Ratcliffe*   3

1.2   Quality in Science Education   *Bob Ponchaud*   13

1.3   The Place of Science in the Curriculum   *Des Dunne*   23

1.4   Science Education and Training beyond 16   *Mike Coles*   33

1.5   Science for All   *Michael J. Reiss*   42

1.6   Science Education from a European Perspective
      Joan Solomon   52

Section 2 Learning Science: Concepts, Skills and Values   **57**

2.1   Learning Science Concepts in the Secondary Classroom
      Phil Scott and John Leach   59

2.2   Children's Thinking and Science Learning   *Philip Adey*   67

2.3   Mapping Concepts in Science   *Paul Hamer, Jasmin Chapman,*
      Barbara Allmark and Jane Jackson   74

2.4   Learning to Investigate   *Rod Watson and*
      Valerie Wood-Robinson   84

2.5   Understanding Scientific Evidence – Why It Matters and
      How It Can be Taught   *Richard Gott and Sandra Duggan*   92

2.6   Learning and Teaching about the Nature of Science
      Jonathan Osborne   100

2.7   Learning about Social and Ethical Applications of Science
      Roger Lock and Mary Ratcliffe   109

2.8   Science and Environmental Education   *Chris Oulton*   118

Section 3 Principles of Teaching and Learning Science 125

3.1 Planning for Teaching and Learning   *Martin Baxter* 127

3.2 Assessment in the Classroom   *Philip Hayes* 138

3.3 Dialogues in the Science Classroom: Learning from Interactions between Teachers and Pupils   *Jerry Wellington* 146

3.4 Explaining with Models   *John Gilbert* 159

3.5 Differentiation   *Stuart Naylor and Brenda Keogh* 167

3.6 Progression and Continuity   *Hilary Asoko and Ann Squires* 175

3.7 Safety in Science Education   *Peter Borrows* 183

3.8 The Use of Information and Communication Technology *Roger Frost* 192

Section 4 Management and Development 201

Introduction: The Professional Development of Teachers *Mary Ratcliffe* 203

4.1 Departmental Management   *Mike Evans* 209

4.2 Inspection and the Evaluation Cycle   *David Oakley* 220

4.3 The Role of Technicians   *David Billings* 228

4.4 Choosing and Using Published Science Schemes *James Williams* 234

4.5 Industrial Links: Purposes and Practice   *Bill Harrison* 241

Index 248

Introduction

This book is for all those interested in secondary science teaching. The book offers guidance for student teachers, teachers in practice and those with management responsibility for science. It is published in partnership with the *ASE Guide to Primary Science Education*, with which it shares several chapters. It covers science education from early secondary through to post-compulsory. Contributors are experienced practitioners and researchers. Each brings an individual perspective and considerable expertise in examining an issue within science education.

The book aims to cover the central issues of high-quality learning and teaching in science, drawing on research evidence. Most chapters are structured to give an overview of important principles, along with practical guidance to help implementation. Case studies, checklists and practical suggestions are highlighted by a bar alongside the text. As it is difficult to predict the future, a central theme is to define the best principles and practice which will stand the test of time. As a consequence attempts have been made to keep current educational jargon to a minimum.

The book is organised into four sections, each with a main theme. Inevitably these overlap but we hope this organisation provides some structure for consideration of important principles and practice.

Section 1 – Setting the Scene – aims to give an overview of the world of science education. The writers discuss such issues as, Why learn science? What are the characteristics of good science teaching? How does science fit in the curriculum? What of the continuum to science education beyond 16? How can we open science fully to all pupils? What science do they do in other countries? The principles discussed in this section set the scene for more detailed discussion of learning, teaching and management which follows in Sections 2, 3 and 4.

Section 2 – Learning Science: Concepts, Skills and Values – includes the development of scientific concepts and the skills of investigation, and discusses ways in which pupils can best learn them. Understanding the nature of science and its social and ethical applications are increasingly important to our lives as a scientifically educated nation and this, together with environmental education, widens the context for science learning. Although these chapters approach the learning from the pupils' perspective, they provide guidance on teaching.

The writers in Section 3 – Principles of Teaching and Learning Science – examine key issues of good science teaching. How can we plan teaching effectively? What are good assessment practices? What can we learn from examining the language of science classrooms? How can we use models effectively in teaching? How do we plan and implement principles of differentiation, progression and continuity? How do we ensure practical work is taught and managed safely? How do we use ICT effectively?

The introduction to Section 4 – Management and Development – highlights the importance of professional development for science teachers as a preface to the themes of organisation and management. Again these chapters overlap with good teaching and learning, particularly with the use of resources and the development of industrial links. The section starts with a consideration of departmental management; evaluation and review as part of an inspection process and the role of technicians in science departments.

The issues discussed are important whatever the detail of the science curriculum being taught. Thus, it is expected that the principles in each chapter will be of value across the UK and internationally. However, it is inevitable in places that the discussion takes place in a particular *context* to illustrate the principles. This context is often related to practice in England and Wales, partly because it is that most familiar to the writers. The most common terminology used to describe age range of pupils is that of Key Stages. Chapter 1.3 contains a description of terminology and age ranges across the UK. We hope you will be able to extend the principles to whatever context you are working in.

Full details of ASE policies to which reference is made throughout the book, are available on ASE's website, along with other valuable information: **http://www.ase.org.uk**

Mary Ratcliffe
August 1998

SECTION 1

Setting the Scene

1.1 The Purposes of Science Education

Mary Ratcliffe

What are the purposes of science education? If you've given this question some thought, it may be in the context of one of the following scenarios:

- As a classroom teacher, justifying the topic being studied. Pupils demand, 'Why do we have to study this? It's boring.'
- As a primary science co-ordinator, dealing with colleagues. 'How are we going to teach science? It's difficult and we've managed perfectly well with little knowledge of science.'
- As a Head of Science, justifying curriculum structures and timetabling to school managers asking, 'Why should science take such a significant part of the school curriculum?'
- As a pastoral tutor discussing career options with an adolescent asking, 'Why should I study any science subject after I've left school?'

All these scenarios raise questions about:

- the place of science in a school curriculum
- the perceived nature of science and its constituent disciplines
- the nature and purposes of science education.

Curriculum structures are dealt with in Chapter 1.3. Here I explore the nature of science and the purposes of science education.

What is Science?

Is science:

- A collection of discrete disciplines – biology, chemistry, physics, astronomy, etc. – with clearly-defined bodies of knowledge?
- *The* method of exploring and extending knowledge about the world?
- Activities conducted by researchers in laboratories in extending and manipulating knowledge?

All these descriptions may be part of the picture but each is flawed in some respect. As soon as we try to pin down what we mean by 'science', different views and values come into play. The conduct of science is an activity – it is a human endeavour.

The Oxford English Dictionary (OED) has five 'definitions' of science reflecting the history of the word 'science' – coming from Old French and Latin 'to know' – through to the interpretation of science as an academic discipline in schools and universities.

The 1725 OED definition, reflects knowledge and processes:

> *A branch of study which is concerned with a connected body of demonstrated truths or with observed facts systematically classified and more or less bound together by being brought under general laws, and which includes trustworthy methods for the discovery of new truth within its own domain.*

However, what is the knowledge base? Is science just 'biology, chemistry and physics'? (See Chapter 1.6 for a discussion of how different European countries view the content of science.) Science is generally viewed as knowledge about the natural and material world. The boundaries are not clear. Is, for example, psychology, pharmacy or biotechnology a science?

There is much written about the nature and purposes of science. I cannot do justice to a consideration of the differing perspectives on the nature of science. Useful reading is given at the end of the chapter. Here, it may be pertinent to consider whether there is a view of science expressed in national curricula. This might help in interpreting the purposes of 'school science'.

The Science National Curriculum orders in England and Wales currently lack a clearly-stated rationale both in terms of the nature of the discipline and of the purposes of science education (DfE, 1995). However, the original non-statutory guidance gives some indication of an underlying view of science:

> *Scientists are curious; they seek explanations. The scientist chooses from the knowledge and ideas which have been previously established to devise systematic studies into scientific phenomena. There are many scientific methods – scientists formulate hypotheses, design and carry out experiments, make observations and record results. There is also an important place for imagination, for inspirational thinking and the receptive mind. ..... A scientist's work can result in the formulation of a new idea or lead to the solution of a problem or the development of a new product. Scientific endeavour produces progressively more powerful ways of understanding the natural world.* (NCC, 1989, p A4)

So far this seems reasonable and in line with other views of science. But what of the next bit:

> *The distinctive nature of science is that it relies more heavily on certain skills than do other areas of human enquiry. Making and testing of hypotheses by observation and experimentation are essential characteristics of science. Another distinction is its general area of interest. Science is a human construction. We define its boundaries and decide what shall count as a science.*

Ah, so the jury's still out as to whether psychology, pharmacy and biotechnology are sciences?

Perhaps the most contentious part of this description of 'what it means to be scientific' is the final sentence:

> *School science is a reflection of science in the 'real' world, where scientists learn from each other and extend the boundaries of knowledge by research.*

It would be interesting to know whether this is a consensus view of 'school science'.

Do we really mirror the real world of research in science classrooms? Do pupils view themselves as explorers or as receivers of agreed scientific knowledge?

The Science Review Group of the Scottish Consultative Council on the Curriculum takes an overarching view of the nature of science:

> *Science is a distinctive form of creative human activity which involves one way of seeing, exploring and understanding reality.*
>
> *Science is not a homogeneous activity generating a single form of knowledge. On the contrary, there is a variety of distinguishable, but interconnected and overlapping disciplines within the scientific domain. All of these 'sciences' are concerned with investigating and understanding aspects of the natural and man-made world, albeit from different perspectives and with variations in the methods of enquiry used. The essential humanness of science is manifested in its modes of working, in its motivations and in the ways it affects and is affected by social and, cultural and historical contexts.*
> (Scottish CCC, 1996)

This has some similarity with NCC's views and that of some, but not all, philosophers of science. There is a variety of perspectives on the nature of science. Nott and Wellington (1993) provide a useful activity to explore your own views. They see a number of elements, with a continuum from one extreme to another, as contributing to an individual's perspective:

- Relativism vs. positivism – truth as being relative or absolute.
- Inductivism vs. deductivism – generalising from observations to general laws versus forming hypotheses and testing observable consequences.
- Contextualism vs. decontextualism – science interdependent with or independent of cultural context.
- Process vs. content – science characterised mainly by processes or by facts and ideas.
- Instrumentalism vs. realism – science as providing ideas which work versus a world independent of scientists' perceptions.

Exploration of the philosophy of science is needed by all teachers of science to ensure that they can articulate a clear perspective of their own. Too often, because we lack an exploration of the nature of science in our own education, our views on the nature of science and, therefore, its translation into school science are underdeveloped.

What is clear is that values are being transmitted in every science classroom, implicitly or explicitly. All school science education is imbued by values; even that which attempts to present scientific processes as uninfluenced by human characteristics. Pupils may be gaining a view of science as a creative, human endeavour influenced by cultures and beliefs or as a collection of objective, value-free facts. Science education which explores the nature of science may assist future generations in dealing with a scientific and technological society (see Chapter 2.6).

Relationship between Science and Technology

The boundaries between science and technology are blurred, particularly in every-day parlance. Note the 'Tomorrow's World' presenter who talks about the programme 'showing the latest in scientific development'. Yet the content of this popular television programme is mainly concerned with *technological* improvements – using existing scientific knowledge and not necessarily exposing cutting-edge research which extends our knowledge of the natural and material world. Similarly, the popular journal 'New Scientist' deals with advances in both science and technology. This raises issues about the relationship between science and technology in the curriculum. Take 'genetic cloning' as an example. This depends on sound scientific knowledge, yet the breakthrough in producing clones comes with increasing technological improvement. It could be argued that science and technology are so closely linked that to separate them in the curriculum is not sensible. Are biotechnology and engineering sciences or technologies?

In Northern Ireland science and technology are integrated into common programmes of study in the primary curriculum, but remain separate in the rest of the UK. The holistic nature of the primary curriculum, however, can allow integration of science and technology even if there are separate programmes of study.

Layton (1993) argues that there is similarity between the design–make–evaluate technology process, a science problem-solving process and a general model of problem-solving. However, Layton also shows that the constraints surrounding the processes are different in a science and in a technology context. Technology might be argued to be 'customer and product' oriented whereas science is 'knowledge' oriented with far fewer constraints on its conduct.

This does not mean, however, that science and technology should be seen as totally separate disciplines within a secondary curriculum. The cloning example shows a fruitful relationship between science and technology. The separation of science and technology in the secondary school may depend more upon the history of the two disciplines in the curriculum rather than the nature of the disciplines themselves. Greater collaboration between secondary science and technology teachers may assist pupils (and teachers) in appreciating the distinctive processes and contexts of each discipline.

Purposes of Science Education

To gain an appreciation of the underlying purposes of the Science National Curriculum, we could again refer to the non-statutory guidance. This offers the following as the contributions of science to the school curriculum:

> *1. <u>Understanding the key concepts</u> of science will allow pupils to use them in unfamiliar situations…*
> *2. <u>Using scientific methods of investigation</u> will help pupils to make successful, disciplined enquiries and use ideas to solve relevant problems…*
> *3. <u>Appreciating the contributions science makes to society</u> will encourage pupils to develop a sense of their responsibilities as members of society and the contributions they can make to it…*

4. *Learning in science contributes to personal development...*
5. *Appreciating the powerful but provisional nature of scientific knowledge and explanation* will bring pupils closer to the process by which scientific models are created, tested and modified...
6. *Giving students access to careers in science and design and technology* is vital ... (NCC, 1989, p A4)

In looking to the future, Scottish CCC suggests that:

> *For individual learners, experience of science education should:*
> *– broaden understanding of themselves, human culture and societies and the natural and made worlds in which they live;*
> *– help to sustain natural human curiosity, develop an enquiring mind and foster an interest in continuing to learn throughout life;*
> *– help to engender a critical way of thinking about phenomena and issues;*
> *– support other aspects of learning across the curriculum;*
> *– develop the potential to contribute in an informed, thoughtful and sensitive way to the enhancement of people's lives and of the environment.* (Scottish CCC, 1996)

The Science National Curriculum in Northern Ireland has the following in the introduction to the Programme of Study at Key Stage 3:

> *Pupils should consider the benefits and drawbacks of applying scientific and technological ideas to themselves, industry, the environment and the community. They should begin to make personal decisions and judgements based on their scientific knowledge of issues concerning personal health and well being, safety and the care of the environment. Through this study, pupils should begin to develop an understanding of how science shapes and influences the quality of their lives.*

All three of these descriptions bring in their respective underlying views of science and, importantly, the personal development of the pupil.

Some science educators have argued for science education as a grounding in 'scientific literacy' or for the 'public understanding of science'. The UK Curriculum Councils' descriptions of pupils' experiences have some similarity to the three strands of 'scientific literacy' agreed by the many commentators (e.g. AAAS, 1989; Driver *et al*, 1996; Millar, 1996). Pupils should gain:

- knowledge and understanding of some science concepts
- an understanding that scientific endeavours are social human activities, involving value judgements and cultural contexts
- an understanding of the processes involved in the conduct of and reasoning about science.

However, we still have to answer the question, 'Why do we consider these three strands so important in pupils' education? Millar (1996) groups the arguments for 'public understanding of science' into five categories:

1) Economic – there is a connection between the level of public understanding of science and the nation's wealth.

7

2) Utility – an understanding of science is useful practically in a technological society.
3) Democratic – an understanding of science is necessary to participate in decision-making about issues with a base in science.
4) Social – it is important to maintain links between science and the wider culture.
5) Cultural – science is the major achievement of our culture and all young people should be enabled to understand and appreciate it.

You might like to consider these arguments in the context of the scenarios at the start of the chapter or carry out the exercise suggested by Millar (1993) in an earlier version of this book. The cultural and democratic arguments are supported by the discussions of the Nuffield Foundation Seminar Series (Reports 1–3).

No simple slogan – 'scientific literacy', 'public understanding of science', 'citizen science'- can adequately convey how these strands interrelate. Fig 1.1A is one attempt to portray the elements contributing to 'scientific literacy'.

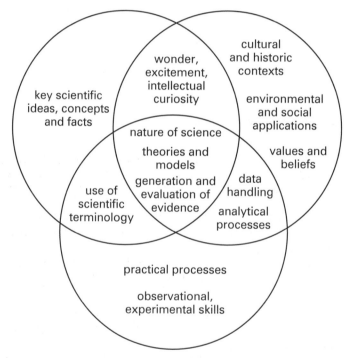

Fig 1.1A Elements of Science

This alone cannot constitute an adequate description of the purposes of science education. The development of the individual pupil is important. Fig 1.1B shows how the elements of 'scientific literacy' could contribute to pupils' personal development.

If any one of the areas in Figs 1.1A and 1.1B is missing, then the individual's education is impoverished. Equally, pupils can miss out if the purposes are skewed in any way through particular methods of curriculum interpretation. This can happen, for example, if acquisition of facts and concepts is emphasised at the expense of development of analytical skills.

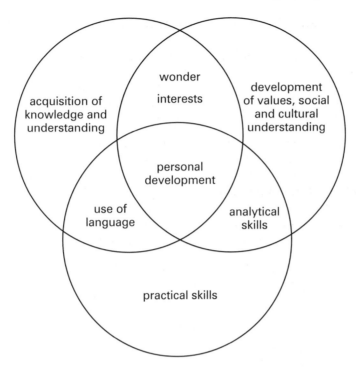

Fig 1.1B Education of the whole person

Jenkins (1997a) recognises the individual in his discussions of 'functional' public understanding of science. He identifies significant features of an individual's approach to science in his discussion of 'citizen science' (Jenkins, 1997b):

a) *The interest of citizens in science and technology is differentiated by science, social group and gender.* Crudely, people may be more interested in medical matters than physical sciences – particularly females.

b) *For most citizens, interest in science and technology is linked with decision-making or action.* We may seek science knowledge for specific social purposes related to health, leisure and local decision-making.

c) *Citizens choose a level of explanation adequate for the purpose in hand.* We hold ideas about science concepts, some of which are misconceptions, which have proved adequate for everyday life.

d) *Citizens consider scientific and technological knowledge alongside other available knowledge.* During our personal, working and social lives, we construct a body of practical knowledge, tested and validated against individual and collective experience.

e) *Citizens consider scientific knowledge alongside its social and institutional connections.* We may ask questions about the source and validity of scientific knowledge, particularly if there are conflicting 'expert' views.

f) *Citizens have complex attitudes to risks associated with scientific or technological issues.* Risk is viewed in different ways according to social, psychological and contextual factors, besides any understanding of probability.

g) *Scientifically informed citizens are more discriminating in their judgements about science- or technology-related issues.* Additional scientific knowledge can help but is not a guarantee of rational decision-making.

If this is how we use science as adults, then the notion of science for specific purposes may be helpful in determining suitable learning experiences for pupils. We do need to be clear about how learning any particular science topic is going to assist the future citizen and also give consideration to the pupils' role in determining the direction of their own learning.

What Science Content?

We have already seen that the boundaries of science as a collection of disciplines are not clear. Both ASE and the Nuffield Foundation Seminar Series, in considering the future of the science curriculum, have had difficulty in identifying the 'essential' concepts of science (ASE, 1998; Millar, 1997; Ratcliffe, 1997). Suggested criteria for determination of which concepts are appropriate for pupils to explore emerged from the ASE consultation, as a modification of those from Project 2061 (AAAS, 1989):

The core content in science should be of:

- *Human and philosophic significance:*
  - contributing to learners' understanding of the world
  - illuminating the way that scientific ideas develop over time
  - showing the impact of scientific ideas on cultural development.

- *Scientific significance*:
  - the content should aim to show how scientists model the world to understand it
  - ideas should suggest explanations and lead to fruitful development
  - the range of ideas chosen should include those currently being used by the scientific community and they should also reflect the history of science.

- *Personal significance.* Relevant content includes:
  - ideas which are immediately accessible
  - preparation for the future as a citizen in a technological world
  - development of ideas within appropriate social, personal and industrial contexts.

You might like to use this list as a checklist for the science content you currently teach.

Science for Whom?

The discussion so far has centred on science education for future citizens. Should the science education for future scientists be any different? This question relates to when, if at anytime, specialisation should appear in the compulsory curriculum through deliberate choice of development in one area of knowledge at the expense of others.

Future scientists are also future citizens. A different core curriculum for future scientists could neglect essential elements of personal and scientific development (Figs 1.1A and 1.1B). However, providing exactly the same curriculum diet for all up to 16 ignores the differences of individuals. (See Chapter 1.3 for further discussion of curriculum structures.)

Science 5–16: A statement of policy (DES, 1985) contains ten principles of science curriculum implementation, which may be useful in considering the implementation of purposes:

1) *breadth* – essentially the three strands of 'scientific literacy'
2) *balance* – across main conceptual areas of science and between knowledge and processes
3) *relevance* – relating to everyday and future experiences
4) *differentiation* – providing essential experience of broad and balanced science yet catering for different standards of achievement
5) *equal opportunities* – particularly relating to gender
6) *continuity* – building on foundations set in earlier phases of education
7) *progression* – developing progressively deeper understanding and competence
8) *links across the curriculum* – links particularly with literacy and numeracy in the primary school; links across the curriculum particularly with mathematics and technology in secondary
9) *teaching methods and approaches* – emphasising practical, investigate and problem-solving activities
10) *assessment* – using methods which recognise skills and processes as well as knowledge and which allow pupils to show what they can do rather than what they cannot do.

These principles hold true today, yet it remains a challenge to fulfil all of these.

Squaring principles of breadth and balance with those of equal opportunities and differentiation is not easy. Yet this has to be tackled if the interests and potential of all pupils in science are to be met.

The rest of this book is about realising the purposes of science education.

About the Author

Mary Ratcliffe was Chair of ASE during 1996/7. She is currently a senior lecturer in science education at the University of Southampton.

References and Further Reading

AAAS (American Association for the Advancement of Science) (1989) *Science for All Americans* (Project 2061), New York, Oxford University Press.

AAAS (1993) *Benchmarks for Science Literacy*, New York, Oxford University Press.

AAAS (Project 2061), website: http://project2061.aaas.org/National Standards – these have been developed for implementation in the USA and relate to achieving goals of 'scientific literacy': http://www.nas.edu

ASE (1998) Science Education 2000+ Summary Report. *Education in Science,* No 176, pp 17–20.

DES (1985) *Science 5–16: A Statement of Policy*, London, HMSO.

DfE (1995) *Science in the National Curriculum*, London, HMSO.

Driver, R., Leach, J., Millar, R. and Scott, P. (1996) *Young people's images of science,* Buckingham, Open University Press.

(Besides reporting on research into primary and secondary pupils' views of the nature of science, there is a very readable overview of perspectives on the nature of science.)

Jenkins, E. (1997a) Towards a Functional Public Understanding of Science. In Levinson, R. and Thomas, J. (Eds) *Science Today: Problem or Crisis,* London, Routledge.

(The whole of this book is worth reading for its range of perspectives on science and science education.)

Jenkins, E. (1997b) Scientific and Technological Literacy for Citizenship: What Can We Learn from Research and Other Evidence. In Sjoberg, S. and Kallerud, E. (Eds) *Science Technology and Citizenship*, Oslo, NIFU.

Layton, D. (1993) *Technology's challenge to science education*, Buckingham, Open University Press.

Millar, R. (1993) Science Education and Public Understanding of Science. In Hull, R. (Ed) *ASE Secondary Science Teachers' Handbook,* Hemel Hempstead, Simon and Schuster.

Millar, R. (1996) Towards a Science Curriculum for Public Understanding, *School Science Review* Vol 77, No 280, pp 7–18.

NCC (National Curriculum Council) (1989) *Science. Non-Statutory Guidance*, York, NCC.

Nott, M. and Wellington, J. (1993) Your nature of science profile: an activity for science teachers. *School Science Review* Vol 75, No 270, pp 109–112.

Nuffield Foundation Seminars *Beyond 2000: Science Education for the Future,* London, Kings College:

Ogborn, J. (Ed) (1996) Report of seminar 1 *Science Education: Is there a problem?*

Millar, R. (Ed) (1997) Report of seminar 2 *Criteria for an appropriate science curriculum.*

Ratcliffe, M. (Ed) (1997) Report of seminar 3 *Towards new models of the science curriculum.*

Scottish CCC (1996) *Science Education in Scottish Schools – Looking to the Future,* Dundee, Scottish CCC.

1.2 Quality in Science Education

Bob Ponchaud

Good progress made by pupils in their learning is a key characteristic of quality education. This chapter discusses the factors contributing to high-quality learning concentrating on the elements of good teaching, particularly subject knowledge, planning and variety. Striving for further improvement, suggestions are given for future developments.

Quality Science – Effective and Affective

In any occupation, professional self-esteem comes in large measure from the belief that one is 'doing a worthwhile job' and 'doing it well'. Few would disagree that teaching science is worthwhile but it is not always quite so easy to be sure that one is 'doing it well' since this involves having clear ideas about what constitutes quality. All teachers know what it is like when things are not going according to plan in the classroom, but a feeling for quality is perhaps less instinctive.

A quality artefact is one which closely meets its specification; a quality tool performs well and lasts; the features of artistic quality are more difficult to define! An essential characteristic of quality education is the *progress* made by children. Only if pupils are making real gains can the purposes of education be considered as being fulfilled. For this reason Chapter 1.1 focuses on the purposes of science education and the rationale for science in the school curriculum. Whatever pupils' individual starting points may be, high-quality science education will carry them forward and extend what they know, understand and can do. This is necessary but not sufficient for surely quality science education will also generate interest, motivation and enthusiasm; it will be both *effective* and *affective*.

As Brian Woolnough (1995) argues:

> It [science] should involve the affective as well as the cognitive aspects of a student's life. It is not sufficient only to be concerned with what students know and can do; one must also be concerned with whether they want to do it. It is of fundamental importance to develop students' emotional involvement with their work; to develop their motivation, their commitment, their enjoyment and creativity in science – for without these any knowledge and skills they acquire in the subject will be of no avail.

Quality in science education, as in everything else, has many dimensions. For all teachers the classroom experience of pupils is itself paramount and will receive their first consideration. All teachers will also wish to contribute to those aspects of the work of a school or department which influence the quality of what takes place in the classroom. The curriculum, its planning and assessment will clearly have a direct effect on what an individual teacher does. Less obvious but equally important are the ways in which pupils' social, moral, spiritual and cultural development is supported; the guidance they are given and how learning relates to the world outside school. Quality in science education cannot just be about science.

The ultimate goal of teachers in any subject must be to produce high-quality teaching all the time. Whilst that remains the ambition it is as well to appreciate that, as Hilary Wilce put it in the TES, '…whatever recipe is chosen, it's all in the end, in the detail. Good teaching is painstaking, tedious stuff…' As she goes on to remind the reader, quality is about doing the routine things consistently and in a way which takes account of pupils' needs as well as on occasions teaching that truly inspirational lesson.

High-quality Learning – What Should Pupils Gain?

What are the science specific features of quality in education? It is useful to decide firstly what pupils should gain from their school experience of science. As a result of their activities in science lessons pupils should be developing the following:

- knowledge and understanding of science which they can apply
- the skills of scientific enquiry
- some appreciation of the nature and limitations of science
- an awareness of how the applications of science affect their lives and others'
- interest in and curiosity about science
- an ability to work safely and show respect for living things and the environment.

This is not a unique representation of the goals of science by any means. It does however represent the breadth of the subject and has implications for the range of techniques, activities and contexts which will need to be utilised if quality is to be achieved. It is, for example, difficult to see how progress can be made in the areas listed without a blend of practical activity, discussion, book-related learning, use of IT and investigation featuring in lessons.

Whilst it is relatively easy to argue that the attributes listed above should be developed in all pupils as part of their science education the discussion continues about their nature and the emphasis which each should be given. Most would agree that a rounded science education should include the development of the 'skills of scientific enquiry', but reaching agreement concerning what these skills are and how they can be developed is not such an easy matter. Teachers, as well as politicians and academics, have a part to play in this legitimate debate for ultimately it is they who will have to translate the resulting curriculum into workable classroom practice. In this chapter it is assumed that the first responsibility of teachers of science is to work towards high-quality delivery of the statutory curriculum whilst taking an active part in discussion of the curriculum organised by the ASE and others.

It is important that pupils also develop within science the ability to:

- communicate scientific findings using appropriate literacy skills
- display, manipulate and analyse scientific data using appropriate mathematical skills

- use ICT to capture, store, retrieve, analyse and present information.

These abilities are important to the development of pupils' scientific literacy and also contribute to the broader curriculum. Quality science education will therefore both utilise and extend these capabilities and make demands on pupils which are consistent with expectations elsewhere in the curriculum.

The Importance of Teaching – Making a Difference

There is little doubt that teaching is the most significant of the factors which contribute to high standards in science education. Analysis of inspection data suggests that the quality of teaching has a four times greater influence on achievement than any of the other 'contributory factors' which are judged in the OFSTED Framework for Inspection. There is certainly substance behind the slogan 'teachers make a difference'.

The criteria for evaluating the quality of teaching which are incorporated into the OFSTED Handbook for Inspection represent a distillation of the experience of HM Inspectors over many years. The criteria are useful pointers for all those seeking an answer to the question, 'What are the features of effective teaching?' Judgements are based on the extent to which teachers:

- have a secure knowledge and understanding of the subjects or areas they teach
- set high expectations so as to challenge pupils and deepen their knowledge and understanding
- plan effectively
- employ methods and organisational strategies which match curricular objectives and the needs of all pupils
- manage pupils well and achieve high standards of discipline
- use time and resources effectively
- assess pupils' work thoroughly and constructively, and use assessments to inform teaching
- use homework effectively to reinforce and/or extend what is learned in school.

These are of course generic criteria which have to be translated in a science context; this is done in much of the rest of this book. There are however important issues of quality particularly in relation to the first two criteria.

Subject Knowledge

As recently as 1994, HMI reported that, *Shortcomings in (primary) teachers' own scientific understanding remain a serious obstacle to achieving higher standards* (Subjects and Standards, 1994–5, OFSTED). It would be wrong to suggest that primary-class teachers have since become science specialists but great strides forward have been made. Teachers have gained familiarity with the National Curriculum requirements and schools have worked hard to make the best use of available expertise in science by strategies such as class swapping and short-term specialist teaching as well as using INSET time to share ideas. The quality of whole-school planning has improved and this has provided valuable support to those teachers with little background in science. Nevertheless there is still much that can be done to further improve subject knowledge and expertise; there is a role here for both primary and secondary specialists. Primary science co-ordinators can do much to pass on their expertise to others by means of support materials, topic workshops and wherever possible working with colleagues. Secondary teachers can contribute their expertise whilst at the same time learning from primary practice and so improving the key-stage transition.

High Expectations and Key Stage Transfer

In order to have appropriately high expectations of pupils it is necessary to know what they have already achieved. Across each key stage boundary there is a danger that continuity will be lost and expectations will be too low. This is particularly true of the transfer from Key Stage 2 to Key Stage 3. Primary science has made massive strides forward so the base on which teachers are building in early secondary school has changed. The appropriate starting points for pupils on transfer to secondary school will depend on individual attainment but also, to some extent, on the way in which science is organised and taught in Key Stage 2. All too often the achievements of pupils are not fully recognised or built upon early in their secondary experience because scientific ideas are encountered in very different contexts to those used in primary school or the language used to describe them is unfamiliar. Curriculum liaison between primary and secondary schools has improved considerably but remains one of the main issues of quality for Key Stage 3 science.

The Importance of Planning – Small Steps towards Big Ideas

The foundations for good science teaching and learning are laid outside the classroom or laboratory. Successful learning is much more likely when teachers have a clear view of what they want children to learn from an activity (objectives), the processes which will carry them towards these goals and what pupils will be able to do as a result (outcomes). It is also becoming increasingly clear from research that it is important to be aware of what ideas pupils have to start with, including sometimes some stubborn misconceptions. (See Chapters 2.1 and 3.6.)

It is also important when planning to take account of notions of continuity and progression (see Chapter 3.6). This is well expressed by Driver *et al* (1994):

> *Teaching science with children's thinking in mind depends upon careful planning in which continuity of curriculum is designed for progression in pupils' ideas.*
>
> *The term 'progression' is applied to something that happens inside a learner's head: thinking about experience and ideas, children develop their ideas. Some aspects of their learning may happen quite quickly and easily, whereas others happen in very small steps over a number of years.*
>
> *Continuity on the other hand is something organised by the teacher: it describes the relationship between experiences, activities and ideas which*

pupils meet over a period of time, in a curriculum which is structured to support learning. Curriculum continuity cannot guarantee progression. Its role is to structure ideas and experiences for learners in a way which will help them to move their conceptual understanding forward in scientific terms.

Our knowledge about the ways in which children's ideas about science develop changes through experience and formal research (see, for example, Chapters 2.1 and 2.2). Fortunately for the teacher in the classroom, much of what experience suggests supports good progression is now enshrined in published schemes and syllabuses. For practical purposes planning will be based largely on established thinking but an awareness of changing ideas is part of professional development, an attribute of the 'reflective practitioner'.

Great benefit can be gained from joint planning of work since experiences of success can be shared, ideas about effective approaches pooled and specialist knowledge utilised. In both primary and secondary science it is common for work to be divided into topics or modules and, especially during times of rapid curriculum change, these have often been planned by individuals in order to make the task manageable. Inevitably there are times when 'the joins show' and the pupils' experience of science is fragmented or involves repetition. There are fertile links between different areas of science which need to be exploited to help pupils gain a coherent understanding of the key ideas. Joint, or at least shared, planning is a means of promoting these connections and enabling teachers to share professional experience and expertise.

Effective planning in science has the following features:

- Work is structured so as to build progressively on pupils' previous knowledge and understanding.
- Opportunities are included for pupils to think about and discuss their emerging scientific ideas.
- Experimental and investigative work is incorporated in such a way that it links with and builds upon pupils' scientific knowledge and understanding.
- Connections between related areas of science are made explicit (see, for example, Chapters 3.1 and 2.3).

Variety – the Spice?

One of the distinguishing features of science education is the emphasis rightly given to practical activity. For many pupils the most memorable experience of their first year of secondary education is lighting a Bunsen burner for the first time. Some, alas, also gain the impression that 'real science' has to take place in a laboratory. Primary science teaching has wider horizons. The interest which most pupils show in practical work is clearly something to be exploited and the good use of experimental work will remain the principal strategy in the effective science teacher's repertoire. Nevertheless there are many other effective and motivating activities and approaches to learning science which the science teacher can draw upon.

Many of the schools and departments that have carried out an 'audit' of their approaches to science teaching have been surprised by the outcomes. It is a common experience to find that the range of activities is large but the incidence of some types is both lower and more variable than anticipated. For example, although IT may feature in schemes of work for science the actual use of this may vary between teachers often depending on their confidence in handling work with computers and perceptions of its value. Most teachers have a 'preferred style' and it is understandable that this predominates especially when they are under the pressures of rapid curriculum change or inspection. Quality science education will however incorporate a range of teaching activities and approaches with the common aim of engaging pupils (see Chapters 3.1 and 3.5).

A useful strategy adopted by some schools with the aim of increasing variety in science is to link an audit of existing practice with the setting of targets for future practice and agreement to try new approaches. Typically this might involve the following:

- making sure that experimental work has clear and specific learning objectives communicated to pupils
- selecting illustrative class practical, investigation or participative demonstration according to the intended purpose
- the use of activities which develop the skills of investigation as well as the carrying out of 'whole investigations'
- giving opportunities for pupils to express and discuss their ideas as well as responding to tightly-framed questions
- providing opportunities for some extended reading about science beyond the double-page spread and, especially in the primary phase, reading fiction as well as non-fiction with a science dimension
- setting science in a social or technological context in which pupils are confronted with issues as well as concepts
- the use of IT (as facilities permit) for research, data logging, display and processing.

This list can, of course, be extended in ways which depend on the interests of teachers and the resources available. The essential elements are clarity of and fitness for purpose and the confidence of teachers in the approach being used. There is evidence that, just as teachers have preferred styles, pupils learn and are motivated in different ways so perhaps variety *is* the spice'.

Science with a Social Life!

When secondary pupils are asked about their reasons for not choosing to study science beyond what is compulsory they often mention the relative lack of discussion and relevance; science is seen to be individual. As one student put it, "Science doesn't have a social life!". There are also strong indications that science thrives where extra-curricular activities are strong and varied. Certainly schools that have broadened their scientific horizons beyond the laboratory report the benefits of doing so. There are also benefits to be gained from involving local employers and those in science-related professions in school-based activities (see Chapter 4.5).

The first responsibility of any teacher must, of course, be to deliver the statutory curriculum in an effective way; but few would wish to stop there. The list of activities which can be used to enrich science is almost endless but includes:

- CREST and other award schemes
- visits to the growing number of 'hands on' science centres
- partnerships with neighbourhood scientists
- science fairs on site
- science 'public understanding' days in the community
- off-timetable enrichment days
- science magazines produced by pupils using school IT facilities
- using secondary pupils to organise science activities for primary pupils.

Recognising and Improving Quality

Teaching is, by its nature and organisation, an occupation in which it is difficult to know how what one is doing compares with what is going on elsewhere. Opportunities to observe colleagues in the same school are few and time to find out about the issues and opportunities for schools other than one's own are equally scarce. How then can the reflective teacher arrive at a professional decision about the quality of their own practice in order to move forward?

The two principal mechanisms by which teachers can gauge their own professional progress and that of their school or department are self-review and external inspection. External inspection carried out by Registered Inspectors working under contract to OFSTED provides a basis for the national evaluation of schools as well as identifying the strengths and weaknesses of individual schools so that they may improve the quality of education provided. In relation to science, inspections will involve evaluation of:

- pupils' attainment in relation to national expectations or standards, drawing on evidence of what pupils know, understand and can do by the end of each key stage
- progress made in relation to pupils' prior attainment
- pupils' attitudes to learning
- any strengths and weaknesses in teaching and other factors which contribute to standards (see Chapter 4.2).

The experience of inspection is inevitably stressful but can also provide valuable information and professional development. As well as generating reports on individual schools, inspection data are used by OFSTED to provide a national overview of subject work and aspects of school life. These are published in various forms including regular booklets about science. These enable teachers to set their own work in a broad context and find out about national issues of quality.

Self review will normally involve both monitoring of what is being done and evaluation of its effectiveness. Targets for future progress will also be set, often incorporated into a departmental development plan. Local Authorities often have their own frameworks for school self-review and for science the ASE has published both primary and secondary self-evaluation documents (NAIGS/ASE, 1996, 1997). These take the main headings of the OFSTED framework and translate the criteria into subject specific terms to aid on-going evaluation. These or other self-review publications can be used to help schools or departments through the five stage cycle of self-improvement:

- How well are we doing?
- How do we compare with other similar schools?
- What more should we aim to achieve – this year?
- What must we do to make it happen?
- How can we review progress?

Is Good 'Good Enough'?

Any discussion about quality is bound to set out high ideals and therefore runs the risk of disheartening those who seek to meet them. It is difficult to balance encouragement and challenge but fortunately where science education is concerned there is much to celebrate; much that will spur all those involved to want even better. The following quotations show both what has been achieved and areas of attention to make what is good even better.

Primary

> *Standards in science have improved and the performance of English pupils in science now compares favourably with that of pupils' in other countries. Four-fifths of pupils achieve or exceed the expected National Curriculum level in science at Key Stage 1 and more than two thirds at Key Stage 2. In a recent international survey Year 5 pupils in England obtained mean science scores which were exceeded by pupils in only three of the other 25 countries which took part.*
>
> *Science in primary schools has made much progress over recent years; standards have been raised and pupils now enter secondary schooling with a better foundation of knowledge, skills and terminology than previously. Inspection shows that this favourable trend is continuing but that there are some persistent variations in standards within and between schools that need to be addressed if primary science is to gain further ground and all children make steady progress. Attention needs to be paid to:*
>
> *– the relative weakness of Years 3 and 4;*
> *– making the best use of available specialist expertise;*
> *– raising expectations by monitoring pupils' progress in science;*
> *– ensuring high standards across the whole Programme of Study;*
> *– making sure that literacy and numeracy are supported by and developed in science.* (OFSTED, 1998a)

Secondary

> *From 1993 there has been steady improvement in standards in science. In particular the sharper focus for lessons, clearer objectives identified by teach-*

ers, and better use of class time has contributed to an improvement in pupils' knowledge base. The proportion of pupils reaching the expected level in science national tests has risen slowly to six out of ten, a similar proportion to other core subjects. International comparisons confirm this broadly positive picture with standards comparing favourably with those in other Western European countries. Results in double award science GCSE have shown steady improvement and at A-level, whilst overall numbers of entries for science subjects have declined, students taking science subjects achieve well and obtain good grades in relation to their GCSE performance. A-level results in modular science courses have also been good, despite the fact that lack of success in early modules has raised questions about the preparedness of some students for these elements of the syllabus. This is a particularly encouraging picture given that the science curriculum has been subject to a number of changes. (OFSTED, 1998b)

There remain some issues for schools to address if science is to continue to flourish and maintain its international standing:

- Pupils understanding of underlying scientific concepts remains insecure, and they are insufficiently able to apply their knowledge to new contexts.
- Standards in experimental and investigatory work have consistently remained below those in other attainment targets.
- More needs to be done to raise the status and popularity of science with pupils at all levels.

About the Author

Bob Ponchaud was an HM Inspector based in London before the establishment of OFSTED. He is now the Subject Adviser for Science and the point of reference for all matters relating to science within OFSTED. Before becoming an HMI he occupied a variety of posts including Head of Science in two large comprehensives. His other experience includes school-based research, writing textbooks and examining science.

References and Further Reading

NAIGS/ASE (1996) *School Science Department Self-Evaluation Document,* Hatfield, ASE.

NAIGS/ASE (1997) *Primary Science Self-Review Document*, Hatfield, ASE.

N.B. These useful publications use OFSTED framework headings but the criteria included reflect interpretations made by the writers (National Advisers and Inspectors Group in Science/ASE) and should not be seen as adding to those in the OFSTED handbook.

Driver, R., Squires, A., Rushworth, P. and Wood-Robinson, V. (1994) *Making sense of secondary science,* London, Routledge.

OFSTED (1998a) *Standards in Primary Science,* London, The Stationery Office.
OFSTED (1998b) *Secondary Review 1993–7,* London, The Stationery Office.
Woolnough, B.E. (1995). *Effective Science Teaching*, Milton Keynes, Open University Press.

1.3 The Place of Science in the Curriculum

Des Dunne

This chapter explores curriculum structures which allow the purposes of science education to be fulfilled. After a review of significant events in the history of the science curriculum in the UK, issues for the future are identified and considered.

Evolution of the Curriculum

The catalogue of events outlined in Fig 1.3A shows the documentation, debates and decisions that have influenced the evolution of the science curriculum over the past 50 years. The context of science is changing, society itself is changing and therefore educational policy is changing. When the pace of change in the scientific world is high and constant this presents a challenge to the teaching of modern science. We could assume therefore that rapid change in the curriculum would take place hand in hand with this ever changing face of the scientific world. This is not the case. The major changes in educational initiatives have reflected social concerns. There has been a move from the education of the elite to education for all.

The involvement of teachers in the Secondary Science Curriculum Review (SSCR) provided the platform for implementation of broad and balanced science and ensured the provision of science education as an entitlement up to the end of compulsory education. Broad and balanced science succeeded in its inclusion of Earth science, astronomy and the investigative nature of science, but clear links with technology were lost. Development of initially CSE and then GCSE courses, such as 'Mode 3' provided opportunities for teachers to develop their professional skills. Some teachers regret the demise of courses which were practically based and allowed them to draw on their own expertise and local conditions.

There is a need to reconcile the pressure in society for flexibility and adaptability to a rapid rate of change with a need for curriculum evolution that will allow it to be 'owned' by the profession and effective in implementation. Prior to the National Curriculum, changes to examination syllabuses and curriculum modifications took place almost annually, and the teaching profession accepted this slow evolution of the curriculum. Indeed this is still the situation in Scotland. A guiding principle should be to recommend a framework for the curriculum whilst recognising the need to allow the flexibility to modify context and content in the light of monitoring and evaluation of implementation.

The curriculum has always undergone a process of change, but it has never been so prominent as in recent years. Change has been brought about in the classroom with reluctance, and generally we prefer the devil we know than the one we are unfamiliar with. There is however some justification that much of the curriculum change over the past ten years has been too rapid (particularly in England and Wales) and too much imposed from above. A succession of ministers and quangos has underestimated the time needed for change to take root and has not understood the processes required for teachers to feel ownership of the curriculum. The speed and style of introduction and imposed change has caused problems in interpretation and implementation.

1951	First examination of the General Certificate of Education (GCE)
1953	1st Report on Secondary Modern Science Teaching – SMA (ASE)
1957	2nd Report on Secondary Modern Science Teaching – SMA (ASE)
	Leybourn and Bailey set up a committee in Manchester – Teaching Science to the Ordinary Pupil
1959	Crowther Report (HMSO)
1960	HMI – Pamphlet No 38 (HMSO) Science in Secondary Schools
1961	First series of policy statements on Science Education Policy (ASE)
1963	John Newsom Half our Future (HMSO) considered the education of pupils aged 13–16 of average or less than average ability
1964	First examinations in the Nuffield Science Projects
	The first period of large-scale curriculum reform
1965	Working Paper No 1, HMI, (Schools Council) – Science should have significance and relevance for the pupils
	Beloe Committee (HMSO) – Certificate of Secondary Education (CSE)
1969	Scottish Integrated Science Project
1970	Nuffield Secondary Science Project (Nuffield Foundation – Longman Group)
	Nuffield Combined Science (Nuffield Foundation – Longman Group)
1973	Raising of the school-leaving age
1974	The Schools Council Integrated Science Project (SCISP)
1976	James Callaghan (in speech at Ruskin College, Oxford) initiated the great debate on education
1977	Education in Schools ('The Red Book') HMI (HMSO) outlined the pattern for a broad curriculum in the first three years followed by all pupils, with an optional structure in the later two years of compulsory education
1979	The Survey of Secondary Schools – HMI (HMSO) introduced the term 'Balanced Science'
	Alternatives for Science Education (ASE) a consultation document which argued the case for a broad and balanced science approach and suggested curriculum models
1980	Education Through Science policy document (ASE)
	Examinations 16–18: A Consultative Paper (HMSO)
1981	The Secondary Science Curriculum Review (SSCR) was established
	The School Curriculum (HMSO)
1982	APU Survey Reports – Science in Schools; Age 15 (HMSO)

Fig 1.3A Selected events in the evolution of science education in England and Wales over the past 50 years

Science Education in Schools (HMSO) – confirmed broad and balanced science

1982 Royal Society proposed a balanced science curriculum leading to a double award

1983 ASE statement of support for a common system of examining at 16+
Curriculum 11–16: Towards a Statement of Entitlement (HMSO)

1984 The National Criteria: Science – GCSE (HMSO) AS level Proposals (HMSO)
SSCR propose a minimum entitlement of science education for all 11–16

1985 The Public Understanding of Science (Royal Society) provides backing for broad and balanced science
DES Science 5–16: a statement of policy (HMSO) ASE endorsed the 5–16 policy 'Better Schools' (HMSO) – endorsed balanced science in first three years of school General Certificate of Secondary Education(GCSE)

1986 Announcement of the establishment of CPVE (Certificate of Pre-Vocational Education)

1987 ASE statement in support of Double Award: Balanced Science
Three into Two Science (ASE)
5–16 consultation document (HMSO) outlined the need for a National Curriculum
SSCR publications (SCDC)

1988 Education reform bill (HMSO)
NCC interim report of the science working group
Higginson report (HMSO) proposals for a review of A-levels

1989 Survey of Balanced Science Courses (HMSO)
Secretary of State announcement about core skills in post 16 examinations
Which Syllabus (ASE)
First version of the Science Curriculum (17 attainment targets – ATs)
Balanced Science for All – ASE Says 'No' to 12.5% Science (ASE)

1990 Moving into balance (ASE) Post 16 examinations – governed by National principles

1991 ASE Investigations in Science Task Group

1992 Second version of the Science Curriculum (4 ATs, 17 strands) Moving Targets (ASE)

1994 Introduction of GNVQ (Science Pilot)

1995 Third version of the Science Curriculum (4 ATs, 17 sub-headings)
ASE – Science Education for the Year 2000 and Beyond Task Group established

1996 Review of Qualifications for 16–19 (Dearing Review), SCAA

1997 ASE Science Education for the Year 2000 and Beyond

1998 QCA makes recommendations to Secretary of State on curriculum review

Fig 1.3A (contd.)

What Curriculum Models Could be Considered?

A useful starting point for considering appropriate curriculum structures is the current curriculum framework across the UK (Fig 1.3B).

There is general agreement that the future curriculum for children aged 3 to 13 should be similar to the current curriculum in breadth and balance. There is greater dissatisfaction with the 14 to 16 curriculum. The evidence collected from the ASE's Science Education 2000+ consultation reveals a growing unease with the same diet for all pupils in the last two years of compulsory education (ASE, 1998). The debate about whether pupils should be able to choose particular aspects of science, as in Scotland, rumbles on.

A major issue is that many pupils are not continuing their study of science beyond the age of 16. There is a measurable decline in the number of higher-education science students. When pupils at age 16 choose to do subjects other than the sciences, what exactly are they positively opting for? Negative experiences of science in their pre-16 education can clearly direct pupils to choose other subjects; but there must remain something in their chosen subjects for which they exercise a positive choice. Many argue that this situation could be addressed by developing a curriculum for 15–16 year olds that is more relevant. A relevant curriculum could include current issues and interesting applications of science, be exciting, and place an emphasis on the creative activity of human culture.

The ASE policy on balanced science strongly supports an appropriate curriculum for all pupils:

> *The Association believes that a child's experience of science should start in the primary school within a broad, integrated curriculum. The Association believes that around 10% of the time in the primary curriculum should be spent on science. The science curriculum in the early years of secondary education must build on the primary curriculum in a continuous and progressive manner. The Association believes that, in the early years of the secondary curriculum, science is likely to be a separate subject area within the curriculum and should constitute between 10 and 15% of curriculum time. The science curriculum in primary and lower secondary should have a balance of content across the disciplines of biology, chemistry and physics along with other areas such as astronomy and Earth science.*
>
> *It is recognised that science knowledge is developing at a rapid rate. A balance of breadth and depth of scientific knowledge and understanding must be maintained, in addition to the development of problem solving, investigative skills and informed attitudes. The Association believes that learners should spend a minimum of 20% of curriculum time on the study of science between the ages of 14 and 16 in order to achieve breadth and depth in each area of science education.* (ASE, 1997)

It is important to note that ASE does *not* suggest that all pupils should have *identical diets*.

Many of the issues arising from ASEs Science Education 2000+ consultation relate to the lack of flexibility for the 14 to 16 age group (ASE, 1998). Outlined below are broad criteria, arising from discussion groups, which could apply to flexible curriculum models able to cope with pupil diversity. A flexible curriculum model should:

• be a broad curriculum encompassing all the sciences

ENGLAND AND WALES

Four key stages 5–16. Specific science curriculum for each key stage.

Key Stage	School years	Age range	Time allocation
KS1	1+2	5–7	54 hr
KS2	3–6	7–11	72 hr
KS3	7–9	11–14	90 hr
KS4	10–11	14–16	10% minimum

The time allocations are those given to the SCAA subject working groups (1994) as guidelines. They are not compulsory. The KS4 curriculum must include English, mathematics, science, physical education, technology and a modern foreign language.

SCOTLAND

Three broad stages 5–14. Science to be included in Environmental Studies. There are five components in Environmental Studies: Science, Social Subjects, Technology, Health Education and Information Technology.

School years	Ages	Time allocation
P1–P3	5–8	25% for environmental studies in years P1–P7
P4–P6	8–11	
P7–S2	11–14	10% Science in S1 and S2
S3–S4	14–16	At least one science

In S3 pupils choose a number of subjects to study from eight curricular modes: language and communication, mathematical studies and applications, scientific studies and applications, social and environmental studies, technological activities and applications, creative and aesthetic activities, physical education and religious and moral education.

NORTHERN IRELAND

4–14 Elementary Education. Science is included in AS3 which covers Science, Technology and the Environment.

Key Stage	Age range	Time allocation for Science
KS1	4–8	10–12%
KS2	8–11	16%
KS3	11–14	10–12.5%
KS4	14–16	10–30%

The time allocations are those given to the Subject Review Groups. They are not compulsory.

Fig 1.3B Current curriculum models

- consist of an identified core or foundation science for all courses
- have different content or emphasis for pupils with different aptitudes and interests
- provide a conceptual base for the further study of sciences post-16 for all students for whom this is a realistic possibility
- provide for a single science certification which maintains breadth and a focus on scientific literacy.

Fig 1.3C shows a range of possible curriculum models that could form the basis of further discussion. Each model has a core or foundation science with optional or modular differences. A structure of nine topics or modules has been chosen for convenience. A range of traditional science models is proposed as well as models which allow greater flexibility to include topics of immediate interest or vocational elements such as building, food, agriculture, etc.

These models require much debate as to their relative advantages and disadvantages.

Another possible model could be a meritocratic model where pupils who achieve a high level of attainment at age 14 are allowed freedom of choice to follow specialist science subjects in depth. This model would stimulate much discussion about the nature of broad and balanced education for the more able child up to the age of 16.

How Should Science Relate to Other Subjects of the Curriculum?

There are many examples of science teachers' contributions to cross-curricular and project activities. The mechanism of how this happens lies with teachers themselves more than the artificial boundaries of separate subjects within the curriculum. Structurally organised approaches were proposed by Black and Harrison (1985). They recommended interdisciplinary timetabling to enable pupils to engage in 'tasks' – i.e. problem-solving and design activities supported by the 'resources' of several subject areas. They also suggested approaches such as termly or annual 'project weeks' where the normal timetable is abandoned and the whole school engages in the theme of the project. Another approach by SSCR (1987) suggested the grouping of four related subject areas such as English, mathematics, science and technology with the blocking of curriculum time on a regular basis. This would enable the pupils to have access to a variety of subject specialists.

During ASE's Science Education 2000+ consultation, many teachers indicated that they felt there was insufficient time to engage in cross-curricular collaboration effectively.

There remain many areas of overlap between subjects. The following sections address each subject in turn and highlight one or two possible areas for development:

English

Communication in both spoken and written form in association with diagrams and tables could form the basis of much discussion between English and science

Core plus option model (science) model

Core Science
Options with specific science topics

Core plus options (science plus interest) model

Core Science	
Science options	Interest options

Restricted choice modular (science) model

A	B	C
Two from three	Two from three	Two from three

Core or foundation modules

Selection of six modules two from each section

Free choice modular (science) model

A	B	C
Selection of six science modules from a total of nine		

Core or foundation modules

Free choice modular (science plus interest) model

A	B	C		
Selection of four science modules from a total of six			Selection of two from four interest modules

Core or foundation modules

Academic/vocational modular model

Core Science	
Science options	Vocational options

Fig 1.3C Possible curriculum models for the 14–16 age group

teachers. Directed activities related to text (DART) are to be found amongst SATIS materials and these could be used as a starting point for discussion (ASE, 1986). The recent emphasis on literacy may also help to fuel this potential area of collaboration. It is evident that science is an important medium for the application of literacy skills. (See Chapters 3.3 and 4.4.)

Mathematics

Mathematics uses precise symbolic and logical language to communicate models and solutions to problems. Mathematics is often regarded as a 'tool' rather than as an integral part of scientific education. There is a great potential in establishing discussions about the uses and applications of mathematics and the common features this has with science. This is particularly true in England and Wales where there are similarities between Attainment Target 1 in both subjects.

Technology

Rapid technological changes mean that the pupils' world is likely to be different in many ways from the present. Although we cannot predict exactly what life will be like in the next century, we can help pupils understand the scientific and technological factors involved in change. Whereas the central purpose of science is the acquisition of better understandings of the world, technology's goal is the production of successful and appropriate artefacts or systems which impinge on people's lives or the environment in practical ways. The relationship between science and technology is one of mutual interdependence rather than a hierarchical dependence of one upon the other.

The public perception is that science and technology are closely associated. However, in practice cross-subject relationships are not as strong as they could be, except perhaps in schools that have a science and technology faculty or have been involved in technology initiatives. The joint ASE/DATA project, Science with Technology, provides one method of making meaningful links (ASE, 1994).

An emphasis on vocational education may enable another route for greater collaboration between subjects since many vocational courses are at the interface between science, technology and other subjects of the curriculum in a work-related context. The emphasis on developing knowledge through applications and problem solving would enable pupils to make career decisions based on firmer, first-hand experience.

History and Geography

There are clear links between physical geography, Earth science and the study of weather. In many schools, departments have worked well together to discuss curriculum coverage and appropriate teaching methods. Links with history are less well explored beyond the study of specific scientists and their lifetimes. A significant number of science teachers seem unaware of the important aspect of 'Enquiry skills' in history and geography. The skills and processes utilised in 'Enquiry skills' have much in common with experimental and investigative science.

Expressive Arts (Art, Music, Drama and Design)

Aesthetic and creative links with the arts can contribute to the solving of techno-logical or environmental problems. The Creativity in Science and Technology (CREST) awards for the 14–19 age group are an important contribution as are science challenge competitions and science fairs. The celebration of pupils' work through display is a particular area of fruitful collaboration in many schools.

Modern Foreign Languages

The development of the Science Across Europe project has led many science teach-ers to collaborate with foreign languages colleagues in their own school. Importantly, the project has allowed pupils to compare local experiences of scien-tific issues with those in many other European countries thereby extending both their knowledge of science and of other cultures.

Religious Education

The influence of religions on the advancement or restriction of scientific develop-ment is an area of possible exploration. Multicultural development in science departments has been helped significantly with the production of *Race and Equality in Science Teaching* (Thorp, 1991). (See also Chapter 1.5.)

Physical Education

PE teachers have always emphasised links with biology and physics in the study of movement, but science departments themselves have not always fully explored PE as a medium for providing variation in the teaching of science.

About the Author

Des Dunne was educated in a Liverpool Comprehensive School before graduating from Durham University. He was a secondary Head of Science in Kent before becoming an advi-sory teacher, adviser and then team leader for the Northampton Inspection and Advisory Service (NIAS) science team. After contributing this chapter he became Principal Subject Officer for Science at the Qualifications and Curriculum Authority (QCA).

References and Further Reading

ASE /BP *Science Across Europe,* Hatfield, ASE.

ASE (1986) *Science and Technology in Society (SATIS),* Hatfield, ASE.

ASE (1994) *Science with Technology,* Hatfield, ASE.

ASE (1997) *Science Education for the Year 2000 and Beyond, A Report from the Task Group,* Hatfield, ASE.

ASE (1998) Science Education 2000+ Summary Report. *Education in Science,* No176, pp 17–20.

Black, P. and Harrison, G. (1985) *In Place of Confusion: Technology and Science in the School Curriculum.* The Nuffield–Chelsea Curriculum Trust and the National Centre for School Technology, Trent Polytechnic, Newgate Press.

Secondary Science Curriculum Review (1887*) Better Science: How to Plan and Manage the Curriculum, Curriculum Guide 5,* London, Heinemann.

Scottish CCC (1996) *Science Education in Scottish Schools, Looking to the Future, A Paper for Discussion and Consultation*, Dundee, Scottish CCC.

Thorp, S. (Ed.) (1991) *Race, Equality and Science Teaching: An Active INSET Manual for Teachers and Educators*, Hatfield, ASE.

1.4 Science Education and Training beyond 16

Mike Coles

Post-16 education is characterised by its non-compulsory nature and close interaction of teachers and students. In this chapter I review the developing policy and the implications for science departments in schools and colleges. Teaching and learning in post-16 settings is discussed in terms of how it is distinct from approaches used with younger students. Feedback on teaching and learning approaches from inspectors and students is described in outline and I discuss features of effective methods. A checklist for evaluating post-16 science teaching is provided.

Background

The most distinctive features of post-16 science education and training are its non-compulsory nature and that students have a degree of choice. Post-16 students can study science as a main or a subsidiary study; their courses can be pure or applied; they may cover science in a broad way or be highly specialist. The learning approach can also vary. Students may be in large classes or in small groups; they may also work as individuals through tutorial systems. Qualifications also vary enormously and may be general or vocational; they may be predominantly theoretical, practice-based (preparation for work) or occupational. Assessment for these qualifications may be through a written 'terminal' examination, examination of modules, course-work, or on-the-job appraisal. To add to the variety of forms of science education, courses may be full time or part time and some will have no fixed mode of attendance.

For teachers in schools and colleges science education of 16–19 year olds will be mainly focused on GCSE, A-levels and General National Vocational Qualifications (GNVQs). In Scotland a more coherent programme exists which can include Highers and vocational qualifications. It is a review of this more restricted provision which forms the basis of this chapter. Current policies, such as the development of a national framework for qualifications, and the impact of information and communications technology (ICT) are likely to widen access to the different forms of science education and training. These will blur the boundaries between provision common in school and the multitude of other science courses and qualifications which are currently available post-16.

Education and training in science forms a significant part of 16–19 studies. There has been a major expansion of student numbers; by 1994 numbers had risen to 75.5% of all 16–19 year olds from 66% some four years earlier. However, students have not been selecting science qualifications in proportion to the expansion.

Numbers of physics students have fallen during this period and chemistry numbers have only been maintained. One of the reasons for this decline in the proportion of students studying science is the fact that students are choosing more diverse study programmes; they are mixing their qualifications across the sciences, humanities and arts. The numbers of students specialising in the sciences has been falling. In 1988/89 the proportion of students following mixed programmes (i.e. a science or maths subject studied with an arts or humanities subject) was 33.2%. This had risen to 37.9% in 1993/4 and continues to rise.

Changes in Courses since 1960

The picture of science education for 16–19 years olds in schools and colleges in the 1960s was monochromatic. A-levels, which had been introduced in 1951, dominated the scene. They were aimed at the most able students who were considering university entrance. Other students studied Ordinary levels (O-levels) and Advanced Ordinary courses (AO-levels). Most colleges enrolled part-time (day-release) students studying science as part of apprenticeships. These colleges also offered full-time vocational courses.

The A-level courses were largely theoretical and were based on the central explanatory concepts of the pure sciences. In most A-level courses the teacher explained ideas whilst students made notes which could be used to answer examination questions. Examination was by written paper and pass rates were set in relation to proportions of the cohort entering the examinations, for example a failure rate of 30% was built-in. The first major change to A-levels began in the late 60s with the development of Nuffield A-levels. These were characterised by a stronger focus on scientific inquiry which was reflected in the examinations. The Nuffield approach grew in popularity and had a significant influence on 'traditional' A-levels. In the 80s a new style of A-level was developed which focused strongly on the teaching of chemistry through its applications. A physics syllabus has also been developed in the late 1990s. These A-levels are known as Salters' syllabuses, reflecting the name of their sponsors. The traditional A-level syllabuses have remained the most popular advanced provision throughout this time.

Advanced vocational qualifications mainly took the form of National Diplomas (full time) and National Certificates (part time). These were administered by the Business and Technician Education Council (BTEC). Numbers of students studying for vocational qualifications have been small (approximately 7% of the total specialist science cohort in 1996) but these qualifications have been growing in popularity, albeit slowly. In the early 90s advanced vocational courses attracted about 2000 students annually compared to the 100,000+ who were studying for A-levels. In 1994 GNVQs in science were launched and ran alongside the BTEC provision. By 1996 the numbers enrolling for these qualifications had reached 5000 per annum for the Intermediate Science GNVQ and 2000 per annum for the Advanced Science GNVQ. In Scotland students were able to select individual vocational modules and it is likely that the proportion of students with some recognised vocational achievement is much higher than in the rest of the UK.

At the same time as the GNVQs were launched the examination boards offering traditional A-levels began to accredit modular schemes for A-levels which provided some choice in content and staged assessment. These syllabuses grew in popularity very quickly. Over half of those centres offering traditional A-levels had switched to the modular alternative in the first year of availability. Approximately 80% of all advanced science students now follow a modular course.

Thus the current situation in schools and colleges offering 16–19 education in science is that the great majority of able students study modular A-levels in the separate sciences with a small but significant number studying for the Advanced Science GNVQ or BTEC (now Edexcel) National. Weaker students repeat their GCSE examinations which they took at 16 or study for the GNVQ Intermediate or the Edexcel First Certificate. Less than 1000 students study the Foundation GNVQ in Science.

Policy for Post-16 Science Education and Training

The 1990s have seen much attention paid to creating a more effective post-compulsory education and training system. The increased participation in post-16 study and government policy on introducing General National Vocational Qualifications has widened the range of science courses available to students. Other policy decisions, mainly connected with new funding mechanisms for institutions and the drive for economic efficiency, have constrained the introduction of new courses in many schools and colleges.

In the early 1990s the ASE established a Post-16 committee charged with developing an ASE position on national developments and responding to national consultations. The committee disseminates information to the membership through its journals, notably the Past 16 Science Issues (PSSI) which is a lively arena for discussion and dissemination.

The ASE Post-16 committee set up a working group in 1994 to consider the issues associated with lifelong learning in science. The group has produced a discussion document forming the basis of ASE policy for science education post 16. The working group has given thorough consideration to issues which all in science education need to address if science is to be a serious and significant part of lifelong learning culture.

The framework for a post-16 education policy could cover the following issues:

- The balance in study programmes of post-16 students. This might cover the nature and extent of specialist scientific studies and of non-scientific studies which allow students to maintain contact with areas outside science. It could also cover approaches to learning.
- Provision of opportunities to select courses which match ability and career intentions. This might include the freedom to choose across 'academic' and 'vocational' approaches to study.
- Provision of opportunities for students to apply what they have learned and to demonstrate their scientific knowledge and skills across a range of scientific contexts.
- The development of key skills through science learning.
- The development of personal skills through scientific work.
- Access to careers advice and to guidance about their studies.

The Dearing Review of 16–19 Education and Training

In 1995 Lord Dearing was asked to take charge of the most serious attempt to reform policy on post-16 education and training since Sir Gordon Higginson's (1988) attempt to broaden A-level study. The reasons for the government's rejection of Higginson's proposals for A-level reform showed through in Dearing's remit. He was asked to propose new policy directions for 16–19 education and training which would maintain the rigour of A-levels and build on the GNVQs in order to increase participation and achievement. This left little room for manoeuvre for designing a system which would have greater coherence and provide each student with breadth of study.

Dearing's recommendations were many and wide ranging and generally well received (Dearing, 1996). However some saw them as too limited in their scope and wanted to see more radical change which would lead to a much more open and less constrained post-16 structure (Royal Society, 1997). The main recommendations that impinged on mainstream science education were:

- Introduction of an AS qualification which is about half way between standards expected in the GCSE and those in A-levels.
- Smaller Advanced GNVQs – a single award (about the size of an A-level) and a part award (about the size of an AS qualification).
- New rules for modular A-levels.
- New 'entry' level qualifications to allow people easier access into the qualifications system.
- Overarching certificate/diploma which would encourage breadth of study programmes (science and technology was included as an essential element).

Lord Dearing launched his report by referring to the economic importance of the education system assisting the development of a more flexible, employable and technically able work force. Some research into ways of increasing greater participation in science, mathematics and technology at local and national level has begun (Osborne *et al*, 1997; Jenkins and Laws, 1998).

Policy changes proposed by Dearing would lead to the options for post-16 science studies in schools and colleges as shown in Fig 1.4A.

At the time Dearing's recommendations were being considered, the general election led to a change in government. The incoming government had previously made its broad policy on education clear through publication of *Aiming Higher* (Labour Party, 1997). This was to inform later developments.

The key points which related to science education were:

- Numbers of post-16 students of science and maths have declined by 40% since 1983.
- Narrow specialisation leads to weak core abilities, poor career choice and high drop-out.
- GNVQs are too bureaucratic.
- There should be work experience for all.
- A unitised system is needed which is part of a national framework.
- A new National Certificate should replace A-levels and GNVQs.
- The Record of Achievement should be used to show full abilities/achievements.

Foundation GNVQs, Pre GCSE courses ('certificate' courses)
GCSEs
Intermediate GNVQ
Advanced GNVQ Double Award (12 units), Single award (6 units), Part award (3 units)
Key Skills units
Additional units from other GNVQs
A-levels
AS
NVQ units
Other vocational qualifications, Traineeships, Modern Apprenticeships

Fig 1.4A Post-16 options from Dearing recommendations (from The Labour Party (1997), Aiming Higher)

The new government decided to consult further on post-16 issues and has endorsed Dearing's structure whilst signaling a longer-term move towards a unit-based framework.

Teaching and Learning Science Post-16

The very wide range of provision in science and science-related qualifications makes good teaching and learning practice difficult to describe succinctly. The breadth of provision does flag up the issue of choice. Students want to learn different things, in different ways and at different times. Practicalities often constrain the curriculum offered to students to the main courses taught and learned in a traditional way. Choice often motivates learners and a student studying in a manner they have determined is likely to perform better.

In a sense good teaching and learning of science post-16 will have much in common with practice in secondary school years. Whatever the age of the student we want to see them engage fully with their studies; show enthusiasm for learning; work well with others; show progress in understanding of key ideas and developing their skills; apply what they have learned, organise their work well and present their thoughts and observations clearly.

However there are some factors which create a need for teaching and learning in post-16 settings to be different. For example the majority of students have opted to study more science, they have at least shown interest in science and are likely to have achieved some success in their previous science studies. These older students are likely to have a baseline knowledge and set of experiences which will support further learning. Often these students have clear career intentions and consequently may be more motivated to work and learn. Finally, the students are likely to be more mature and demonstrate self direction. More mature learners are likely to have a more consistent self knowledge and will be aware of how they like to learn; they might be expected to want to negotiate a profile of learning styles which suits them rather than accept a common style determined by the teacher. Students may select courses by considering the way teaching and learning is structured – and not just by considering the content of courses. All students have preferred learning styles. The main characteristics of preferred learning styles across post-16 courses has been investigated in depth by Meagher and his colleagues at the University of Newcastle (Meagher, 1997; see also Chapter 3.1).

In summary then, we would expect post-16 students to:

- show more independence of action (in planning work, developing ways of learning and in evaluating what they have learned through use of assessment criteria)
- be more confident in handling data, drawing conclusions and tolerating uncertainty.

How Do Post-16 Students Judge Effective Teaching?

One of the research exercises which underpinned Lord Dearing's review of education and training of 16–19 year olds involved gathering student opinion about what makes good teaching. As students transferred to post-16 studies they felt that their teachers found it easier to communicate with them and respond to them as equals. Typically students appreciated their new-found independence and felt more inspired and encouraged to learn and work independently The report of this work summarises the students response under five headings. These are discussed below.

Teacher skill in imparting knowledge was important to students because some teachers found it easier to bring relevance to lessons. Students noted that this was easier in vocational subjects. Students wanted to judge teaching skills in terms of method, pace and tone of lessons. They described how they easily became lost by teachers who raced through lectures and left insufficient time for making notes.

Students identified *quality of interaction with students on a personal level* as a second area. They were more motivated to learn by staff who were respectful, honest, trustworthy and friendly. Teachers who were enthusiastic also had a positive effect on learning.

The third area of good teaching was the *level of support provided by the teacher*. Students wanted a good balance between teacher direction and independent learning. They stated a need for clear direction about what was required of them.

The fourth area was *knowledge of course content and structure* with students feeling more comfortable with staff who knew the qualification and its requirements and procedures.

Finally students identified *continuity of teaching within courses* as a criterion for good teaching. Students had experienced courses where changes of staff had led to inconsistencies of approach.

A Checklist for Judging the Quality of the Teaching of a Topic

Teachers engaging with teaching and learning in post-16 settings for the first time notice the difference in ambiance which smaller classes, deeper study and more mature students brings. It might be helpful for teachers to evaluate their own teaching using the following checklist. This list has been adapted from several sources of evaluative criteria. Before using the list it will need to be adapted to suit the courses or topics being taught. It might be useful to jot down how you would know if your teaching matched each criterion.

1) Were the aims and purpose of the topic explicit?
2) Were the context(s) used for the topic interesting to students? Did the students show increased motivation?
3) Was the range of learning activities balanced and did the activities combine to promote effective learning? Was there some scope for students to develop their own approach to the work?
4) Were explanations from the teacher (and students) clear and accurate?
5) Was questioning of students skillful?
6) Was the pace and challenge of the work appropriate?
7) Were resources used effectively?
8) Were students applying their knowledge and skills?
9) Were relationships good?
10) Did students make progress (in terms of knowledge and skills)?
11) Were students evaluating what they had done?

Findings from Inspection of Lessons in Schools and Colleges

In recent years OFSTED has commented on the fact that in teaching and learning in the A-level sciences:

> *there is a tendency in too many classes to 'spoon-feed' rather than encourage students to speak for themselves. In some cases there is an over reliance on dictated notes and duplicated hand outs.*

The problem of perceived examination requirements leading to a rather narrow learning experience is identified as one cause of this problem. Notwithstanding this criticism of some lessons the quality of teaching of post-16 lessons has been consistently the highest of that for all secondary years. OFSTED singles out the high quality of science knowledge and the good relationships in science classes for special comment.

In the GNVQs the same problem of over direction of students was identified by OFSTED and seen in about 10% of the lessons observed by FEFC inspectors. The report from these inspectors stated that generally GNVQ lessons contained a variety of methods which included:

> *assignments, group work, oral presentations, simulations, case studies, practical work, independent study, role play, educational visits and work experience*

In general, feedback from inspection of post-16 courses is positive. However the relatively lower take up of science subjects post-16 might signal a need for a review of teaching approaches and course structures.

Progression to Post-16 Studies

Continuity of learning across the 16+ interface has always been an issue for teachers, even teachers in 11–18 schools. The broadening of the curriculum through balanced science has produced a strong consensus that students (even the most able) are not as well prepared as previously for A-level study. Many schools and colleges have developed special arrangements to ease the transition. Research commissioned by QCA has concluded that the situation is not specifically due to weaknesses in balanced science provision and needs to be tackled on a broader basis. The researchers noted that the great majority of the schools in their sample make some kind of special provision to ease the transition from pre-16 to advanced level study. These measures include careful A-level syllabus selection, additional personal tuition or bridging or induction courses at the beginning of year 12. Research carried out by the Royal Society of Chemistry into changes in GCSE chemistry 1988–95 also supports the conclusion that it is not only balanced science through a double award GCSE which is leading to poor progression to A-level. These researchers found evidence that in some ways balanced science examinations were superior to single subject chemistry as a preparation for A-levels. Principles of teaching for progression are discussed in Chapter 3.6.

Employer and HE Tutor Perspectives

There has been a growing consensus of opinion between employers and tutors in higher education about ways in which 16–19 science education can better meet their needs. In an extensive study carried out for the Dearing Review of 16–19 education employers from science-based organisations and higher education science tutors were asked to state the topics they wanted to see taught (Coles and Matthews, 1995). The research methodology was designed to avoid the trap of producing 'wish' lists which would require everything scientific to be included in syllabuses. The essential requirements of employers and tutors were matched to A-level syllabuses and the specifications for the Advanced Science GNVQ. The conclusions of the researchers were that neither the A-levels nor the GNVQs wholly satisfied the needs of employers. The A-levels did not place sufficient emphasis on important skills such as communication, working with others and information seeking and handling. The Advanced Science GNVQ did not include sufficient background knowledge in some areas. More research work needs to be done to ensure post-16 qualifications better match the needs of those who use them in recruitment. This would be in the best interests of all concerned, especially students.

Science as a Means of Developing General Skills

Without a good range of general skills students are unlikely to make good progress in their studies or in the work place. There is much written on this subject and a strong consensus that students should be encouraged to develop good general skills. The skills which receive most attention are communication skills, numeracy and use of ICT. There are other skills which are high on the agenda of recruiters of people for jobs and courses. These are abilities to work with others, problem solving and management of study or projects. Research shows that these skills are best learned in context and scientific learning is capable of providing rich settings for these skills to develop. Good examples are collaboration with others during practical work and the presentation of findings of investigations. The experience of GNVQ Science centres is that the key skills, which are part of the qualification, can be accommodated within the normal learning and assessing of work.

Summary

The late 1990s are seeing post-16 science undergoing significant change at policy level; schools and colleges are seeking ways of responding to the increasing diversity of courses they can offer and the choices students might want to make. A key issue for science education post 16 is how to make science accessible to all students especially those who may not plan to take up a scientific career and those with relatively weak pre-16 achievement. The decline in numbers of students opting for specialist science courses is also a concern.

The range of teaching and learning methods used in post-16 science is limited, especially in A-level classes. The range may need to be expanded so that the preferred learning styles of individuals are more likely to be met for part of their studies. This diversity of methods may attract more students into post-16 study.

About the Author

After teaching in comprehensive schools in Cheshire and a period as science adviser in Suffolk, Mike Coles became lead officer for science at the National Curriculum Council. In 1993 he joined the University of London Institute of Education as NCVQ Research Fellow, managing work on science GNVQs and researching vocational aspects of science education and training. He is currently a Principal Research Officer at QCA and visiting fellow at the Institute of Education.

References and Further Reading

Coles, M. and Matthews, A. (1995) *Fitness for Purpose – a Means of Comparing Qualifications*, London, SCAA and NCVQ.

Dearing, R. (1996) *Review of Qualifications for 16–19 Year Olds*, London, SCAA.

Higginson, G. (1988) *Advancing A-levels*, London, HMSO.

Jenkins, E.W. and Laws, P. M. (1998) *The Transition from GCSE Double Award Balanced Science to A-level in the Sciences*, Centre for Studies in Science and Mathematics Education, School of Education, University of Leeds.

Meagher, N. (1997) *Methods and Effectiveness in Advanced GNVQ Teaching and Learning*, Department of Education, University of Newcastle Upon Tyne.

Osborne J., Black P., Boaler J., Brown M., Driver R., Murray R. and Simon S. (1997) *Attitudes to Science, Mathematics and Technology: A Review of Research*, London, QCA.

Royal Society (1997) *Re-appraising Post-16 Education*, London, Royal Society.

Stanton, G. and Richardson W. (1997) Qualifications for the Future: a Study of Tripartite and Other Divisions in Post-16 Education and Training. *FEDA Report*, 2, 5.

1.5 Science for All

Michael J. Reiss

Pupils differ with respect to such characteristics as gender, ethnicity, class, the extent to which they may have special needs, their preferred learning styles and other aspects of their personality and home culture. Not only do pupils differ in all sorts of ways, but you, their teacher, will have differing expectations of them from your previous knowledge of pupils. What is a science teacher to do with this diversity? Teaching to match pupils' differences in ability is discussed in Chapter 3.5. This chapter argues that to take account of other aspects of this diversity leads to teaching that is both just and a better form of science education. I begin by asking two questions: 'To what extent do we need to provide different curricula, resources and teaching approaches for different categories of pupils?' and 'Do we present some pupils with an understanding of science that makes them feel it is not for them?'. After a review of relevant policy statements, I examine practical work, the use of narrative, language issues, assessment issues and how to challenge racist, sexist and other discriminatory behaviours. Finally, I look at possible ways to teach the topics of separating and purifying mixtures, nuclear power and human reproduction.

Science for All

To what extent do we need to provide different curricula, resources and teaching approaches for different categories of pupils?

Should the same resources be provided for a pupil with a physical disability (such as severe sight impairment) and a pupil without such a disability? Of course not. But should both pupils receive exactly the same curriculum? This question is a harder one. And what of girls and boys? Should they receive identical teaching approaches? I will discuss these questions below. Here it is sufficient to state the two fundamental *criteria* by which such questions will be answered, namely a combination of what is in each pupil's best interests and what is fair. Both criteria are needed: it might be in an individual pupil's best interests to hog a teacher's attention but that wouldn't be fair to the other pupils.

Do we present some pupils with an image of science that makes them feel it is not for them?

Throughout the UK primary age range, pupil enthusiasm for science remains high. During secondary schooling, though, it falls off sharply in physics and chemistry (Osborne, Driver and Simon, 1998). Is this because we provide an image of science that causes many pupils, quite validly, to conclude that such a science is not for them? To ensure that pupils find school science interesting we need to provide science lessons which:

- encourage pupils to believe that they can succeed at science
- are perceived by pupils as relevant
- capture pupils' diverse interests.

One very positive feature of the last fifteen years or so has been the extent to which science educators have taken on board issues to do with equality (Thorp, 1991; Cobern, 1996; Guzzetti and Williams, 1996). Pupils are now exposed to far less bias with regard to the nature of science than was the case until recently. However, much still remains to be done in terms of equality (Thorp, Deshpande and Edwards, 1994; Aikenhead, 1997; Solomon, 1997). While gender inequalities in the UK are considerably less than in many other countries (Harding and McGregor, 1995), girls continue to be several times less likely than boys to continue with the physical sciences once they have the option, while boys are more likely than girls to leave school with no qualifications. In many education authorities, certain ethnic minority pupils, notably African Caribbean, Pakistani and Bangladeshi pupils, continue to underperform relative to other pupils, whereas in other education authorities these patterns are reversed (Gillborn and Gipps, 1996). Though underresearched, differences in educational attainments in science and other subjects are very strongly related to class (Croxford, 1997; Robinson and White, 1997).

Policy Statements

Many organisations have produced policy statements relevant to the notion of science for all. The ASE policy on 'Gender and Science Education' includes the following recommendations:

- *Teaching and learning styles should explore and build upon the personal experiences of learners of both sexes, and provide compensatory experiences to avoid reinforcing existing bias.*
- *Assessment schemes should support equal opportunities policies, enabling all young people to recognise their own strengths and weaknesses and thus to influence their own learning.*
- *Resources and displays of learners' work should reflect the principles developed in equal opportunities policies. Display and other materials should ensure that stereotypical views relating to adult roles and to aptitude and ability in science are not reinforced. Opportunities should be provided for girls and boys to interact with women and men in employment areas with a scientific and technological base. Both traditional and non-traditional roles should be represented. Role models in the form of secondary sources about the place of women in science in past ages should also be promoted.* (ASE, 1997a)

A number of these recommendations about gender are echoed in the ASE's policy on 'Race, Equality and Science Education' which also adds its own perspectives:

The science curriculum should emphasise that:

- *science is not neutral; scientists and the pursuit of science are influenced by the environment in which they operate;*
- *people from all societies now and in the past have been involved in scientific exploration and discovery;*
- *there is an interplay between science, technology and society;*
- *there is no scientific or genetic evidence to support racism.*

The teaching and learning of science should:

- *help learners to question the reasons underlying the inequalities between peoples and nations, and relate such issues to those of global interdependence;*
- *question and challenge racist attitudes and assumptions;*
- *provide positive images and avoid stereotypes of people, places and times;*
- *show science as a world-wide human activity;*
- *encourage a global awareness of environmental issues;*
- *build on the cultural background and experiences of learners;*
- *provide specific support for the language development of bilingual learners.* (ASE, 1997b)

Finally, the ASE's policy on 'Access to Science Education' addresses issues that follow from the fact that pupils arrive at science lessons with different levels of physical, sensory, cognitive and emotional development:

Learners can be isolated by sensory, physical, cognitive and emotional problems. Choosing familiar contexts and providing appropriate activities motivates and stimulates learners.

Appropriate science experiences will involve:

- *using a range of teaching and learning strategies*
- *developing concepts and skills gradually*
- *matching the demands of the activity to the learner*
- *allowing different outcomes for different individuals*
- *building on the learner's strengths*
- *allowing time for learners to reflect on their work*
- *using a range of methods to monitor progress*
- *ensuring written material is at an appropriate level for each learner*
- *explaining new vocabulary*
- *using first-hand examples to reinforce understanding*
- *using a range of communication methods*
- *adopting a consistent presentation style for written work*
- *ensuring safe working conditions*
- *making effective use of learning support assistants.* (ASE, 1997c)

Exemplification of Practice

The intention of this section is two-fold. First some general guidelines are suggested – with examples – on:

- practical work
- the use of narrative
- language issues
- assessment issues
- challenging racist, sexist and other discriminatory behaviours.

Secondly case studies are provided of possible ways to teach about the topics of:

- separating and purifying mixtures
- nuclear power
- human reproduction.

Practical work

Practical work is an important element of science education. Girls and boys often interact differently with their teachers. Girls are more likely to ask for help or reassurance about what to do next. Teachers may accept girls' dependence on them, tell them what to do and thus reinforce feelings of relative helplessness (Murphy, 1991). Boys may get more attention than girls, at least partly because teachers spend time with them attempting to ensure that they don't misbehave, get injured or damage equipment. However, to every generalisation there is at least one exception. Precisely because some teachers strive to be fair to girls, some silent boys can go for months without ever having a science teacher spend any time with them at all (Reiss, in press).

When arranging practical work for pupils with special educational needs, including pupils with severe learning difficulties, it often helps to break down practical activities into small steps. At the same time, consider how apparatus or other facilities in a laboratory can be modified to provide the maximum opportunity for relevant practical work. For further details and excellent case studies see NCC (1992) and Jones (1993). An attractive environment which displays and values pupils' practical activities works wonders.

The use of narrative

Many pupils find much of school science impersonal. It helps to give a human face to science if you tell your pupils some of the wonderful stories about scientists in action. For example:

Marie Curie (1867–1934) worked on radioactivity. She won her first Nobel Prize for Physics with her husband, Pierre Curie. In 1906, after Pierre was knocked down by a horse-drawn wagon and killed, Marie was appointed to fill his vacant chair at the Sorbonne and so became the first woman professor in France. In 1911 opposition by some of her colleagues led to her being refused election to the French Academy of Sciences. Soon after, however, she was awarded her second Nobel Prize, this time for Chemistry. Marie Curie was the epitome of a dedicated scientist. The four years it took her to purify polonium and radium from pitchblende consisted of four years of continuous hard physical work, often spending day after day stirring the great quantities of material. She and Pierre refused to take advantage of the lucrative industry that grew up around their discovery and isolation of radium, believing that investigators should not profit from the results of her research. During the First World War, she and her daughter, Irene, worked in what became known as 'Little Curies', mobile X-ray cars set up by Marie Curie to take X-rays of soldiers injured by lodged bullets.

Ibn al'Haitham *(c.* 965–1038) was an Egyptian Islamic scholar. In the West he is generally known as Alhazen. He rejected the accepted belief that light was emitted by the eye, and took the view that light was emitted from self-luminous sources, was reflected and refracted and then entered the eye. He wrote a book called *The Treasury of Optics.* In this he discussed lenses, plane mirrors, curved mirrors and the workings of the camera obscura. He had a lathe on which he made the lenses and mirrors for his experiments. He studied spherical aberration and realised that in a parabolic mirror all the rays are concentrated at one point so that it is the best type of burning mirror. His work on refraction led him to the principle of 'least time' in the determination of the path taken by a light ray. Al'Haitham only turned to physics in middle age as he spent much of his early adulthood pretending to be mad. This was to avoid being punished (possibly even put to death) by the Caliph al-Hakim whom he had upset by his failure to devise a method of controlling the annual flooding of the Nile. Once the Caliph died in 1021, al'Haitham promptly regained his health and started work again.

Charles Drew (1904–50) was an Afro-American doctor who invented blood banks. He was born in a Washington ghetto and in 1933 received his Master of Surgery and Doctor of Medicine degrees. During the Second World War, Drew was approached by the British government and asked to start a blood-bank programme for use on the battlefield. It was so successful that he was asked to organise an inter-national blood-bank project and to become the first Director of the American Red Cross Blood Bank. Although he received many awards and honours, Drew experi-enced racism all his life. In 1941 he resigned his position with the American Red Cross Blood Bank after it was decided that blood from black donors should not be mixed with blood from white donors. In 1950 he was seriously injured in a car acci-dent in North Carolina. He needed a blood transfusion but the hospital he was rushed to refused to treat him because he was black. Drew died before reaching a hospital that would treat him.

Pupils can be encouraged to write imaginatively. What would it have been like to be Marie Curie or Ibn al'Haitham or Charles Drew? For further biographies of scientists and examples of how the history of science can be used to enrich science teaching see Solomon (1991), Ellis (1992) and Reiss (1993).

Language Issues

Chapter 3.3 deals with the language of science classrooms. Here it is useful to consider approaches which allow all pupils access to science:

• Encourage pupils to talk about science with one another in the language and terms they want (whether or not they are bilingual).

- Label shelves and cupboards where equipment is kept in the language(s) familiar to pupils. Pupils themselves can help provide these labels.
- Provide a copy of the Laboratory Rules in each pupil's home language.
- Ensure that all writing intended for pupils is sufficiently large and clear to be visible.
- Ensure that all relevant oral contributions, whether by pupils or yourself, are audible.
- Keep alert to the possibility that some pupils would benefit from specialist equipment (e.g. glasses, hearing aids, Braille transcripts, pocket tape recorders).
- Liaise well in advance of lessons, even if only briefly, with language and other classroom assistants.

Assessment Issues

It is probably impossible to come up with a single assessment instrument that is universally fair to all pupils. For example, gender bias is accentuated by having science tests that are either all essays (generally favour girls) or all multiple choice (generally favour boys). The best practice is to adopt a range of assessment procedures (see Chapter 3.2). Care also needs to be taken when setting and marking homework. While it is excellent practice to enable pupils to make use of their home environment, tasks that require access to books or home computers may severely disadvantage low-income families.

A subtler problem is that valid contributions may not always be recognised. In one instance, pupils aged 8 to 15 were given the task of designing boats to go around the world:

> *The pupils' designs covered a wide range but there were striking differences between those of boys and girls. The majority of the boats designed by boys were powerboats or battleships of some kind or another The detail the boys included varied but generally there was elaborate weaponry and next to no living facilities. Other features included detailed mechanisms for movement, navigation and waste disposal. The girls' boats were generally cruisers with a total absence of weaponry and a great deal about living quarters and requirements, including food supplies and cleaning materials (notably absent from the boys' designs). Very few of the girls' designs included any mechanistic detail.* (Murphy, 1991, p 120)

It was clear that if a teacher had in mind that what was crucial was the mechanical ability to go round the world, then the girls' designs would do less well. Related to this is the Pygmalion effect, i.e. teachers tend to give work higher marks if it is from pupils whom they expect to get high marks. Experiments have shown that science scripts with boys' names on them are sometimes marked significantly higher than identical scripts with girls' names on them (Spear, 1984).

Challenging Racist, Sexist and Other Discriminatory Behaviours

There should be a whole-school policy on this and it should be followed. Any teacher, ideally any adult on school premises, should make it clear to the perpetrator of the discrimination, the person/people discriminated against and any onlookers that such behaviour is completely unacceptable. In addition, any offending literature should be confiscated and graffiti quickly removed. If these procedures are adopted, and if your school has appropriate sanctions in place, discriminatory behaviours including name calling should be less frequent than otherwise. Good sex education and good tutorial work can help reduce sexism, sexual harassment, racism and other sorts of unacceptable behaviour, e.g. towards pupils with disabilities. It is possible that science education could play a distinctive role in helping pupils scientifically to examine whether such discrimination is reasonable.

Case Studies

Separating and Purifying Mixtures

The very diversity of ways in which mixtures can be separated and purified makes a pluralist approach particularly straightforward. I remember seeing one very successful lesson where much of the time was spent looking at various objects used for separating things that had been brought in by the 12- and 13-year-olds from home. Such an activity could then lead into a discussion of the principles behind the various approaches to separation and purification. It is worth getting pupils to think about why people separate and purify mixtures:

- Why do people want pure salt?
- What can be got from distillation?
- What use is it that iron can be separated from aluminium through the action of magnets?
- How can the fact that different substances have different melting points be used to good effect?
- When is it a nuisance that mixtures separate out? (e.g. salad dressings, paints)

For the historical roles in the separation and purification of mixtures played by such people as Mary the Jewess, the Islamic alchemists and others see Reiss (1993, pp 82–3).

Nuclear Power

Here are some possible classroom activities for pupils to tackle when learning about nuclear power:

- Research the roles played by such scientist as Henri Becquerel, Ernest Rutherford, Marie Curie and Lise Meitner.
- Plot a map of the distribution of nuclear power stations around the globe and suggest reasons for the results observed.
- Plot graphs of the decrease in radioactivity in vegetation in Cumbria in the years after Chernobyl and compare the results with government predictions.
- Explain how carbon dioxide emissions from electricity-producing stations in France fell by two-thirds from 1980 to 1987.

- Write to both pro- and anti-nuclear power organisations asking them the same specific questions, e.g. 'How safe is nuclear power?' and 'How important is it for electricity generation?'
- Examine the medical evidence for and against an increase in the incidence of leukaemia around certain nuclear power stations.
- Design and use a questionnaire to investigate fellow pupils' knowledge of and attitudes towards nuclear power.
- Role play a Cabinet meeting trying to decide whether to extend a country's nuclear power programme or to scrap it.
- Write an imaginary letter from one of the servicemen or indigenous people on test islands like Bikini Atoll.

For a fuller discussion see Wellington (1986).

Human Reproduction

The topic of human reproduction is obviously one best dealt with sensitively. Here are some suggestions to reduce the likelihood of discriminating against certain pupils:

- Ensure that your school's sex education policy is followed and that parents (and, ideally, pupils) are involved in the design of your science department's contribution to the school's sex-education programme.
- Tell pupils about the range of ages over which people reach puberty.
- Help pupils to examine the degree to which the treatments of human reproduction in their science textbooks are sexist. (Many science textbooks fail to mention the clitoris though all mention the penis; mention of female orgasms is often omitted; contraception is often presumed to be the responsibility primarily of females.)
- Avoid stigmatising certain religions (e.g. Islam and attitudes to differences between the sexes; Roman Catholicism and contraception).
- Help pupils to explore what it would be like to have a gender, sexual orientation or religious faith different from their own.

For a fuller discussion see Reiss (1997) and Reiss (1998).

Concluding Remarks

There are two main reasons for ensuring that one's science teaching is 'Science for all'. One is that such teaching is just; the second is that such teaching is better science teaching. Two main things hold back some teachers from teaching in the ways advocated in this chapter. One is that such teaching requires a continual degree of reflection – 'Which pupils haven't I dealt with yet?', 'Are certain pupils dominating practical work?', etc. The second is that if such teaching is something to which you aren't yet used, it requires a certain effort. One needs, for example, to learn up about the contributions made by different cultures to science and to be firm in ensuring that all pupils in a class are treated fairly. However, such teaching is worth it.

About the Author

Michael J. Reiss is Senior Lecturer in Biology at Homerton College and a Priest in the Church of England. After a PhD and post-doctoral research in evolutionary biology he taught in schools before returning to higher education. His research and writing interests are in science education, sex education and bioethics.

References and Further Reading

Aikenhead, G. S. (1997) Toward a First Nations Cross-cultural Science and Technology Curriculum. *Science Education*, No 81, pp 217–38.

ASE (1997a) *Gender and Science Education: Policy Statement,* Hatfield, ASE.

ASE (1997b) *Race, Equality and Science Teaching: Policy Statement,* Hatfield, ASE.

ASE (1997c) *Access to Science Education: Policy Statement,* Hatfield, ASE.

Cobern, W. W. (1996) Constructivism and Non-western Science Education Research. *International Journal of Science Education*, No 18, pp 295–310.

Croxford, L. (1997) Participation in Science Subjects: the Effect of the Scottish Curriculum Framework. *Research Papers in Education*, No 12, pp 69–89.

Ellis, P. (1992) *Science Changes!* Hemel Hempstead, Simon and Schuster.

Gilborn, D. and Gipps, C. (1996) *Recent Research on the Achievements of Ethnic Minority Pupils*, London, HMSO.

Guzzetti, B. J. and Williams, W. (1996) Gender, Text and Discussion: Examining Intellectual Safety in the Science Classroom. *Journal of Research in Science Teaching*, No 33, pp 5–20.

Harding, S. and McGregor, E. (1995) *The Gender Dimension of Science and Technology*, Paris, UNESCO.

Jones, A. (1993) *Science Education for Pupils with Special Needs,* Nottingham, Nottingham Trent University.

Murphy, P. (1991) Gender Differences in Pupils' Reactions to Practical Work. In: Woolnough, B. E. (Ed.) *Practical Science: The Rule and Reality of Practical Work in School Science,* Milton Keynes, Open University Press, pp 112–22.

NCC (1992) *Curriculum Guidance 10: Teaching Science to Pupils with Special Educational Needs*, York, National Curriculum Council.

Osborne, J. F., Driver, R. and Simon, S. (1998) Attitudes to Science: Issues and Concerns, *School Science Review*.

Reiss, M. J. (1993) *Science Education for a Pluralist Society*, Buckingham, Open University Press.

Reiss, M. J. (1997) Teaching about Homosexuality and Heterosexuality. *Journal of Moral Education,* No 26, pp 343–52.

Reiss, M. J. (1998). The Representation of Human Sexuality in Some Science Textbooks for 14–16 Year-olds. *Research in Science and Technological Education*.

Reiss, M. J. (In press) *Understanding Science Lessons*, Buckingham, Open University Press.

Robinson, P. and White, P. (1997) *Participation in Post-Compulsory Education,* Twickenham, Centre for Education and Employment Research, School of Education, Brunel University.

Solomon, J. (1991) *Exploring the Nature of Science,* Glasgow, Blackie.

Solomon, J (1997) Girls' Science Education: Choice, Solidarity and Culture. *International Journal of Science Education*, No 19, pp 407–17.

Spear, M. G. (1984) The Biasing Influence of Pupil Sex in a Science Marking Exercise. *Research in Science and Technological Education*, No 2, pp 55–60.

Thorp, S. (Ed) (1991) Race, Equality and Science Teaching: An Active INSET Manual for Teachers and Educators, Hatfield, ASE.

Thorp, S., Deshpande, P. and Edwards, C. (Eds.) (1994) *Race, Equality and Science Teaching*, Hatfield, ASE.

Wellington, J. J. (1986) The Nuclear Issue in the Curriculum and the Classroom. In Wellington, J. J. (Ed), *Controversial Issues in the Classroom*, Oxford, Basil Blackwell, pp 149–68.

Useful addresses

Access to Information on Multicultural Education, AIMER, Reading and Language Information Centre, University of Reading, Bulmershe Court, Earley, Reading RG6 IHE, Tel 01734 857123 extn 4871.

National Association for Gifted Children, Elder House, Milton Keynes MK9 1LR, Tel 01908 673677.

Oxfam, Oxfam House, 274 Banbury Road, Oxford 0X2 7DZ Tel 01865 311311.

Women into Science and Engineering, The Engineering Council, 10 Maltravers Street, London WC2R 3ER; Tel 0171 240 7891.

For a good web site about women in every field of science see http://scienceweb.dao.nrc.ca/can/women/

Science Education from a European Perspective

Joan Solomon

This chapter explores the differences and similarities in science education across Europe.

Can Science Education really be Different?

Science is an international endeavour; it is almost an ethic of science that it will ignore differences of nationality, creed and race in those who contribute to its work. Apart from during the period of the Second World War, young scientists have always been free to study first in one European university and then in another, and they found the research being done in their field both complementary and continuous. They all read then, and still do, the same scientific journals. With that in mind it is not surprising to find that the content of the science curriculum is effectively the same in almost all the countries of Europe, especially in the secondary schools. Pupils everywhere have to learn about photosynthesis and Ohm's Law, the Periodic Classification of the elements, and all the other great ideas of science. There is some variation in the age at which they meet the different topics because of variations in the number of lessons given, when they start school, and the amount of choice and specialisation that pupils are allowed. These variations depend on several very broad factors:

- the perceived *purposes* of science education
- the national attitude to how *school education* should be carried out
- the national attitude towards *science as a system of thought*.

National curricula rarely stipulate exactly *how* science lessons are to be conducted in the schools, although they offer advice on the subject (and inspect rather less than in England!) and this is clearly crucial to the formation of pupils' attitudes towards science. Not only is the conduct of lessons affected by the teachers' perceptions of the nature of science as a system of thought – abstract and mathematical, or empirical and technical – it will also depend on educational traditions, such as whether children should be positively encouraged to co-operate in their study, and what is a suitable activity for a school teacher to perform (in France, Italy and many other countries no supervisory duties are carried out by secondary teachers).

A curious factor is the way that the boundaries of 'science' change from country to country. In Portugal, for example, Social Science, History and Geography are all included under the heading 'Science', and in France, Science and Mathematics are taught together in the upper secondary school. While the overall content learnt by pupils is generally unchanged by variations in these subject boundaries, attitudes towards 'science' may well be affected.

The Purposes of Education

The cultural diversity within Europe may be denser and richer than that in any other continent. First we may find quite general differences which affect broad *institutional factors in education* such as national and political attitudes towards:

- standardisation and uniformity (e.g. France)
- efficiency and market forces (e.g. UK)
- school autonomy (e.g. Sweden)
- a legal edict against labelling by ability (e.g. Denmark).

In addition there are differences in preferred *regulative principles of thought* which affect all education. These are naturally interesting to teachers since, without being mutually exclusive, they identify some very deep-seated motivations for education and for teaching, especially perhaps in science. They first arose as educational philosophies within Europe at different times and places, and the emphasis placed on each now varies from country to country. The major strands are called humanism, rationalism and naturalism.

Humanism

This focuses upon education for the formation of character. Sweden, and other Scandinavian countries, believe strongly that the purpose of education is to develop character and citizenship, just as the British public schools believe in developing character and leadership. Therein lies a substantial difference. While Swedish schools in the 1960s were already comprehensive and providing wide-ranging sex education for pupils according to their interpretation of the humanist precept, in our country other humanist arguments were still used to support grammar school selection to pick out able children and train them for the more responsible positions in society. Norwegian education, for example, favours small village schools which keep in close contact with their communities, while British educational authorities try to close small schools on the grounds of economics and lack of competition. Nevertheless both countries share a humanist vision of education's mission to cultivate the whole child – moral disposition as well as intelligence, and even bodily well-being, where that is thought to be connected with character.

Rationalism

This strand in European education is usually traced back to the philosopher Rene Descartes but it stands equally firmly in the tradition of mediaeval scholasticism. Here it is only the intellect of the child which is being trained, and not the character. In some ways, the French would argue, it leads to an 'égalité' in education which matches a deep principle in their national aspirations. It leads, however, to a curriculum of largely abstract topics, especially in mathematics and science, and an assessment method which is rigorous and positivist. Indeed the humanist educational systems mentioned before may look towards those of the rationalists with some envy. Who, after all, can hope to assess the character-forming objectives of a humanist system as rigorously as the logical ones of rationalism?

Sometimes selection by ability sits comfortably within rationalism since those who succeed in competitive examinations in school are likely to go on succeeding in them, and skill in the kind of problem-solving required in examinations is very easily equated with high intelligence when the latter is measured in a similar way. Teachers within this kind of system are also selected from amongst those who score well in degree examinations and are not thought to need much extra training, if any at all, before starting to pass on their science expertise to pupils. This sort of education is essentially a transmission process and teachers are *not* considered to be *in loco parentis*, as in the British system, nor burdened with responsibility for the moral development of their pupils. Thus it is only within the last ten years that France, Spain and Italy have required their science graduates to train at all before entering the teaching profession.

What is likely to work less well in the rationalist tradition is a mixed ability comprehensive system which still tries to teach in this tradition, as many of the modern French lycees are doing. This problem has been the subject of a recent OECD report and it results, in the worst cases, in *wild children and desperate teachers*. This is not because the system is marking out some children for a lower status, but because the curriculum, especially in Science and Mathematics, is intellectually demanding and presented in an abstract mode. French schools still teach Mathematics as the 'Queen of Sciences', usually avoid any discussion of social issues, and may offer their pupils limited practical work in the laboratory.

Linked with this intellectualism is the encyclopaedic tradition of the Enlightenment. In education this produces a tendency towards systematisation, which at its best makes for a wide respect for knowledge, and at its worst for rote learning.

Naturalism

The basic contrast between this tradition, and the other two mentioned, is that naturalist education is seen as an interior process, rather than one received (some of these radical educationalists might well have substituted the word *inflicted*) externally from school teachers. From Rousseau to Illitch, and William Morris to Pestalozzi and Steiner, there have been voices raised for the last two centuries which questioned whether the school as institution, with its top-down delivery of knowledge, was the right way to educate children. The argument still continues, but it should be stressed that if naturalism were no more than a radical de-schooling movement it would have no place in the educational literature. Its thinking is much more complex and constructive than this, and in some countries, such as Denmark, its influence is to be found right at the heart of school and college teaching.

Many of the themes that later naturalist educators developed were already to be found in Rousseau's *Emile* first published in 1762. These include respect for the 'natural state' of the child coupled with freedom to observe natural objects, a deep suspicion of all institutions including schools, and a dedication to the principle that children should make their own steps forward when they were ready to do so. The prime educational objective is the cultivation of creative thought.

The long continuing German debate about the nature of 'bildung' – education in the sense of 'forming the whole individual personality' – ensures that their educational systems are, at least in part, a nurturing process which brings out the inner potentiality of the child. In England the influence of Continental naturalism arrived late, and then came into conflict with H.E.Armstrong's more structured heuristic practical methods of teaching science. His account of *The Heuristic Method of Teaching, or the Art of Making Children Discover Things for Themselves* (1898), showed its distance from more radical naturalism by the use of the word making.

Naturalist approaches have always been a reaction against the formalism of school teaching. They are no longer confined by national frontiers because of their transformation and re-introduction from America in two successive waves during the present century. The earliest brought over were the ideas of John Dewey and focused on project work which is to be found all over Europe and is particularly strong in England and Denmark. The second wave brought the inspiring ideas of Jerome Bruner which included discovery learning.

Primary Science

Science is being taught in primary schools across almost all of Europe, and often by non-specialist teachers. Of course all the teacher educators bemoan the lack of scientific knowledge in their teachers, none more so than in the rationalist countries who have a vested interest in 'getting the concepts right'. These are the countries most likely to employ specialist teachers as early as possible (Poland and France). In terms of 'connectedness' it is the non-specialist teachers and the cross-curriculum teaching which is most likely to supply the transferability of scientific knowledge which lies at the root of popular culture. British pupils are the only ones to be assessed on their skills of investigations. In most other European countries the primary curriculum is less specific. Often practical investigations rarely take place at all, and no mention is made of topics in either physics or chemistry.

There is anxiety about how primary science is being taught. Most EU member states have decided that 'The Environment' is the most suitable topic for primary science. Sometimes it seems to comprise all of what is taught, and in countries such as Sweden and Spain, voices are questioning whether just feelings for animals and preserving the countryside might not be swamping out the teaching of scientific concepts. There is also worry in the more rationalist countries that 'Integrated Science' might be dissolving away the old science disciplines. Even the pun about school science *disintegrating* is common. Nevertheless science is usually much enjoyed by young children and this may provide a promising growth point for science as popular culture.

Practical Work and Technology

These are two ways in which British science education differs from that in most other European countries. We have compulsory assessed practical work and although many other countries exhort teachers to get their pupils to perform investigations, it does not happen regularly. The poorer countries, like Ireland and Greece, often blame this on to their lack of well-equipped laboratories but even when there is the latest apparatus, as in Germany, it may be used more for teachers' demonstrations than by the pupils, and mostly for rather routine practical work than for pupils' own investigations.

Finally there are unresolved controversies about the inclusion of what is variously called 'Technology' or 'Technics' in the school curriculum. In different European countries it may be:

- a study of the main *industrial means of production* (e.g. Italy) with or without a discussion of social effects
- only *Information Technology* and the use of computers
- acquisition of *workshop skills for the designing and making of technological artefacts* (e.g. the Netherlands, Denmark and the UK at junior secondary level).

In Poland and Italy technology is linked with physics. It is based within the science curriculum at various levels of secondary school in Greece, Denmark and the Netherlands. In Spain, Portugal, Belgium and the UK is it a separate subject. In Switzerland, Ireland, France and most German lander, technology does not figure at all for mainstream pupils except as IT. In Sweden technology now has all three of the meanings mentioned above, as a separate curriculum subject. Elsewhere it may be confined to a vocational stream.

Despite the English placing of Design and Technology as an important subject for all primary and secondary pupils, its natural successor – Engineering – is probably less popular here than in almost any other country. Our legacy of a humanistic view of education, as fitting children for their place in life, may have encouraged practical work only in the Victorian Trade Schools, and the 1944 Technical Schools, and that low status has dogged its progress ever since. Be that as it may, some Europeans look to our curriculum demands for Design and Technology with a rather inflated admiration. In Portugal and Hungary admiration may run the other way when we find that Engineering is the university goal of a large number of their school pupils and attracts almost as many girls as boys!

About the Author

Joan Solomon taught Science, Physics, and Science Technology and Society in a number of secondary schools for more than 25 years. While teaching she authored one of the first STS school courses and obtained a PhD at Kings College, London. She became a PGCE Tutor at Oxford and carried out many commissioned research projects. She is now Professor of Science Education at the Open University.

SECTION 2

Learning Science: Concepts, Skills and Values

Learning Science Concepts in the Secondary Classroom

Phil Scott and John Leach

Imagine the scene: a Key Stage 3 science class is learning about gas pressure. The teacher is asking the pupils to think about, 'How you are able to drink through a straw'. Most pupils in the class explain the drink moving up the straw in terms of their own personal action: 'You suck it up'. Air is not mentioned. By contrast, the teacher draws upon the concept of air pressure. She explains the same phenomenon in terms of the relative air pressure at the surface of the drink and at the top of the straw.

In this chapter, we shall consider how such differences in explanations arise and discuss the implications of these differences in 'ways of knowing' for teaching and learning scientific concepts.

Everyday Knowledge and Scientific Knowledge

Scientific explanations of phenomena such as drinking through a straw are based on a formal concept, explicitly defined by a particular community to serve an agreed function following a process of careful testing and checking. Here we are concerned with the scientific community, and the scientific explanation for drinking through a straw is based upon the formal concept of air pressure. This single concept is used to explain many disparate phenomena such as the inflation of balloons, the action of rubber suckers, how sink plungers work and so on. In science the idea is that explanations based on particular concepts should be generalisable, in a consistent way, to as broad a range of phenomena as possible.

Things are often different with everyday explanations. In everyday situations there is no need for explanations of different phenomena to be consistent with one another: everyday explanations often draw upon a range of ideas. Thus you can drink through a straw by the physical action of 'sucking', balloons stay inflated because they are 'full of air', the sink plunger works because it 'sticks to the sink'. An important point here is that everyday ways of talking about objects and events have different purposes from scientific explanations. When someone says that they are sucking orange juice through a straw, everybody understands what is meant, and in the sense that the main purpose of everyday talk is communication the 'explanation' has worked.

Formal scientific concepts such as air pressure cannot be 'seen' by simple observation of drinking straws, balloons and sink plungers; they are not there to be 'discovered' in the objects and events which they are used to explain. Ideas such as air pressure provide new 'conceptual tools' which can be used by people in talking and thinking about objects and how they work. Some ideas, of course, fit the available evidence better than others. Science teachers have the task of teaching their pupils how to talk and think about the world using scientific concepts, with their specific purposes and associated limitations. This task can be complicated by the fact that everyday and scientific views of a single phenomenon may draw upon the same words (such as 'pressure', 'air') but with very different meanings attached. As we shall see in the next section, the word 'air' is sometimes used to mean 'nothing' in everyday situations, whereas in a scientific context 'air' is a substantial medium which is capable of exerting large pressures.

One Example of Pupils' Everyday Thinking

A great deal of research has been carried out internationally to probe the content and nature of pupils' everyday thinking or 'alternative conceptions' about natural phenomena. The research into alternative conceptions is well documented (see, for example, NCC 1993; Driver *et al,* 1994). Here we shall consider the nature of students' everyday thinking about 'air'.

Everyday Thinking about Air

Much of the science studied by secondary school pupils draws upon concepts relating to the structure of matter in some way. The basic notion that matter is fundamentally the same 'stuff' irrespective of what state it is in, is a seemingly trivial point which is actually fundamental to scientific explanations. It enables us to understand, for example, how gaseous carbon dioxide and liquid water can be used in the synthesis of solid wood during photosynthesis.

Secondary school pupils' everyday notions about matter, and especially gases, are often significantly different from the scientific models introduced in school. For example, the work of Brook and Driver (1989) suggests that many secondary age pupils think of air as weighing nothing, or as having 'negative weight' and making things lighter (see Fig 2.1A).

Formative Assessment and the Notion of 'Learning Demand'

In the previous section, some of the differences between scientific and everyday thinking about air have been outlined. An important job for teachers is to be clear about the demands that specific curriculum content is likely to make on pupils as they attempt to move from their existing ideas to the scientific point of view.

In some learning situations the task is simply a matter of getting pupils to draw upon familiar knowledge in one context and to use it in another. For example, by the secondary years most pupils know about the existence of micro-organisms and that they can cause disease; it is probably a relatively simple matter to persuade such pupils that micro-organisms can do many other things, including causing decay. In other cases, the task is more difficult as it involves introducing students to a whole new 'way of knowing' about familiar phenomena. An example of this is introducing

Pupils aged 5–16 were asked to explain what would happen to the balance beam as air was added to, and removed from, the balloons:

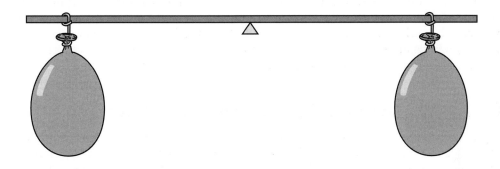

The frequency of different types of reasoning about the effect of air on the mass with age is shown on the graph below:

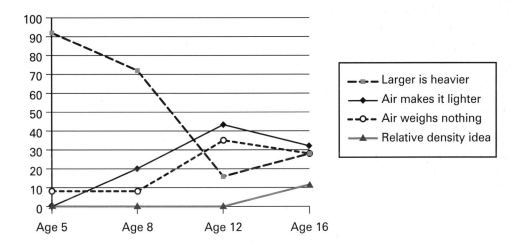

Fig 2.1A The weight of air (from Driver and Brook (1989))

pupils to the idea that air is substantial (and composed of matter) in the same way that solids and liquids are.

In the introduction to a seminal book on educational psychology, David Ausubel made the now well-known statement:

> *The most important single factor influencing learning is what the learner already knows. Ascertain this and teach him accordingly.* (Ausubel, 1968)

This point of view is consistent with more recent ideas of *formative assessment* where on-going assessment of pupils is drawn upon in planning and implementing subsequent teaching steps (see Chapter 3.2). What we are advocating in this chapter perhaps goes one step further in suggesting that the teacher needs to be aware not only of the child's present understandings in planning teaching but the nature of any *differences* between those existing understandings and the scientific view. We have previously (Leach and Scott, 1995) referred to this difference between pupils' every-day ways of knowing, and the scientific ways of knowing that are being taught, as the *learning demand* of a particular topic for pupils.

Given the notion of starting where the pupils are at, a key question is still left hanging. What might 'teach accordingly' actually involve? Of course, there is no simple algorithm to guide the teacher, many different teaching approaches can be successful. However we believe that a view of science learning as taking on new concepts or 'ways of knowing' by pupils with well-developed everyday knowledge does have some implications for teaching and these are considered in the next section.

Implications for Teaching: Activities, Explanations and Talk

The first obvious point to make is that if learning science involves taking on new ways of knowing (as developed and validated by the scientific community) then the teacher has the job of introducing those new ways of knowing. Pupils will not 'discover' them for themselves. The key challenge for the teacher is to make the scientific view available to pupils whilst being sensitive to any differences between everyday and scientific ways of knowing.

In many respects introducing the scientific view can be likened to telling a story (Scott, 1996). The teacher is presenting a particular story or explanation based on scientific concepts. We can think of the teacher as 'performing' the science story, making it available to all of the pupils in the class. During the presentation of the science story pupils are likely at different times both to take part in, and to act as an audience to, the performance. The teacher who is sensitive to pupils' thinking will respond to their ideas as the story unfolds; their comments and questions can alter the way in which the story develops. The skill of the teacher is to control the inter-actions so that the performance retains its coherence and leads to the portrayal of the science way of knowing (see Chapter 3.3).

Talking through a Scientific Explanation

How might a science teacher set about introducing a scientific explanation? On first consideration this appears to be a trivial question: doesn't the teacher just *tell* the pupils?

In the following paragraphs a brief episode from a science lesson is analysed; the analysis suggests that maybe things are not quite so simple as the teacher 'just telling'.

The teacher (who we shall call Jim) is working with a Year 8 class on air pressure explanations for various phenomena. Jim has already introduced the idea that reducing the amount of air in a fixed space reduces the air pressure in that space. Now he is about to show how that rule can be applied to a new context. Jim calls the class to the front of the room where two partially inflated balloons are positioned under a bell jar which is connected to a vacuum pump (Fig 2.1B).

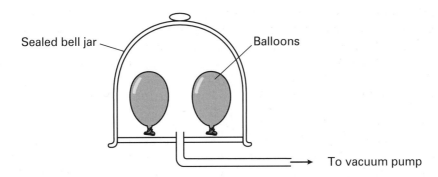

Fig 2.1B

Jim first describes the apparatus to the class (the underlining of certain words indicates points of <u>emphasis</u> by the teacher):

Teacher: *This big jar's [the bell jar] got two bungs in. One of them's got a little valve in it so we can connect the pump to it...inside it, it's just air – we hope – and the're two balloons which have got a <u>tiny</u> bit of air in. They're partly blown up but then there's been a knot tied in the neck of the balloon...and then put a bung in the top [of the jar]...fits so it's quite tight and we're going to connect it to the air remover.*

As Jim describes the apparatus he thus draws attention to various practical features (inside the bell jar, 'it's just air'; the two balloons 'have got a tiny bit of air in').

He switches on the pump and the balloons begin to slowly inflate, much to the amusement of the class:

Pupils: *They're going up. Yeah, Yeah they <u>are!</u> They're floating...*[much laughter]*...they're going to pop! I hope they do!*

Jim now draws attention to something which one pupil, Michael, has been muttering to him during the demonstration:

Teacher: *Hang on, hang on. Just you hang on a minute Michael. Alright I'm going to have to stop this now.*
Pupils: Look, look ...[laughter].
Teacher: [teacher switches off the pump] *Michael's just told me that if we suck all the air out of this jar, the pressure in the jar is less. There's <u>low</u> pressure 'cos there's <u>less</u> air in the jar. Now what's the next bit Michael? Why should that make the balloons go up?*
Michael: *Cos the balloons, erm, have got the same air pressure as outside still, so that when there's less air pressure in the jar there's more air pressure in the balloons and, cos the pressure is more, it, inflates.*

Michael's ideas are consistent with the scientific view. Jim therefore repeats what Michael has said, then pauses and asks Michael to continue, 'Why should that make the balloons go up?'. Michael continues with the explanation and Jim responds:

Teacher: *Good lad! We haven't affected the air in the balloon because the air in the balloon is fixed, it's been sealed in when somebody tied a knot in the balloon, so* *we're only taking air away from inside the jar. We're not taking air out of the balloons. The air in the balloons stays the same, that's the same air pressure as they are right <u>now</u> before we started connecting the pump.*

Jim thus reacts positively to Michael's explanation ('Good lad!') and then reviews the scientific explanation drawing particular attention to the fact that the air inside the balloons has *not* been disturbed.

Jim finally repeats the full explanation once more, speaking in a *slow* and *deliberate* voice thus marking the importance of the ideas:

Teacher: *So if we make <u>less</u> air in the jar, there's <u>less</u> air pressure in the jar, the pressure in the balloons is still the <u>same</u> as it was before and so the balloons inflate.*

Talking around the Phenomenon

This brief episode focuses on a memorable demonstration which constituted just one small part of a teaching sequence in which an air pressure explanation was first introduced by the teacher and then used to explain various phenomena.

In doing so Jim first drew attention to features of the apparatus (such as the balloons being knotted) which are central to presenting the pressure difference explanation and which might also act as a source of confusion for pupils (perhaps extra air gets into the balloons). Jim then focused upon the ideas of one of the pupils, Michael, in presenting the scientific view and making it available to the whole class. There was a very strong sense of 'public performance' as Jim repeated Michael's words and then invited him to continue with the explanation – 'Now what's the next bit Michael?' In this way Jim was able to break down the presentation of the scientific explanation into its main parts and jointly perform the explanation with Michael in front of the class. The performance was further elaborated through Jim: adopting a 'special voice' to signal the importance of key passages of talk; emphasising key words in the explanation; repeating the scientific explanation; summarising the key ideas.

An important general point to recognise here is that the actual physical phenomenon cannot stand by itself in providing an introduction to the scientific view. It is the 'talk around the phenomenon' which is crucial to making the scientific view available to pupils. The phenomenon itself does not, and of course cannot, 'tell the scientific story'. In subsequent lessons the pupils themselves were given the opportunity to engage in talking through the science way of knowing as they were asked to apply it to a range of different phenomena. In this way they were given the chance to make sense of the air pressure explanation (and how to apply it) for themselves.

Recognising the Learning Demand

The context of teaching and learning about air pressure is an interesting one in that the 'learning demand' involved in coming to the scientific view includes a number of different facets.

A fundamental aspect of learning in this context (and many other areas of science) concerns the idea that the scientific view is *generalisable* to a range of different phenomena. Indeed this particular lesson sequence was planned so that the teacher first introduced the scientific view by means of demonstrations and then directed the pupils to apply the new ideas to further different situations. The notion of the *generalisability* of scientific explanations therefore provided a guiding rationale for the lessons and part of the learning demand for this context involves coming to appreciate this powerful feature of scientific knowledge.

A further important aspect of the learning demand concerns coming to understand and to accept the scientific point of view. The point was made earlier that some pupils may consider air as being 'nothing' or lacking substance. For such pupils the notion that the surrounding air can exert pressures of sufficient magnitude to crush plastic bottles or to force drink up through a straw must seem odd to say the least! There is a potential problem relating to the *plausibility* of the scientific explanation. The teacher who is sensitive to the differences between everyday and scientific views will recognise this and acknowledge the point in their teaching, rather than presenting the scientific view as though it were the most obvious thing in the world (which clearly it is not).

Final Comments

Clive Sutton (1996) refers to science learning as 'learning to talk in new ways' and also suggests that part of the job of the science teacher is 'to persuade pupils of the value and reasonableness of those new ways'. This notion of *persuading* pupils resonates with the ideas which are laid out above, where: a sequence of lessons is planned to gradually draw pupils into the scientific view; demonstrations are used as devices to introduce and to practice applying a scientific explanation; key aspects of the *nature* of the scientific knowledge being presented are made explicit; issues relating to the plausibility of the scientific view are directly addressed; opportunities are provided for pupils to talk and think about new ideas for themselves.

In teaching science concepts to pupils we are encouraging or persuading them to take on the ways of talking and thinking of the scientific community.

About the Authors

Dr. Phil Scott is a Lecturer in Physics and Science education at the University of Leeds. Prior to this he was Head of Science in a large comprehensive school in West Yorkshire. He has particular interests in the area of language and learning in science classrooms.

Dr. John Leach is a Lecturer in Science education at the University of Leeds. Previously, he taught chemistry and science in secondary schools. His research focuses upon the role of understanding of the nature of science in science learning. Both Phil Scott and John Leach are members of the Learning In Science (LIS) Research Group at the University of Leeds.

References and Further Reading

Ausubel, D. P. (1968) *Educational Psychology: a Cognitive View*, New York, Holt, Rinehart and Winston.

Brook, A. and Driver, R. (1989) *Progression in Science: The Development of Pupils' Understanding of Physical Characteristics of Air across the Age Range 5–16 Years,* CLIS Research Group, CSSME, University of Leeds.

Driver, R., Squires, A., Rushworth, P. and Wood-Robinson, V. (1994) *Making Sense of Secondary Science,* London, Routledge.

Leach, J. and Scott, P. (1995) The Demands of Learning Science Concepts: Issues of Theory and Practice. *School Science Review,* Vol 76, No 277, pp 47–51.

NCC (1993) Knowledge and Understanding, Chapter 3. In *Teaching Science at Key Stages 3 and 4,* York, National Curriculum Council, pp 56–79.

Scott, P.H. (1996) Social Interactions and Personal Meaning Making in Secondary Science Classrooms. In Welford, G., Osborne, J. and Scott, P. (Eds) *Research in Science Education in Europe,* London, Falmer Press.

Sutton, C. (1996) The scientific model as a form of speech. In Welford, G., Osborne, J., Scott, P. (Eds) *Research in Science Education in Europe.* London, Falmer Press.

2.2 Children's Thinking and Science Learning

Philip Adey

Children's ability to learn depends to an important extent on their ability to process new information. This information-processing capability can be enhanced by a carefully constructed intervention programme which sets challenges and encourages pupils to become conscious of their own thinking. Science provides an excellent context in which such challenging problems can be set, but adopting such an intervention programme requires stepping back from a 'delivery' view of teaching, and recognising that time spent in the early years of secondary schooling to the development of higher-level thinking repays itself later in significantly enhanced learning capability.

How Children Process Information

Passing information from one person to another is a lot more complicated than it may seem. People outside education sometimes believe that if a teacher knows something, and a child does not, then all the teacher has to do is to tell the child what she knows. Anyone who has been a teacher knows that information does not get transferred that easily. And in fact, if anyone were to reflect for a few minutes, they could gain an inkling of what the problem is.

"Daddy, where does rain come from?"

"Well, water from the sea gets evaporated by the sun's heat, it goes into the atmosphere, but when the air is blown over high ground it gets colder, and cold air can hold less water than warm air, so the water condenses, forms drops, and rain falls."

Terrific. 99/100 of children switch of at this point. The 1/100 says, "What's evaporation? What's condensation? Why does the air get colder? Why doesn't cold air hold water?" Either way, not a lot of information has been transferred.

Knowledge is a funny thing. Where is knowledge? In people's heads? In books? In the collective unconscious? Knowledge is in all of these places but, unlike water, it cannot simply be poured from one place to another. This is because knowledge actually consists of an incredibly complex network of understandings deeply embedded in social and cultural assumptions. Knowledge is never a set of isolated items or 'facts' which one person or book can pass to a learner. Even apparently trivial bits of knowledge such as the correct number bus to get from Harrods to Buckingham Palace cannot simply be 'given'. The tourist in London who asks the question may be told, "Number 14 goes nearest". But in which direction? Is there a single fare? Where do I buy the ticket and how do I know when I am there? Only the Londoner who takes all these peripheral pieces of information *for granted* can use the simple answer '14' to any effect.

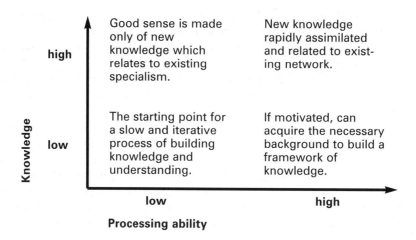

Fig 2.2A Knowledge and processing ability

All information needs to be processed by the receiver. The effectiveness of this information processing depends on a) the existing network of understandings that the receiver already has, and b) the power of her information-processing capability. If these are the two main controlling factors, there are four possibilities, summarised in Fig 2.2A. (See Chapter 2.1 for the role of existing knowledge on learning.)

Our ability to process information develops with age and experience. It involves a qualitative shift in the type of thinking available, a growth in the number of variables that can be held in the mind at once and acted upon. This is the basis of the stages of cognitive development described by Jean Piaget. Children using what he describes as concrete operations are able to understand relationships between two variables, and simple cause – effect relationships. But it requires a higher level of thinking – formal operations – to be able to handle fluently 3 or 4 variable problems. This is what is needed to understand how to control variables. If you cannot hold in mind at one time the possible values of the variables length, mass, and angle of swing of a pendulum, you cannot understand why it is necessary to hold two constant while you change the third. Likewise, proportional thinking requires that a ratio (two variables) be multiplied by a third variable to increase or decrease it by a given proportion. All three variables have to be held in the mind at once and manipulated independently, and such a demand on working memory is what characterises formal operations.

Demand for such formal thinking starts to be made about levels 5 and 6 in the National Curriculum. These form something of a natural barrier of difficulty for progression through the curriculum.

But what exactly is the status of these different levels at which children process information? Do they form some sort of staircase up which all children ascend under the control of pre-determined maturational development of the central nervous system? No, they do not. Although there certainly is an element in the process which depends on maturation, progress is importantly influenced by the child's experiences. In other words, as teachers and as parents, we can have a real influence on the process of cognitive development.

We need to distinguish here between the ideas of *instruction* and of *intervention*. The meaning of instruction is unproblematic: it is the provision of knowledge and understanding through appropriate activities. Instruction can be categorised by topic and by domain and the end product of instruction can be specified in terms of learning objectives.

Intervention here is used in the sense of intervention in the process of cognitive development, that is in manipulating experiences aimed at maximising the rate of progression through the different levels of thinking. Both instruction and intervention are necessary to an effective educational system, but instruction has been emphasised to the neglect of intervention. It could be claimed that intervention actually offers the only route for the further substantial raising of standards in an educational world which has spent the last forty years concentrating on improved instructional methods.

How Much Does It Matter?

For at least 15 years there has been a national campaign under successive governments to 'raise standards' of education. Whilst politicians tend to focus on assessment, goal-setting, inspection, and other essentially external pressures on schools, education professionals are more interested in the mechanisms of learning and teaching. We believe that if we can better understand how children learn, then we can certainly raise academic achievement by improving our professional practice. This is an approach which owes more to research, to theoretical models of learning, and to the professional expertise of teachers than it does to external controls. Here I want to focus on models and research which over the last 20 years have led to a fuller understanding of how children's ability to process information can be enhanced.

The Theory and Practice of Increasing Pupils' Ability

To address directly the development of pupils' ability to process data does not mean trying to teach thinking skills like a set of rules. What we have to do is to provide the conditions under which the complex process of high-level thinking is most likely to develop. The term 'constructivism' is now well known in science education circles, meaning the need for pupils to construct their own knowledge and understanding. In cognitive intervention theory, we also depend on constructivism, but we broaden its meaning to include the pupil's construction of their own higher-level thinking abilities.

Here are some of the principles which are features of intellectually stimulating activities:

- *Challenge*, and the management of support to children in their problem-solving
- *Reflection*: encouraging pupils to become conscious of their own thinking strategies

- Questioning which aids children in the *construction* of 'reasoning patterns' – ways of thinking which have broad application
- *Bridging* the use of reasoning patterns from special contexts to science in general, and to life in general.

I will illustrate each of these principles with specific activities.

Dialogue 1	Dialogue 2
T How do you know the width affects the note?	**T** How do you know the width affects the note?
P The wide one gives a deeper note.	**P** The wide one gives a deeper note.
T But look at the tubes, they have different lengths as well as different widths.	**T** Look at the tubes. How are they different?
P Oh yes.	**P** They are different widths.
T How can you tell whether it is length or width, or both?	**T** Anything else?
P ???	**P** Different lengths.
T You can't, can you? If you change two things, you don't know which is having the effect, do you?	**T** How do you know it is not the length that affects the note?
P I suppose not.	**P** Both the length and the width affect the note.
T OK, go away and choose two tubes which have the same length, but different widths, and try those.	**T** Maybe. But maybe it is just the width, or just the length. How could you tell whether it is length or width, or both?
	P ???
	T Go away and think about it, and try to find a pair of tubes that will prove whether it really is just the width that affects the note.

Fig 2.2B Two dialogues

Take the idea of *challenge*, otherwise known as 'cognitive conflict'. Presented with a bunch of tubes varying in length, width, and material, and asked to find which variable affects the pitch of the note you get when you blow across the tube, a typical 11 year old will choose a short wide one and a long narrow one. He may come to you and say, "I've found that narrow tubes give lower notes than wide tubes". This statement needs to be challenged, but the method of challenge is critical. It should be designed so that the pupil has the best possible chance of constructing the control of variables strategy for himself. Which of the two dialogues shown (Fig 2.2B) do you think is most likely to achieve this?

Let us look now at *reflection*, known in the trade as 'metacognition'. A pupil has been investigating the load and lift forces in a 'wheelbarrow' made of a notched stick, with one end of resting on a table edge, and a load hung from one of the notches (Fig 2.2C). A force meter is hung from the other end to measure the lift. She has recorded the lift as successive loads are added and calculated the ratio of load to lift for each. With quite a bit of help and discussion, and comparing results from other groups she has established that the ratio is approximately constant, and has gone so far as to predict what the lift would be for a load that is too heavy to actually try.

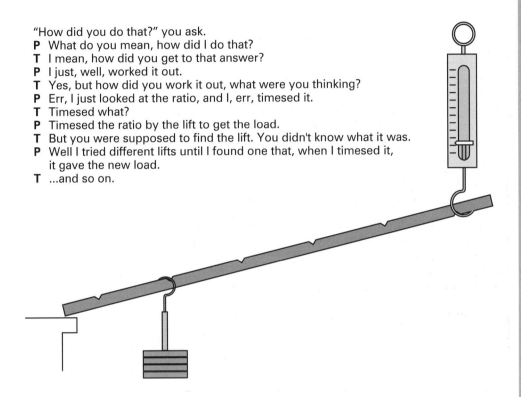

"How did you do that?" you ask.
P What do you mean, how did I do that?
T I mean, how did you get to that answer?
P I just, well, worked it out.
T Yes, but how did you work it out, what were you thinking?
P Err, I just looked at the ratio, and I, err, timesed it.
T Timesed what?
P Timesed the ratio by the lift to get the load.
T But you were supposed to find the lift. You didn't know what it was.
P Well I tried different lifts until I found one that, when I timesed it, it gave the new load.
T ...and so on.

Fig 2.2C The wheelbarrow

The child is being encouraged to unpack her own thinking, to put on the table the process by which she reached an answer. This makes working explicit, so it becomes available for use again, and it emphasises that the reasoning process is as important as the answer, although there may be many legitimate reasoning pathways to the same correct answer.

Our fourth principle was *construction*. This is discussed in Chapter 2.1. Teaching for cognitive acceleration involves, above all else, putting the pupil in the position where she has to construct for herself – slowly and often painfully – the type of thinking needed to tackle all sorts of scientific problems and investigations.

Bridging is the process of drawing attention to the many other contexts in which a reasoning pattern, developed in one particular context, can be applied. So, from the examples above, the bridging phase of a cognitive intervention lesson might involve a discussion of other times when the control of variables or proportionality 'ways of thinking' might come in useful.

CASE

All of these principles have been incorporated into the methods of 'Cognitive Acceleration' developed at King's College London, with demonstrable effects on their pupils' academic achievement. CASE (Cognitive Acceleration through Science Education) has introduced a method of teaching which focuses not so much on good instruction leading to the development of content knowledge, but rather on intervention in children's ability to process information. In other words, CASE is a programme designed to help children to think more effectively. When they think better, they learn better, because they are better equipped to make better sense of their regular science instruction.

The CASE programme consists of a set of 32 activities (called Thinking Science) designed to be used at the rate of one every two weeks instead of a regular science lesson, during the early secondary years. They are quite specifically signalled to pupils as 'special' lessons. It may seem that setting aside a special lesson once every two weeks for Thinking, when direct attention to covering curriculum content is set aside, makes it even more difficult to deliver the National Curriculum. But reflect for a moment on those words 'covering' and 'deliver' in the last sentence. What view of knowledge do such words imply? They imply that knowledge is a packet which can be delivered, or a set of topics and material which can be covered in the sense of going over it. This is precisely the view of knowledge against which I argue and which has been discredited by the constructivists. Pupils who process information more efficiently will learn more efficiently. Time spent in encouraging the development of the general processing mechanism may immediately be lost from 'covering' the curriculum, but it provides learners with the tools with which they can learn more effectively in the future.

Does It Work?

In a word, yes, it does. In our original research we asked 10 schools to try CASE teaching in just one or two early secondary classes for two years, and to identify one or two matched 'control' classes who would follow their normal science curriculum. The CASE pupils made significantly greater gains in cognitive development over the two years of the experiment. More importantly, they demonstrated long-term effects on their ability to learn. Overall pupils who had experienced CASE teaching in the early years of their secondary education gained higher grades in GCSE than matched control children who had not had CASE.

We published this data in 1991, and it attracted many schools who wished to find out how they could adopt the methods. At that time we started to run two year professional development courses for CASE, and also to train CASE Trainers who have been working in many parts of the UK ever since. In 1996 we got the first GCSE data from these schools with whom we started to work in 1991. This confirmed the original research results: CASE schools produced significantly higher 'value added' effects. After taking account of the intake level of their pupils, CASE schools get much higher proportions of pupils with level 6 or above at Key Stage 3, and of pupils with grades A–C at GCSE, than non-CASE schools. And this is not only in science, but in maths and English as well. It seems that the pupils' enhanced processing ability is general, and can be applied across the curriculum.

CASE is not a 'silver bullet'. There is nothing magic about the particular set of activities published as Thinking Science. What is magic is the use that teachers make of them, and learning how to do this is not a straightforward matter. Teaching for cognitive stimulation requires an unusual amount of concentration on questioning skills, managing group and whole-class discussions, and provoking reflective thinking in pupils, but these are strategies that can be learned by any teacher prepared to commit some time and energy to developing the new skills.

About the Author

Philip Adey taught chemistry in Barbados before embarking on a curriculum development and teacher education project where he learned that what worked with bright grammar school boys doesn't work generally, since which he has been exploring cognitive barriers to learning and how they can be surmounted. He is now Director of the Centre for the Advancement of Thinking at King's College London.

References and Further Reading

Adey, P. S. (1993). *The King's–BP CASE INSET Pack*, London, BP Educational Services.

Adey, P. S. and Shayer, M. (1994). *Really Raising Standards: Cognitive Intervention and Academic Achievement*, London, Routledge.

Adey, P. S., Shayer, M. and Yates, C. (1995). *Thinking Science: The Curriculum Materials of the CASE Project* (2nd ed.), London, Nelson.

CASE has a website: http://www.thenerve2.com/ca/index.html

For more information about CASE, including a list of CASE trainers, contact: King's College London School of Education, Waterloo Road, London SE1 8WA. Tel 0171 872 3134.

The CASE network is a user group which publishes a termly newsletter. Write to: Denise Ginsburg, 16 Fen End, Over, Cambridgeshire CB4 5NE.

2.3 Mapping Concepts in Science

Paul Hamer, Barbara Allmark, Jasmin Chapman and Jane Jackson

In this chapter we define the term cognitive mapping, outline types of cognitive map, detail some of our own, and other reported, experiences of using cognitive mapping and indicate the utility of these techniques in improving pupil learning.

Cognitive Maps

Our definition of cognitive mapping is:

> *any format which attempts to physically represent an individual's / group's thinking processes on paper or screen.*

Types of Map and Their Application

We have found some confusion about the various types of cognitive map. This confusion is not surprising as forms of map are constantly being developed by groups or individuals working in isolation, then disseminated via journals and training sessions. Subsequent development by recipients then incorporates idiosyncrasies or refinements as they, in turn, apply what they have learnt in their own unique context. We propose the following taxonomy outlined below to assist in dialogue about mapping techniques:

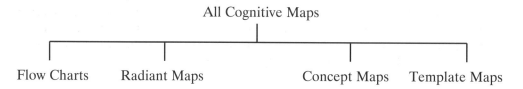

All Cognitive Maps

Flow Charts   Radiant Maps   Concept Maps   Template Maps

Flow Charts or Flow Maps

These are a familiar tool, used to summarise subject content in science. Continuity maps are another form of flow map concerned with curriculum structure rather than subject content. These have been presented elsewhere as 'learning maps' (NIAS, 1995). Mindful of the distinction between continuity and progression (see Chapter 3.6), we have developed a set of continuity maps for National Curriculum science 11–16 that were intended as a learning framework around which we could design progression routes for pupils.

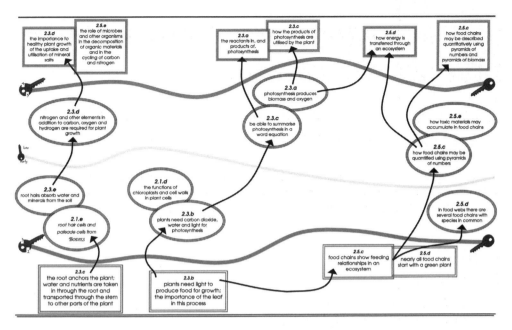

Fig 2.3A KS3 continuity map for plants (from The Learners' Co-operative Ltd)

A continuity map (Fig 2.3A) can be placed on a larger piece of paper and further details added alongside such as: equipment; resource needs; experimental work; cross-curricular planning. We have found this to be a very useful way of evaluating topic load, avoiding repetition within and across key stages and auditing existing courses. We have also used continuity maps for differentiation, in deciding 'cut-off points' for classes and individuals – allowing them to concentrate on learning more fundamental ideas thoroughly.

Although we originally designed our continuity maps for teacher use we have found some applications for learners. Some Key Stage 3 pupils, given a choice of a variety of starting points for revision work, selected our continuity maps and used them as the basis for producing their own summaries – as flash cards; wordlists; audio tapes; other forms of map. Other pupils have used continuity maps in a similar way to staff, placing their map on a larger piece of paper and adding columns for information such as notes on relevant experiments, diagrams and key word definitions.

Radiant Maps

> *Each bit of information entering your brain … can be represented as a central sphere from which radiate tens, hundreds, thousands, millions of hooks. Each hook represents an association and each association has its own infinite array of links and connections.* (Buzan, 1993).

Radiant maps not only allow learners to organise and summarise information in a way which mirrors the significance of association in thinking and memory, they also:

• save time in taking or making notes

- emphasise key words (which convey important ideas)
- stimulate creativity by obliging the brain to make associations as a map is designed
- aid memory, as they can be made visually interesting more readily than linear notes
- facilitate and articulate chunking of information.

Chunking is grouping bits of information into larger clusters and is an essential aspect of the initial processing of information by our working memory.

> *Extensive brain research, starting with George Miller's 'Magic 7' in the 1950s, has shown that the more students are able to 'chunk' information, the greater the chance for retention of this information.* (Hyerle, 1996)

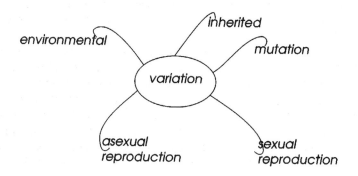

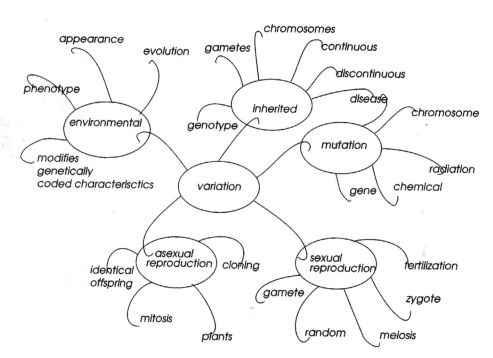

Fig 2.3B A burr and a 'burr of burrs' for the concept of variation at Key Stage 4 (from Deirdre Lucas)

A key point deriving from Miller's work is that the size of the chunks should be small enough to avoid overloading the working memory. We feel that this particularly applies to new learning situations. Enormous value lies in following up early exploration and subsequent familiarisation with chunks by chunking them to form larger maps.

We currently perceive two classes of radiant maps: consequence maps (see Chapter 2.7) and memory maps. Our taxonomy for memory maps distinguishes between burrs and larger maps. Burrs (Fig 2.3B) are consistent with chunking down to Miller's 'Magic 7'. Larger maps, such as learning maps and Mind Maps[TM]* are consistent with our own notion of 'chunking up' the curriculum to facilitate holistic learning. All memory mapping methods have a sound basis in semantic network theories – *theories of memory organisation that assume concepts are stored in long-term memory within hierarchically organised networks of meaningful associations.* (Good and Brophy, 1995)

Word burrs (Osborne, 1993; Sutton, 1992) are a fun vehicle for brainstorming and provide a useful introduction to radiant (and concept) mapping techniques which avoid overloading working memory. Once learners are used to working with word burrs they can be modified to form visual burrs by adding key/memorable images around the burr. Similarly, the addition of numerical data around the burr converts it into a number burr. Osborne and Sutton both describe other ways of beginning to impose structure on a basic word burr by coding with colour, line thickness or line length. Both also indicate how learners' progression can be monitored by using burrs at the start and finish of learning episodes.

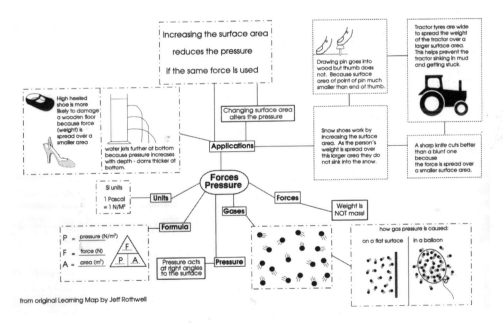

from original Learning Map by Jeff Rothwell

Fig 2.3C (from original Learning Map by Jeff Rothwell)

Mind Maps are trademarked to Tony Buzan

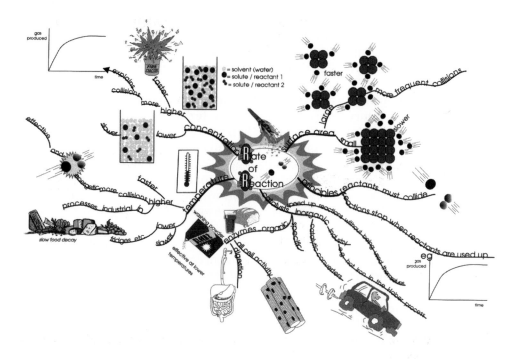

Fig 2.3D KS4 rates of reaction memory map (from The Learners' Co-operative Ltd (1996))

Learning maps (Fig 2.3C) and mind maps (Fig 2.3D) are both ways of 'chunking up' and also differ from burrs because these maps allow greater structuring of information. Learning maps, as described by Rose and Goll (1992), are less rigidly defined than maps produced in strict adherence to Buzan's rules for mind mapping. The more closely these rules are followed, however, the closer the map approaches a visual mnemonic for an area of learning.

Concept Maps

(Sometimes referred to as semantic nets.)

> *Concept maps are intended to represent meaningful relationships between concepts in the form of propositions. Propositions are two or more concept labels linked by words in a semantic unit ... A concept map is a schematic device for representing a set of concept meanings embedded in a framework of propositions.* (Novak and Gowin 1984).

Like memory maps, concept maps (Fig 2.3E) clearly have a sound basis in semantic network theories of learning. Unlike memory maps, concept maps do not necessarily radiate outwards from a central main idea, through "sub-concepts" to detail. If drawn hierarchically (as described by Novak), however, a concept map can look very similar to a single major branch of a learning map or mind map. A key distinction between mind maps and concept maps lies in their basic structure – in mind maps linking is conveyed by branch structure; in concept maps linking is

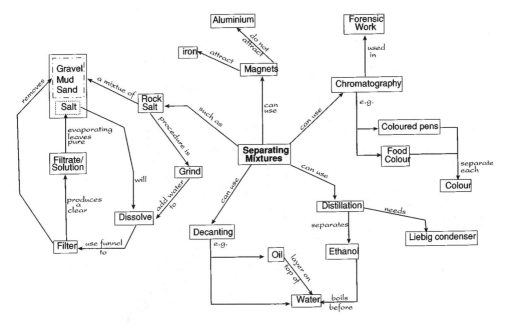

Fig 2.3E Separation of mixtures (from The Learners' Co-operative Ltd and Bedfordshire Science Team (1996))

conveyed by a written word or phrase placed on the link line between the associated concepts. In hierarchical concept maps spatial relationship (above and below) is used to indicate the direction of the relationship between concepts, with arrowheads being used only when the subordinate concept is not positioned below the superordinate concept. In non-hierarchical maps arrowheads are used to indicate the direction of the relationship between concepts.

Many articles illustrate the wide range of applications for concept maps (see References and Further Reading). Adamczyk *et al* (1994) describe how concept maps can be used for:

- assessment of pre-knowledge of a topic to be taught/post knowledge of a topic that has been taught/long term knowledge retention/understanding
- consolidating a learner's knowledge base
- constructing differentiated/flexible learning programmes
- evaluating the effectiveness of whole teaching programmes; and even
- determining the Inset requirements of colleagues.

They go on to describe useful variants of the basic concept map (see below).

Readers teaching proficient concept mappers may wish to extend their pupils' mapping skills by the introduction of coded links, such as those used in the 'Multirelational Semantic Maps' developed by Lambiotte *et al* (1989) at Texas Christian University.

As with other forms of map *concept maps are most useful if produced entirely by the student(s); however, there is a learning curve for their production and there is therefore much to be gained by providing students new to the technique with starters, fragments and exemplars in a way which encourages progressive development of the skills involved.* (Jackson *et al*, 1996).

We have produced differentiated sets of concept maps for KS3 science. Each set comprises a range of maps, progressively easier to complete than others (differentiation by task demand). Even with classes familiar with concept mapping, use of one of the easier versions of a completed map can be a time-saving review device.

The most demanding map is generated by the pupil(s) from the list of object words (concepts) provided – this corresponds to Adamczyk's 'free range map'; the learner(s) must come up with their own links. Easier variants are:

1) Concepts already arranged on the page to provide a spatial cue.
2) An 'object only' map, as above, with the extra help of the links drawn but not written.
3) A 'link only' map showing only the links and leaving the pupils to think of appropriate object words to go in each box.
4) A 'link only' map, as above, with the list of object words provided.
5) A 'link only' map, as above, with shape cues incorporated into the object word boxes and matched in the list of provided objects – similar to Adamczyk's 'propositional map'.

A list of enrichment words is provided with each set for use with pupils as appropriate. The variants described above, although producing a concept map as the end product, could also be classified as template maps.

Template Maps

> *Representational systems such as tables, graphs, flow charts or diagrams possess many of the same features that characterise semantic maps; that is, they all incorporate abbreviated verbal information within non-linear spatial layouts.* (Lambiotte *et al*, 1989)

To Lambiotte's list we would add assessment continua, causal chains, Vee diagrams, Venn diagrams and any partly-formed map (Fig 2.3F).

Most of these template maps are, of course, tools which are extremely familiar to science teachers; we hope that their inclusion here will provoke fresh consideration of their utility and relationship to the process of learning. Only Vee diagrams, as a sophisticated and less familiar format, will be considered in any detail.

> *The Vee heuristic is a tool for acquiring knowledge about knowledge and how knowledge is constructed and used.* (Novak and Gowin, 1984)

Gowin invented the heuristic in 1977 as the culmination of two decades' searching for a method to help pupils (and instructors) clarify the nature and purpose of practical work in science. It has subsequently been developed into a tool which can also be used to analyse the content of presentations or texts and as an aid in problem solving. As with concept maps (which should, according to Novak and Gowin, be introduced first), Vee diagrams (Fig 2.3G) can be used as formative assessment devices and scoring systems have been developed to help this application.

1 Assessment continuum:

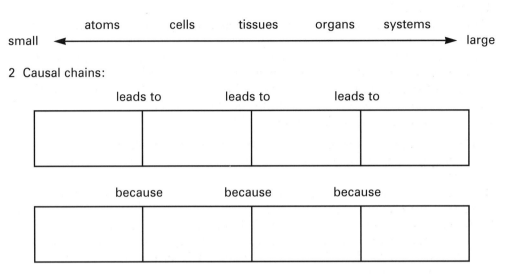

2 Causal chains:

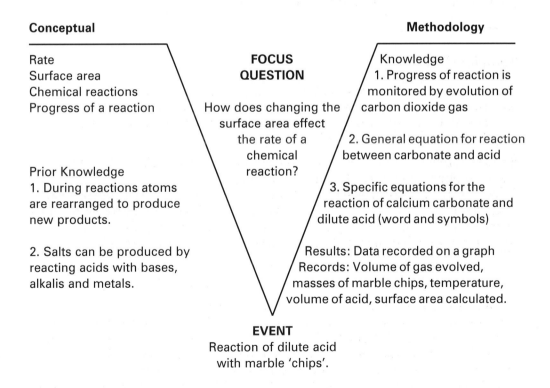

Fig 2.3F Less familiar template maps

Conceptual   **Methodology**

Rate   **FOCUS**   Knowledge
Surface area   **QUESTION**   1. Progress of reaction is
Chemical reactions   monitored by evolution of
Progress of a reaction   How does changing the   carbon dioxide gas
                                     surface area effect
                                         the rate of a   2. General equation for reaction
                                          chemical   between carbonate and acid
Prior Knowledge   reaction?
1. During reactions atoms   3. Specific equations for the
are rearranged to produce   reaction of calcium carbonate and
new products.   dilute acid (word and symbols)

2. Salts can be produced by   Results: Data recorded on a graph
reacting acids with bases,   Records: Volume of gas evolved,
alkalis and metals.   masses of marble chips, temperature,
                                              volume of acid, surface area calculated.

                                    EVENT
                              Reaction of dilute acid
                               with marble 'chips'.

Fig 2.3G Vee diagram example

An Evolving Methodology

The authors are practising teachers and members of a group established to develop and disseminate strategies for maximising learning (The Learners' Co-operative). The initial stimulus that led to the creation of the group was the challenge set to two of us charged with introducing the (first) National Curriculum into an inner city comprehensive. At the same time, we were trying to synthesise an integrated, pupil centred methodology that would allow us to:

- develop learning activities to lower the 'literacy barrier' we had identified as a key cause of pupil disaffection and consequent poor performance
- reduce time spent transmitting knowledge from teacher to class
- increase the effectiveness of the "independent learning" which was purportedly taking place
- increase the variety of learning experiences and effective differentiation
- restructure the curriculum to maximise efficiency of delivery and give time for remediation and enrichment
- make the learning process explicit to our pupils.

Our early trials of various activities, and dialogue with colleagues, resulted in *non-judgemental differentiation* (Chapman and Hamer, 1998). In this approach (based on Howard Gardner's theory of multiple intelligences (Gardner, 1994)) we encourage learners to process and review taught information in ways matched to their preferred learning styles. The range of activities includes the maps described. We feel that memory maps and concept maps, in particular, are powerful learning tools as they facilitate 'parallel processing' – that is, they engage more than one intelligence simultaneously.

In the course of disseminating these techniques we have received intriguing feedback from trainee mappers. Some report greater ease in assimilating a particular style of map and have related this to a metacognitive insight into their own teaching style. This, in turn, has raised their appreciation of the need to use a variety of approaches to match pupil diversity. There appears to be a consensus that there is significant potential for future development of mapping techniques. While some types of map are well researched, there is a need for empirical research into those forms which are not. It is important to note that these are accelerated learning strategies and that their assimilation is consistent with DfEE's desire to *see more examples of accelerated learning, based on the latest understanding of how people learn, which has enabled pupils to progress at greater speed and with deeper understanding.* (DfEE, 1997)

Summary

Using mapping tools allows learners to communicate their inner cognitive world in readily accessible formats. A variety of methods exist, each with a variety of applications already described. These allow us to bridge the gap between learning theory and classroom practice. As practitioners try out new methods, further applications and formats evolve.

References and Further Reading

Adamczyk, P., Willson, M. and Williams, D. (1994) Concept Mapping: a Multi-level and Multi-purpose Tool. *School Science Review,* Vol 76, No 275, pp 116–124.

Bishop, K. and Denley, P. (1997) The Fundamental Role of Subject Matter Knowledge in the Teaching of Science. *School Science Review,* Vol 79, No 286, pp 65–71.

Botton, C. (1995) Collaborative Concept Mapping and Formative Assessment Key Stage 3: Understanding of Acids and Bases. *School Science Review* Vol 77, No 279, pp 124–130.

Brodie, T. (1992) Concept Mapping for Differential Assessment. *School Science Review,* Vol 74, No 267, pp 130–133.

Buzan, T. with Buzan, B. (1993) *The Mind Map Book*, BBC Books.

Chapman, J. and Hamer, P. (1998*) The Learners' Co-operative Differentiation Manual 2nd Ed*. The Learners' Co-operative Ltd., PO Box 69, Plymouth, PL4 6YP.

DfEE (1997) *Excellence in Schools*, HMSO.

Gardner, H. (1994) The Theory of Multiple Intelligences. In Moon, B. and Shelton Mayes, A. (Eds) *Teaching and Learning in the Secondary School*, London, Routedge/Open University Press, pp 38–46.

Good, T. L. and Brophy, J. (1995) *Contemporary Educational Psychology* 5th Ed. New York, Longman.

Hyerle, D. (1996) *Visual Tools for Constructing Knowledge*, Association for Supervision and Curriculum Development, Alexandria, Virginia.

Jackson, J., Allmark, B.E., Bretherick, M., Chapman, J., Fildes, C., Hamer, P., Hodges, A., Jarvis, A., Marchione, A. and Rothwell, J. (1996) *Science Thinking Maps for Key Stage 3*, Bedfordshire Science Team and The Learners' Co-operative Ltd.

Lambiotte, J.G., Dansereau, D.F., Cross, D.R. and Reynolds, S.B. (1989) Multirelational Semantic Maps. *Educational Psychology Review* 1, 4, pp 331–367.

Novak, J.D. and Gowin, D.B. (1984) *Learning How to Learn*, CUP.

Osborne, J. (1993) Alternatives to Practical Work. *School Science Review,* Vol 75, No 271, pp 117–123.

NIAS (1995) *The Differentiation Book*, Northamptonshire Inspection and Advisory Service.

Rose, C. and Goll, L. (1992) *Accelerate Your Learning; Action Handbook*, Accelerated Learning Systems Ltd.

Sizmur, S. (1994) Concept Mapping, Language and Learning in the Classroom. *School Science Review,* Vol 76, No 274, pp 120–125.

Sutton, C. (1992) *Words, Science and Learning*, Open University Press.

Willson, M. and Williams, D. (1996) Trainee Teachers' Misunderstandings in Chemistry: Diagnosis and Evaluation Using Concept Mapping. *School Science Review*, Vol 77, No 280, pp 107–113.

2.4 Learning to Investigate

Rod Watson and Valerie Wood-Robinson

This chapter discusses the educational aims of investigative work in school science and highlights a mismatch between pupils' and teachers' understanding of the aims. The ways in which investigations can be manipulated to meet different needs of different pupils are discussed. Finally, a structure for investigational lessons presented and various approaches to help support pupils' thinking and decision-making are introduced.

The Role of Investigative Work

This chapter is about enabling children to learn, using practical investigations. So, what are investigations? Why are they used?

The teachers who have worked with the ASE–King's Science Investigations in Schools (AKSIS) project (Watson, 1997) have identified the following two characteristics of investigations:

- In investigative work pupils have to make their own decisions either individually or in groups: they are given some autonomy in how the investigation is carried out.
- An investigation must involve pupils in using procedures such planning, measuring, observing, analysing data and evaluating methods.

Not all investigations will allow pupils to use every kind of investigational procedure, and investigations may vary in the amount of autonomy given to pupils at different stages of the investigative process.

Most teachers believe that investigations are worth doing to help pupils learn science. Groups of teachers working with the AKSIS project named pupil motivation, collaborative working and opportunities for discussion as indicators of successful investigations, leading to the learning of scientific concepts and procedures. The strong emphasis on this area of work in the UK is reflected in international comparisons where England (and Singapore) scored significantly higher than other countries (Harmon *et al*, 1997).

The AKSIS project compared teachers' aims for specific investigation lessons with what their pupils thought they learned (Watson, Goldsworthy and Wood-Robinson, 1998). Over 50% of the teachers' aims were procedural, such as proposing hypotheses or planning a fair test, compared with 20% of pupil responses. The majority of pupil responses (74%) were about learning content compared with 33% of teachers' responses. The mismatch between teacher and pupil perceptions is striking. Pupils concentrate on more obvious features of investigations: if they are given a task 'to investigate the factors affecting the rate of sugar dissolving in water', they tend to see the purpose of the lesson being to learn about the dissolving. Similarly when they mentioned procedures half their responses were very specific (e.g. to learn to operate a balance). It is more difficult for pupils to recognise the gradual learning of processes such as developing better fair-testing strategies or approaches to planning.

The ASE policy statement on learning and teaching (ASE, 1997) states that:

> *Teaching and learning science should provide opportunities for learners to:*
>
> - *take responsibility for their own learning, and to contribute to deciding short term goals and objectives*
> - *reflect on and appraise their own work and progress.*

Autonomous learners need to understand the educational aims of investigative lessons.

A major aim for investigations must be to develop pupils' competence in relevant processes. The ASE policy on learning and teaching emphasises ...*opportunities for learners to: enquire, predict and hypothesise; explore, observe, investigate and discover; solve problems; and to discriminate, judge and evaluate.* Experimental and investigative work in the UK curricula offers opportunities for developing these aspects of science learning.

A second aim of investigations is to develop pupils' knowledge and understanding of scientific concepts. Although less dominant in teachers' aims for investigative work, it is still an important aim for many teachers.

A third possible aim is to develop pupils' understanding of the relation between empirical data and scientific theory (Driver *et al*, 1996) – doing investigations which examine just what evidence can be used to refute or support different theories, rather than just explaining patterns in results in terms of pupils' current knowledge.

The range of kinds of investigations which fit easily with the national curricula has been criticised as being limited, having an over-heavy emphasis on fair testing. This is to the detriment of other kinds of investigations such as classifying, identifying, pattern seeking, exploring, investigating models and making things and developing systems (Goldsworthy, Watson and Wood-Robinson, 1998).

Matching Investigations to Pupils

In designing investigations there are three inter-related considerations:

- curriculum needs: how the investigation fits into the scheme of work, relating to previous and subsequent experiences
- the objectives of the activity
- presentation of the activity to meet pupils' learning needs.

Curriculum Needs

Most schemes of work reviewed by the AKSIS team are organised around knowledge. Some included opportunities for doing investigations, but there is usually no framework for progressively developing specific skills or procedures. There is a need to develop schemes which describe opportunities for progression in investigative work.

Objectives

The AKSIS team found that most teachers' objectives for a lesson were similar for all pupils in the class. The teachers had a clear picture of a successfully completed investigation and aimed to get all pupils to that end point. They differentiated by differential support amongst the whole class tackling the same investigation presented in the same way and they spend a lot of time with weaker students, supporting them to do an investigation which was really too difficult for them.

An alternative is to alter the difficulty of the investigation by changing the task description. The following example is based on the work of the OPENS project (Fairbrother, Watson *et al*, 1992). The six investigations listed below are suitable for a similar topic area (plant growth).

A.1 Place a batch of seeds in a dark cupboard, place another batch in the light. Control all the other factors. Which produces the greenest shoots after a week?
A.2 Find out whether light and temperature affect plant growth.
A.3 Discover the factors affecting plant growth.

B.1 Find out if light affects the production of starch in a leaf of this plant.
B.2 Find out how light affects the process of photosynthesis.
B.3 Investigate the factors affecting the process of photosynthesis.

The openness of the investigations increases going down the two lists. In A.1 the variables are specified and some guidance is given on altering the independent variable, in A.2 the variables are specified but no guidance is given on manipulating them and A.3 is left open. The openness changes the opportunities to develop specific skills and procedures. More decisions have been taken by the teacher in investigation A.1 than in A.3 affecting the opportunities for independent planning by pupils. Investigation A.3 may be suitable for pupils with much experience and understanding of planning investigations. Investigation A.1 treats light as a categoric variable (light or dark) and so limits the kind of data produced and hence limits the opportunities for interpretation of the data. Investigation A.3 is more open and so pupils can interpret it in a variety of ways and some may decide to treat light as a continuous variable. Set B is different from set A in that all the investigations include a higher conceptual demand.

Presenting Activities

The AKSIS project found that teachers were often unaware of the extent to which they were making most of the important decisions. Teachers sometimes frame an investigation very heavily, leaving little for pupils to decide. It is very difficult to strike the right balance between providing a structure which supports pupils to work through their own ideas in an open situation, and providing a structure which drives the pupils towards producing a experiment which is predetermined by the teacher.

Decision to take	What was decided	Who took the decision
Question, hypothesis	What could you change, about the wire, that affects the amount of current that flows through the wire?	Teacher
Independent variable	Different groups chose: Gp(a) type of wire Gp(b) length Gp(c) thickness Gp(d) type; length	After a class brainstorm, pupils in groups. Less able groups were guided by the teacher to choose 'type' (a categoric variable)
Range	Gp(a) 4 kinds of wire Gp(b) 5–100 cm Gp(c) 0.5–2.5 mm ✓ Gp(d) 2 kinds; 30–230 cm	Pupils in groups
Interval	Gp(a) Not applicable Gp(b) 25 cm (5 values) Gp(c) 0.5 mm (5 or 6 values) Gp(d) NA; various	Pupils in groups
Dependent variable	The amount of current that flows through the wire	Teacher
Measuring dependent variable	Gp(a) Bulb brightness and ammeter Gp(b) Bulb brightness Gp(c) ammeter Gp(d) Bulb brightness	Pupils (Teacher reminded some groups of ammeter)
Repeat readings	Most groups not. Some repeated where reading appeared anomalous	Pupils; time limitations
Control variables	Gp(a) length Gp(b) type; thickness supplied; pupil Gp(c) type; length Gp(d) each factor varied separately, others controlled	Gp(a) Pupils with teacher guidance Gp(b) Determined by wires Gp(c) Pupil Gp(d) Teacher guidance
Value of control variables	Length as convenient	Pupils
Design of circuit	Circuit built on circuit board	Determined by circuit boards. Some teacher guidance
How to process the data	Gp(a) Bar chart Gp(b) Table, graphs Gp(c) Table, graphs Gp(d) Table	Pupils

Fig 2.4A Decisions table: what affects the amount of current that flows through wires?

One teacher varied the openness of an investigation, which was limited by the specific apparatus involved (circuit boards). This enabled him to match the wide range of pupil needs within his year 7 class and to encourage a variety of pupil decision-making and response. The balance between the decisions of the teacher and pupils is shown in Fig 2.4A.

A Lesson Structure for Investigations

Based on teachers' reporting in the 'diaries' phase of the project, the AKSIS team has identified different stages common to many investigation lessons. The stages do not necessarily occur in the order given in Fig 2.4B and sometimes different stages merge. For example, during stage 4, an anomalous result may stimulate a pupil to question the emerging evidence (stage 8) and decide to take repeat readings (revisiting stage 3). Making explicit the educational aims and focus, and giving a picture of good performance in these procedures, is not shown on the Fig. This is sometimes included in stages 1, 2 and 3 and could be followed up with stronger emphasis on stage 9 'Reflections on learning'.

Stage of investigation	Purpose
1. Focusing	Pupils are encouraged to make links to previous knowledge and understanding: either school knowledge or everyday knowledge. The aim is to set a context for the investigation and to engage pupils' interest.
2. Defining the problem	The problem is introduced to the class and pupils clarify what they are investigating.
3. Planning	The pupils plan what they are going to do.
4. Doing: obtaining evidence	Pupils carry out practical activities, making measurement and/or observations.
5. Describing method	Pupils write what they have done.
6. Recording and describing results and patterns	Pupils examine their results, describe them, and look for patterns. They may construct tables and graphs to record and display their results.
7. Interpreting: conclusions from patterns linked to knowledge and understanding	Pupils draw conclusions from their results and make links to their knowledge and understanding. They explain their results.
8. Evaluation of methods used	Pupils critically evaluate the data that they have collected and evaluate procedures used to gather the data.
9. Reflections on learning	Pupils reflect on what they have learnt: what knowledge they have gained, or what skills or procedures they have improved.

Fig 2.4B Stages of investigation lessons

On average 3–4 hours was spent on each whole investigation. They usually involve lengthy periods, often a whole hour, for thinking about and clarifying the problem and planning (stages 1, 2, 3) before starting practical work (stage 4). This is not matched by similar time to reflect on the investigative process after carrying out the practical work. Even when teachers planned longer evaluation and reflection sections, the time for these was eroded by earlier parts over-running.

To define, plan and report their investigations, pupils need to use the special language of investigations. Teachers and pupils need to understand that many words used in investigative work have a special meaning. Different teachers use the same words in different ways. For example, 'fair' test has a restricted meaning of controlling variables, yet we have found that many teachers and pupils use it with a variety of different meanings such as accuracy in measurement, repeating readings and making sure the apparatus is working properly. In some of the planning stages, the phrase 'what we will measure' is used as pupil-talk for the dependent variable. This attempt at simplification does not help situations where the independent variable and control variables are also measured. For example, in a thermal insulation investigation, the dependent variable (the temperature of the water) was 'what we measure', but the independent variable (the thickness of the insulating material) and control variables (the volume of water used and the size of the beaker), also needed measuring.

One way of providing guidance for pupils, in stages 2 and 3, is by asking a particular sequence of displayed questions. The AKSIS project has found that such scaffolds (variously called planning sheets, prompt sheets or planning boards) are very common, with many teachers using them most or all of the time. A minority of teachers use a variety of sheets within one class, to match different learning needs. The effectiveness of such scaffolds depends on how they are used. They can be used like a traditional worksheet, detailed to take the students through stage by stage. Used in such a prescriptive way there is little opportunity for pupils to make decisions and take the initiative.

Another aid to planning is the use of a variables table. The pupils have to identify the key variables relevant to their investigation as headings to columns on a blank table. Having 'brainstormed' all the 'things' that could be changed in their investigation, they write the variable they want to find out about (the outcome or dependent variable) on the last column. All the other variables that might affect the outcome are used as headings for the other columns. They then choose one of these as the independent variable and choose different values for it. The remaining columns represent control variables. Fig 2.4C is, therefore, useful in helping pupils to organise their thoughts.

These two devices are not merely supports for pupils, as substitutes for teacher's attention in a busy class. They are tools to expose pupils' thinking. With a quick glance at the sheet of an individual or group, the teacher gets an idea of what the pupil is thinking and provides appropriate guidance, according to her aims matched to the pupils' learning needs.

The variables table can provide a structure for systematically taking and recording readings during stages 4 and 6. Prompt sheets may serve as frames to help pupils

Water	Soil	Plants (grass seedlings)	Amount of light	Growth
20 ml a day 20 ml a day 20 ml a day	Bag of soil Bag of soil Bag of soil	2cm 2cm 2cm	Dark cupboard Natural light 40 W bulb on 24 hrs	

Fig 2.4C Example of a pupil's variable table

structure their writing (stages 5, 6, 7). A sheet with stems of statements, to be completed by pupils can induct them into using the language of investigations. Such frames provide support for pupils learning in open situations but should become unnecessary as the pupils learn how to investigate scientifically. Teachers must help pupils decide when they can dispense with such aids.

The AKSIS project has found the use of graphs to be underdeveloped. Graphs are often seen as a key feature of stage 6, as simply a way of representing the results at the end point of an investigation. There is value in translating tabulated data into graphs, but more value when pupils use them to interrogate the accuracy of individual readings and to make new quantitative predictions which could them be tested (stages 7 and 8). Sketch graphs can be used in making preliminary predictions, to express the relation expected between two variables (stage 2).

In order to make learning through investigations more explicit, and to promote the learning of rational argument more time is needed in reflecting on the procedures used: for example challenging pupils to defend the quality of the evidence that they present. Discussing results and arguing from evidence requires specialised use of language. Pupils need time in investigative lessons exploring the use of this language of argument (see also Chapter 3.3).

Summary

We would like to highlight three important points:

- Investigations involving practical work are essentially thinking activities. It is important to provide time for discussion and to encourage pupils to make their ideas explicit.
- Explicit teaching can enhance learning through investigations. There is, however, a difficult balance to be struck between providing support which gives students enough freedom to make decisions for themselves, and imposing a structure in which the teacher has made most of the important decisions.
- Autonomous learners need to be aware of the educational purposes of activities in which they are engaged.

About the Authors

Rod Watson is a senior lecturer in the School of Education, King's College London. His work has included the direction of three major research and curriculum development projects; the Open-ended Work in Science (OPENS) Project, the National Environmental Database (NED) Project and the ASE–King's Science Investigations in Schools Project.

Valerie Wood-Robinson has been a Head of Biology, Head of Science and a Science Adviser. She has interspersed her teaching with work on curriculum development projects. She is currently a Senior Research Assistant in the AKSIS Project.

References and Further Reading

ASE (1997) *Learning and Teaching: Policy Statement,* Hatfield, ASE.

Driver, R., Leach, J., Millar, R. and Scott, P. (1996) *Young People's Images of Science*, Open University Press.

Fairbrother, R.W., Watson, J.R., Black, P., Jones, A. and Simon, S. (1992): *Open Work in Science: an INSET Pack for Investigations,* Hatfield, ASE.

Goldsworthy, A., Watson, R. and Wood-Robinson, V. (1988) *Interim Report of the AKSIS Project to the QCA*, London, King's College London.

Harmon, Smith, Martin, Kelly, Beaton, Mullis, Gonzalez and Orpwood (1997) *Performance Assessment in IEA's Third International Mathematics and Science Study (TIMMS)*, Boston, MA, USA, Boston College.

Watson, J.R. and Fairbrother, R.W. (1993) Open-ended Work in Science (OPENS) Project: Managing Investigations in the Laboratory. *School Science Review,* Vol 75, No 271, pp 31–38.

Watson, R. (1997) ASE–King's Science Investigations in Schools Project: Investigations at Key Stages 2 and 3. *Education in Science,* No 171, pp 22–23.

Watson, R., Goldsworthy, A. and Wood-Robinson, V. (1998) Getting AKSIS to Investigations. *Education in Science,* No 177.

Understanding Scientific Evidence – Why It Matters and How It Can Be Taught

Richard Gott and Sandra Duggan

Understanding evidence has been accorded an increased emphasis in experimental and investigative science. This chapter suggests how we might define what we mean by an 'understanding of evidence' and why it matters not only to those who work in science-based employment but also to the informed citizen. We suggest that the ideas underpinning scientific evidence constitute a knowledge base in their own right and that they are central to science. We believe that this knowledge base must be taught explicitly and we put forward some suggestions as to how teachers might do so.

Background

Investigative work has been an official part of the National Curriculum since its birth in 1989. Generally, investigative work has been found to be popular with pupils but has received a mixed reaction from teachers. Foulds *et al* (1992) report that most pupils find investigations interesting and enjoyable and Watts (1991) comments on the sense of empowerment and enjoyment that this type of practical work engenders. More recently, a report from Northern Ireland (Jones *et al*, 1997) showed that pupils find investigative work both challenging and rewarding, giving them a sense of achievement. They also appreciate the freedom of working out problems for themselves away from the direct guidance of the teacher. Conversely, if investigative work is carried out infrequently and only in association with formal assessment, then it becomes onerous because pupils associate it with examinations.

While the best practice has resulted in enjoyment and motivation on the part of the pupils, some research done in the early days of the National Curriculum (Foulds *et al*, 1992), produced some worrying findings. This study found that although pupils were successful at carrying out investigations in terms of designing an investigation and collecting measurements, they had little understanding of the meaning of the data or of evaluation. Indeed the authors report that:

> *The most striking feature of pupils' work is their lack of understanding of the nature of evidence.*

What was happening was that pupils were busy 'doing' but not understanding what it was all about. This can make the task seem pointless and contributes to the frustration that some teachers have expressed – they are uncertain or unconvinced of the value of investigative work (Jones *et al, op cit*).

Originally, this part of the National Curriculum, was called 'Scientific Investigation' but it was changed in 1995 to 'Experimental and Investigative Science' with a strong emphasis on evidence – 'obtaining', 'analysing' and 'evaluating'. This emphasis attempts to address the earlier problems revealed by the introduction of investigative work. At the same time, it puts an onus on teachers to help their pupils understand evidence while offering little in the way of detailed guidance as to how this is to be done. Perhaps more importantly there is no attempt at defining what exactly constitutes an understanding of evidence.

Understanding Evidence – What Does It Mean?

We shall focus here on a definition of the understanding required which would allow the *quality* of the evidence to be evaluated – i.e. so that the question 'is the evidence good/sound?' can be answered. We recognise that there are other factors in making decisions *about* evidence and we shall refer to these in the next section.

In 1995 we published a tentative list of constituent ideas which, we suggest, need to be understood in order to comprehend scientific evidence. Fig 2.5A shows a very brief version. We have called these ideas 'concepts of evidence'. We were driven to this term by the need to avoid the term 'skills' which has a flavour of 'drill and practice'. All of these ideas about evidence can be subsumed under two headings: *reliability* (ideas to answer the question, 'Are the measurements to be trusted?') and *validity* (ideas to answer the question, 'Will the data allow the question to be answered?'). To judge, weigh up or evaluate evidence we need to be able to understand the ideas which underpin reliability and validity. This list is a much abbreviated version of a more extensive list on our website (http://www.dur.ac.uk/~ded0www/evidence_main1.htm).

Associated with design	Variable identification and establishing links. Categoric, continuous and discrete variables. Fair tests and control experiments. Sampling design. Tables as organisers.
Associated with measurement	Relative scale of quantities. Range and interval of measurement. Choice of instrument and the accuracy of a scale. Calibration and instrument errors. Repeatability of measurements. Sampling/number of readings. Accuracy of a measurement. Sensitivity of a measurement. Precision of a measurement. Types of error.
Associated with data handling	Using and interpreting simple and complex tables. Graph type. Patterns/relationships in data. Multivariate data.

Fig 2.5A Ideas to understand evidence

We believe that these concepts of evidence are best viewed as a knowledge base in their own right equivalent to the more familiar concepts that are traditionally associated with science. Solving any problem in science involves an interaction of these traditional science concepts with concepts of evidence. If pupils are evaluating either their own evidence about a problem or second-hand evidence, then they need to employ both.

Why Understanding Evidence Matters

An understanding of scientific evidence matters because it is an essential part of scientific literacy and employment in science and science-related occupations.

Scientific Literacy

Science relies absolutely on evidence. This is its defining characteristic – theory must accord with reality. But what of the wider relevance of evidence outside the confines of pure science?

Science and technology play an increasing part in our everyday lives. We are all confronted with issues from time to time about which we have to make decisions be it birth control, or weighing up the pros and cons of a particular medical drug treatment or deciding whether to eat irradiated foods. Factors other than scientific evidence affect our decision (see Chapter 2.7).

In some instances, such as BSE or global warming, it may well be that the scientific evidence is limited, in which case we need to acknowledge this and make the best use we can of the available evidence. But if the evidence does exist, the evaluation of the quality of the evidence should be a central feature in decision-making about a scientific issue. Cross (1993) writes:

> *Whether a citizen is able to take action when confronted with the data depends on many factors, two of which are undoubtedly understanding the arguments involved, and being able to judge the quality of the evidence.*

Public awareness of what does and what does not constitute sound scientific evidence lies at the heart of scientific literacy. Issues such as knowing how to handle inconclusive evidence, risk assessment and acknowledgement of the absence of scientific certainty or truth all play a part.

We do not wish to suggest that making such judgements is a simple matter – it is not – but encouraging pupils to collect and handle their own evidence and to deal with 'messy' data must be an essential first step on the way towards this kind of decision-making. We believe that developing a critical awareness of the status and reliability of evidence should be a crucial aim of science education. Pupils should leave school with, at the very least, a belief in their ability to understand data and make judgements based upon it, if they so wish, or make quite different judgements based on other criteria but accepting, knowingly, the consequences of so doing.

Employment in Science and Science-related Occupations

Much existing research on employers' requirements of its workforce, and in particular of its new recruits, are cast in general terms rather than in terms of the specifics of what might be taught in the reality of the science classroom. The Council of Science and Technology Institutes (CSTI, 1993) sought the views of over 1000 employers in industries where science and maths are used and found that some 30% of the workforce uses science or maths in some aspect of their work. Of those, a relatively small fraction (4%) are engaged in 'pure science' compared to the rest who are employed in applied science and engineering.

The report examined what it is that industry requires of employees. Employers identified communication skills, management skills and a central core of skills concerned with the doing of science. The latter, which is of most relevance here, is defined as the ability to: generate own ideas, hypotheses and theoretical models and/or utilise those postulated by others; design and conduct experiments, trials, tests, simulations and operations; and evaluate the resulting data.

Coles (1997) interviewed scientists employed in the private and public sector across a wide range of scientific fields and at different professional levels. He came to broadly similar conclusions as the CSTI which can be summarised as an understanding of major scientific concepts, an understanding of scientific evidence and personal and interpersonal skills. He found that general capabilities were often expressed ahead of any specific scientific knowledge, understanding or skills. These capabilities he describes as practical techniques, problem-solving by experimentation, decision-making by weighing evidence and scientific habits of mind (such as logical thinking, scepticism).

Although the above research is informative, we believe that it remains at too general a level to be useful in terms of what is to be taught. For example, we can exhort schools to 'encourage scientific habits of mind', but how is that to be done?

Our own research has attempted to delve below 'the things that scientists do' in a search for the understandings which are necessary, if insufficient, pre-conditions. Our aim is to determine what *understandings* must be *taught* so that pupils can better fulfil the requirements of the workplace.

We have carried out a pilot study in a local biotechnology industry. Using our list of concepts of evidence as a guide, we set out to determine what understanding is needed at two levels of employment: the most basic technician level and at a higher level (called the supervisory level in this company). Details of this study are in a separate publication (Gott *et al*, 1997).

In brief, we studied the documentation concerning one of the company's key products to determine the extent of the understanding that might be required. We then used interview and observation techniques to probe the understanding necessary at the two levels of employment sampled.

Our results have enabled us to extend and modify our list of concepts of evidence to include such concepts as precision and specificity. The study has also shown that many of our list of ideas concerning evidence are indeed significant, albeit in this one example of the workplace.

One point of interest is the response of the workforce to questions about what science they did. Their response covered mainly ideas such as buffer solutions, pH and so on. When asked about the things we are calling here concepts of evidence, they recognised their central importance but referred to them as 'procedures'. The point here is that all our experience of science in schools and university gives us a working definition of what science is and it is a definition that focuses on traditional scientific concepts. It does not include ideas about evidence: perhaps because they have never been explicitly part of science education but have come up under the realm of on-the-job training.

But How Can It Be Taught?

Understanding evidence matters to those who work in science-based employment and to the ordinary citizen. If we accept that the ideas associated with evidence comprise a useful knowledge which is not well understood by pupils, then it follows that we must devise ways of teaching such ideas.

It has been argued that such ideas are within every science course. That may be so, but are they explicit? Are they considered, sequenced and planned for systematically? Or are we expecting children to pick them up by a process of osmosis, as maybe we ourselves did? We suggest that it is currently the latter.

Part of the problem in teaching about evidence may stem from not recognising that there *is* something to know and understand. This is exacerbated by the lack of any text-based materials to encourage that recognition. When we look at the curriculum and see a topic labelled 'Newton's laws', then we see far more than that. All our experience in science education, the many textbooks available, indeed all the acculturation of becoming a physics teacher means that such a simple phrase conjures up a whole host of ideas, teaching activities, questions and explanations. By contrast, there is very little in the way of similar material for investigative science outside a list of well-tried investigations, often used for assessment purposes.

In some schools, the list of ideas about evidence (outlined in Fig 2.5A) has proved to be more important than we had imagined. Because these ideas are written down in detail they become a part of the 'syllabus'. That means they can be cut and pasted into schemes of work and treated in exactly the same way as the more traditional bits of science understanding. We can now argue about the best way to teach about evidence.

In our earlier writing (Gott and Duggan 1995), we suggested some ways in which concepts of evidence might be taught. More recently, we have developed and trialed more extensive materials for schools (Foulds *et al.,* 1997, 1998), GNVQ (Gott *et al,* 1998) and university-level teaching. Another set of materials, although coming from a quite different perspective, can be found in Thinking Science (Adey *et al,* 1989) (see Chapter 2.2).

This developing bank of materials uses a wide variety of approaches including investigative and other forms of practical work, group work, the use of information technology (e.g. to produce graphs), quizzes, written exercises and applying ideas about evidence to 'second-hand' evidence and to press articles.

We would not wish to prescribe the method of teaching, leaving it to the teacher to select appropriately for a particular group of pupils. At the same time, the aim should always be to enable pupils to apply their understanding *frequently* within *whole* investigations: it is only in whole investigations that the impact of different aspects of evidence can be seen together. They can also be used as a method of formative assessment enabling the teacher to establish the level of understanding of particular ideas.

Our local schools have found that integrating teaching evidence alongside the rest of the science curriculum is most easily done by maintaining continuity of context. Hence, if a class is studying dissolving, then after the basic concepts have been taught, the teacher might use the same context but use it to teach a particular idea about evidence, e.g. the relationship between continuous variables and line graphs. With experience, teachers have found that it is possible to change the context of a 'text book' investigation but still use it to target the same concept of evidence.

We illustrate the integration of teaching concepts of evidence in the following example.

An Example of Teaching about Evidence: the Concept of Sampling in Biology Investigations

Biology investigations are complex. There are so many variables to be considered. And, because of inherent biological variation, there is the added complication of sampling. We might approach such issues in a series of lessons along the lines shown in Fig 2.5B.

Idea/purpose	Activity
Investigations involving living things have many variables. They have to be recognised. Then the important ones must be isolated.	**Teacher-facilitated introduction:** Think about this question: 'What affects the number of robins in your garden in winter?' • Brainstorm all the variables that might affect it. • Put them in a big circle on the board. Make a class list on the board of variables that matter: • a lot • a little • not much at all.
Putting these ideas into practice ...defining the independent variable	**Investigation** • Now try this in your group with one of these questions, e.g. Investigation: 'What affects the amount of lichen on a gravestone?' In your group: • Draw a circle. • Brainstorm all the possible variables involved and put them in the circle. • Put a circle round the dependent variable (the amount of lichen). • Decide what factor you will investigate first – this will be your independent variable (e.g. the aspect of the gravestones; or gravestones in highly polluted and relatively unpolluted areas; or gravestones of different types of stone, etc.) and highlight it.

...isolating the effect of the independent variable by controlling other relevant variables ...deciding on the sample size	• Decide all the variables that could be controlled – put a star next to these. Decide which ones matter – put two stars against them. Think about how you will control them. • How will you measure how much lichen there is on one gravestone? • How many gravestones should you choose? • Carry out your investigation and report back.
Discuss the idea of choosing and isolating pre-existing values for the independent variable as compared with actively manipulating them as you would in, for example, a physics investigation. Discuss the idea of an adequate sample size.	**Teacher-facilitated class discussion** • What question did each group investigate? • How many gravestones did each group choose? • How did groups control the variables to make the test as fair as possible? • How important were the variables that couldn't be controlled?
Consolidation	**Follow-up** Plan (or criticise an existing plan for) other investigations in which it is necessary to: • choose pre-existing values for the independent variable • decide on and give reasons for choice of sample size. or Use a quiz with questions about biological sampling. or Ask pupils to look in the press or on the Internet for some examples of how sampling is reported.

Fig 2.5B An example of one possible way of focusing teaching on sampling design and sample size in biology

Concluding Remarks

Understanding evidence is a central part of science and of informed decision-making in everyday life. As technology advances and more 'critical thinkers' are required, science education has a duty to enable students to examine the quality of scientific evidence effectively.

About the Authors

Richard Gott is Professor of Education in the School of Education, University of Durham. Sandra Duggan is an experienced researcher, currently working in the School of Education, University of Durham.

References and Further Reading

Adey P.S., Shayer M. and Yates, C. (1989) *Thinking Science: the Materials of the CASE Project,* Nelson.

Coles, M. (1997) Science education – Vocational and General Approaches. *School Science Review,* Vol 79, No 286, pp 27–32.

Council of Science and Technology Institutes (1993) *Mapping the Science, Technology and Mathematics Domain,* The Council of Science and Technology Institutes.

Cross, R.T. (1993) The Risk of Risks: a Challenge and a Dilemma for Science and Technological Education. *Research in Science and Technological Education,* 11, 2, pp 171–183.

Foulds K., Gott, R. and Feasey R. (1992) *Investigative Work in Science,* University of Durham.

Foulds K., Gott, R. and Johnson, P. (1997) *Science Investigations 1*, Collins.

Foulds K., Gott, R. and Jones, M. (1998) *Science Investigations 2*, Collins.

Gott, R.and Duggan, S. (1995) *Investigative Work in the Science Curriculum,* Buckingham, Open University Press.

Gott, R., Duggan S. and Johnson P. (1997) *What Do Practising Applied Scientists Do and What Are the Implications for Science Education?* Internal working paper, University of Durham.

Gott, R., Duggan, S. and Jones, M.(1998) *Evidence in Science*: materials in 15 sessions written for pilot project on Skills, Competence and Capability in GNVQ Science funded by Nuffield Science in Practice, University of Durham.

Jones, M., Gott, R. and Jarman, R. (1998) *Investigations as part of the KS4 science curriculum in Northern Ireland*. Internal working paper, University of Durham.

Watts, M. (1991) *The Science of Problem-solving: a Practical Guide for Teacher,* London, Heinemann/Cassell Educational.

2.6 Learning and Teaching about the Nature of Science

Jonathan Osborne

For pupils, who will become our future citizens, understanding the nature of science is possibly more important than scientific knowledge *per se*. The reasons for this view and methods of assisting pupils in understanding the nature of science are the subjects of this chapter.

Why Teach about the Nature of Science?

Today, all sciences are taught to all pupils from age 5 to 16. Yet, as we become increasingly dependent on the service sector of our economy, our society needs fewer and fewer individuals with a scientific knowledge or technical skills (DfEE, 1996). Even in our daily lives, scientific knowledge becomes less and less useful with the ever increasing technological sophistication of our homes. We can no longer fix our domestic appliances without expert help. In such a context, what is the use and value of learning science?

Paradoxically, scientific issues are now increasingly permeating our daily lives. Whether it is the disposal of nuclear waste, the beef we eat, the warming of the climate, the effects of pollution or the cloning of humans, the relentless advance of science and technology has implications for the choices that confront us both personally and as a society. In this context, individuals do not require an extensive knowledge of science, nor even the ability to make practical use of it. Rather, what they need is an understanding of the nature of science – an ability to assess the level of certainty of scientists' claims; to appraise risks; to understand how scientists produce reliable knowledge; to distinguish correlations from causes; and an ability to translate and interpret common scientific reports presented by the media. In short, what science education should seek to develop is a public who will be able to 'read' and understand the discourse of science in a 'critical' way. Consequently, teaching about the nature of science, is not an additional extra or an element to add variety, but a fundamental requirement of a science education for the next century.

Yet as science teachers we are often ill-prepared to address such issues. Ask yourself how we know any of the facts in Fig 2.6A and what evidence do we have to justify their assertion to children?

Moreover, how would you argue with someone who said that the correlation between smoking and cancer does not show any relationship as all the people who get cancer are genetically disposed to the disease developing? Hence, smoking is an irrelevancy.

100

> Day and night is caused by a spinning Earth.
> All stable matter is made of combinations of 92 atoms.
> We live at the bottom of a 'sea' of air.
> Plants produce 'food' by using energy from sunlight.
> The Earth is over 4500 million years old.

Fig 2.6A Common ideas taught in school science

Correlational studies, such as that which established the link between smoking and cancer, are a substantial part of the scientific enterprise. However, correlations are not causes and one of the most common fallacies in logical reasoning is inferring the existence of a causal connection from a known correlation. Hence the relationship between smoking and lung cancer has never been 'proved' – we have simply eliminated all the alternative hypotheses that have ever been suggested. Science progresses by constructing new ways of seeing the world and eliminating those ideas which are false rather than 'proving' or deriving them from observations. The failure to establish any alternative hypothesis leads us to believe that there is a causal connection between smoking and lung cancer.

The National Curriculum specifically requires that the nature of science is addressed in science teaching. At KS3 pupils should be taught about the importance of evidence in supporting scientific knowledge. Moreover, examples should be related to the social and historical context by providing the opportunity to study how at least one idea has changed over time. At KS4, teachers are asked to take this further by exploring how scientific ideas are accepted or rejected on the basis of evidence; how scientific controversies can arise; and how scientific ideas are affected by the social and historical context in which they occur.

How then, can such aspects be taught? The starting point has to be recognising that scientific knowledge is an enormous intellectual achievement – the fruits of the work of some very creative, imaginative and determined individuals. After all, it is only 400 years since Giordano Bruno was burned alive in Rome for proclaiming that stars are suns – and that around them are other planets on which live other people. Galileo was only spared a similar fate because he recanted his assertions and, only in 1992, did the Pope finally pardon Galileo and admit that the church was wrong! When Charles Lyell and colleagues first began to argue in the 1830s that the fossils they were unearthing were evidence for an Earth much older than the version to be found in Genesis, it was very difficult for people to change a lifelong belief. In fact, Edmund Gosse, a reputable scientist of the time, went so far as to argue that the fossils had been placed there by God to deceive mankind! Similarly, Wegener's hypothesis, proposed in 1915, that the continents of Africa and South America were once joined seemed absurd for what force could have separated two such massive and solid bodies?

What then, is it about science that has made it so enormously successful at transforming our conception of the world we inhabit, despite such opposition? Valuable as the previous anecdotes are, teaching about the nature of science requires a more systematic approach and a good understanding of the nature of the subject we teach. Unfortunately, our own education has commonly ignored the nature of the subject and considered the philosophy of the subject simply extraneous. As a consequence, science teachers often hold naive views of the subject which would now be considered outmoded by most philosophers (Koulaidis and Ogborn, 1995). An essential remedy is some further reading and Couvalis (1997) offers a useful contemporary interpretation of the nature of science.

When children are asked, 'What do scientists do?', they commonly answer that scientists 'do experiments and find out things'. Science education should aim to show the range and variety of methods of doing science and that there is no singular method. In simple terms, scientists collect evidence from observations that lead to conjecture about the real world and its nature. Such conjectures – the theories and ideas of scientists – are subjected to experimental test and either survive or fail. Initial ideas are always tentative and disputed but as they survive experimental tests, the model becomes more generally accepted. It is these processes – the commitment to evidence, the testing of the models and theories, and the significance of refutation that need to be highlighted to pupils.

Highlighting the nature of science requires good examples. Although contemporary science provides many exemplars of the tentative nature of scientific ideas and the contested nature of evidence, e.g. whether global warming is happening or not, such science is not a strong feature of the curriculum. Rather much of the knowledge taught in schools is historical and the stories of its discovery are a rich vein that can be mined to illustrate the nature of the subject. A selection of examples is offered in what follows.

Example 1: Doing Science

Historical case studies provide an invaluable means of focusing on what it means to *do* science. In a note to the secretary of the French academy on 1 November 1772, Lavoisier reported the findings of the experiment which led him to believe that the phlogiston theory was incorrect. Lavoisier used the Sun's rays focused by a magnifying glass to heat mercury in a floating tray in a bath of liquid covered by a glass dome. The phlogiston theory predicted that the mercury should weigh less afterwards and that the water level should drop because of the phlogiston gained by the air when the mercury was heated. Pupils can be given the account as a jumbled DART (Fig 2.6B) (see also Chapter 4.4).

He covers the floating tin with a glass dome.
He heats the mercury using a magnifying glass and the Sun's rays.
He repeats the experiment using phosphorus.
He weighs the ash left behind and finds it weighs more.
Lavoisier now thinks that there is something in the air which combines with the burning substance to weigh more.
Lavoisier places mercury on a tin and floats it in a bath of water.
Lavoisier suspects that the phlogiston theory is wrong.
The phlogiston theory predicts that heated substances will lose their phlogiston and weigh less afterwards.
The residue left by phosphorus after burning also weighs more.

Fig 2.6B Scrambled story of Lavoisier's work

After that the pupils can then be asked to label each statement with one of the standard process words or phrases: *observing; making a hypothesis; doing an experiment; predicting; reaching a conclusion.*

This method can be applied to any story of a scientific discovery. Crucially, what it shows is that scientists do not just derive their ideas from their observations. Rather they speculate and dream up theories which they then test.

Example 2: What Counts as Evidence?

Here, the focus is on the evidence and its relationship to theory. This is a very important critical skill to develop because at the heart of science is a commitment to the value of evidence. Pupils will be increasingly confronted with reports in the media such as that shown in Fig 2.6D.

Pupils need opportunities to examine evidence for and against theories as school science tends to reinforce the view that science is either unambiguously right or wrong. Contemporary science, in contrast, confronts us daily with findings that are *uncertain;* either lacking sufficient data, e.g. global warming, or alternatively, have a poorly developed theoretical mechanisms, e.g. AIDS and BSE.

Therefore, it is important to introduce exercises into the class that require pupils to evaluate theories against evidence. For instance, when Darwin put forward his theory of evolution it was based on evidence he gathered from his trip to the Galapagos. There he discovered an enormous number of unique species of animals and plant. However, there was other evidence that contradicted his arguments and supported the biblical account. Pupils can be asked to examine the evidence (Fig 2.6C) and sort them into those which:

a)   support Darwin's theory
b)   oppose Darwin's theory
c)   support the biblical account
d)   oppose the biblical account
e)   support neither theory.

---

1. Darwin finds an enormous number of new animal species on the Galapagos Islands.
2. The Galapagos Islands are very remote and cut off from other land masses.
3. Many fossils of extinct animal species were found on the Dorset coast and elsewhere in the early 1800s.
4. Kelvin estimates the age of the Earth from its rate of cooling to be 15000 years.
5. Edmund Gosse suggests that the fossils were put there by God to deceive mankind.
6. Horses are selectively bred for racing or strength.
7. There are no fossils or animal remains that link mankind to its nearest similar looking species – the ape.
8. Evolution has never been observed actually happening.

Fig 2.6C Some evidence in considering theories of evolution

Long-haul flights may pose risk for babies

A study of how babies react to the air inside aeroplanes has raised questions about whether they should be taken on long-haul flights, particularly if they have coughs and colds.

Some very young babies can experience reduced blood oxygen levels and 'may be at risk of cot death when suffering from a lung infection during a long air flight' according to the research carried out by the North Staffordshire Hospital in Stoke-on-Trent.

In the experiment, which was roughly equivalent to letting the babies fly at 6000 feet above sea level, 34 healthy, sleeping babies breathed air containing six per cent less oxygen than usual. Four suffered unexpectedly low levels of oxygen saturation in their blood and did not wake up naturally. Researchers could not explain why

the four babies reacted 'dramatically differently' from the rest. They were immediately withdrawn from the trial, the hospital said. The changes in a baby's blood caused by a flight were found to linger for some time afterwards.

Thirteen of the babies had brothers or sisters who were cot death victims. This research is part of work into the causes of sudden infant death and the team was led by Dr David Southall, a professor at the hospital.

He said yesterday: 'The four babies were removed from the trial before they were in any danger. It is impossible to know what would have happened had they continued to breath the air with reduced oxygen.

The new research is published today in the British Medical Journal which carries three other related reports. A

leading article by Professor Anthony Milner, who specialises in the health of very young infants at St Thomas's Hospital, London, concluded that flying appears to be 'perfectly safe' for healthy babies. He says that British Airways, which carries 34 million passengers a year, has never seen a cot death on a flight. He estimated that it flies 750,000 babies per year.

Professor Southall states that his team was aware of some unconfirmed reports of a small number of cases of sudden infant deaths after air travel.

He adds: 'We considered that information on this important issue should ideally be gathered before infants were permitted to travel by air. We found no evidence that such studies had been done.

Questions for discussion
1. What is the evidence that letting babies fly in aeroplanes may cause a problem?
2. What is the evidence that it does not harm them at all?
3. How sure are you about this evidence?
4. What reasons might there be for the difference between the findings of the researcher and the fact that no babies have been known to die whilst flying with British Airways?

Fig 2.6D Media report

Another good example can be found in Solomon *et al* (1992) where pupils are asked to examine the evidence that confronted Alfred Wegener who proposed that the continents were floating on the rocks beneath.

Too often the science we teach in schools is what has been termed a 'rhetoric of conclusions' and pupils are never exposed to the idea that new scientific knowledge is tentative and that scientists are often *equivocal* about their claims using words like 'may' and talk in terms of probabilities. Such examples help to illustrate this vital point.

Example 3: Conjecture and Refutation

New scientific ideas are often disputed and there may be legitimate theoretical objections. For instance, the thesis that global warming is caused by human activities is contradicted by the argument that the effect is caused by the natural warming between ice ages. Moreover, the period for which we have been collecting data is just too short to make any sensible prediction from. When the idea was first put forward that day and night were caused by a spinning Earth that moved around the Sun, many arguments were put forward against the idea – many of which are again theoretical objections rather than evidence-based arguments. A valuable approach for illustrating the role of argument in science is role play. Pupils can be asked to act out an imaginary dispute between Galileo and his opponents. Each character has a role card with questions at the end. A typical example is shown in Fig 2.6E.

A Defender of Ptolemy

You are an intelligent man and enjoy a good debate. You are a priest and are rising up in your career very rapidly and are now quite senior at the Vatican. You have read about the young Galileo's ideas and think they are absurd.

You believe that the Earth is clearly the centre of God's Universe. Rather than the Earth moving, there is a perfectly good theory that Ptolemy, a Greek, devised to explain the movement of the heavens. This has worked well for 1500 years. Moreover, you have a number of points to make that you think Galileo's ideas can not explain:

- The Earth is large and immovable whereas the Sun is small and appears to move.
- A spinning Earth would throw objects off into space.
- Birds and clouds above a spinning Earth would drift steadily westwards.
- If the Earth moved through space at the speed necessary to travel around the Sun in a year, the resulting wind would blow people off the Earth.

Discussion questions:

- How do you explain the movement of stars near Jupiter, which Galileo has shown appear to go round Jupiter rather than the Earth?
- Some stars (the planets) wander backwards once a year. Ptolemy's explanation is very complicated. Galileo's would be a lot simpler as all the movements of the stars could be explained by only one object moving. Doesn't this make it a better theory?

Fig 2.6E Role play character card

Such 'dramas' highlight the importance of attempts to refute ideas as a means of establishing them and can be used with any controversial idea in the past such as Darwin's theory of evolution or Torricelli's idea that we live at the bottom of a sea of air. Many attempts, are made to refute new ideas – when they have all failed we believe ideas to be 'true' – by that we mean we think it is very unlikely that they will be found to be fallible.

Example 4: The Social Construction of Science

Scientists do not do their work in isolation. They are normal human beings and their thoughts and ideas are influenced by the culture they inhabit and events happening in the world around them. Therefore, when talking about scientists it is useful to give an impression of what was happening in the society at the time. What wars were being fought? What great books were being written? What major historical events have just happened? Reading about science offers an opportunity to explore the influence of the culture on science, and also, of science on our culture.

Two examples picked from everyday science texts illustrate the potential of such resources. Firstly a portrayal of reproduction in sticklebacks in a biology textbook for 16-year-old students.

> *In the mating season, the male stickleback develops a red breast and builds an underwater nest out of pieces of weed which he glues together with a substance made by his kidneys. He then lures a ripe female to his nest by showing her his red breast. The female enters the nest and lays her eggs. She leaves the nest through the other side. The male may persuade several other females to lay eggs in the same nest.* (Roberts, 1986, p 323)

Surely, innocuous enough? However, a closer, critical reading raises several questions. The picture here is of the male seducer, 'persuading' and 'luring' the female almost against her will to engage in the process of reproduction. The possibility that the female may contribute as much to this process, that she may entice the male remains totally unconsidered. Moreover, the anthropomorphic notion that the male 'persuades' the female demonstrates the social and cultural notions which are being used to construct the 'scientific' version of events. This version of stickleback courtship is developed from the classic account of Tinbergen (1951) which shows females as the passive recipients of males' attention. However, more recently his account has been challenged by the work of scientists who found exactly the opposite of what Tinbergen had reported – adding colour made the male stickleback less likely to be attacked by another territorial male. Moreover, the work of other scientists, who chose to study the behaviour of *female* sticklebacks found that females defended their territories and their encounters were more aggressive than those in the all male sticklebacks. Commenting on this research, Reiss (1984) points to the fact that it demonstrates that 'the way scientists see the world depends very much on the way previous scientists have seen it' and 'that even the most famous piece of research is not necessarily correct' – surely both understandings that science education should aspire to communicate?

Secondly, contrast Richard Dawkins' version of the function of genes and DNA in his book *The Selfish Gene* (1976) with the standard view that the function of the genes is to transmit the characteristics from one generation to the next (Mendel's First Law).

It is raining DNA outside. On the bank of the Oxford canal at the bottom of my garden is a large willow tree, and it is pumping downy seeds into the air. There is no consistent air movement, and the seeds are drifting outwards in all directions from the tree. Up and down the canal, as far as my binoculars can reach, the water is white with floating cottony flecks, and we can be sure that they have carpeted the ground to much the same radius in other directions too. The cotton wool is mostly-made of cellulose, and it dwarfs the tiny capsule that contains the DNA, the genetic information. The DNA content must be a small proportion of the total, so why did I say that it was raining DNA rather than cellulose? The answer is that it is the DNA that matters. The cellulose fluff, although more bulky, is just a parachute, to be discarded. The whole performance, cotton wool, catkins, tree and all, is in aid of one thing and one thing only, the spreading of DNA around the countryside. (Dawkins, 1976)

The distinction may be subtle but it is important. From Dawkins' point of view, the organism is merely the means by which the gene replicates itself – put simply, the chicken is the egg's means of reproducing itself. Secondly, together with others, Dawkins' thesis has given rise to a controversial body of thought known as evolutionary biology. This sees human behaviour as genetically determined and which significantly reduces the role of free will in the account of human behaviour. The classical position limits the role of genes to the acquisition of the physiological characteristics of the organism. One might ask – which of these interpretations is more appropriate or even correct? But that would be to miss the essential point of such an approach which is to expose that, even in science, there exist multiple interpretations of similar data and that interpretations are made in the social and cultural context in which the scientists are situated.

Conclusion

Just as understanding the game of football requires a knowledge of the procedures and rules by which it is played, understanding the incessant stream of scientific claims prominent in the media, requires some knowledge of what the 'game' of science is all about. If developing a scientifically literate populace, who will have the critical faculties to begin to assess the significance of scientific evidence and ideas, is to be an aim of science education, then teaching about the nature of science is not an indulgence but an essential act fundamental to a contemporary science education.

About the Author

Jonathan Osborne is a senior lecturer in science education at King's College London. Prior to that he was an advisory teacher and taught physics and science in Inner London schools for 12 years. He has a wide range of research interests from primary science through to alternatives in practical work, informal science education and the impact of contemporary science on the curriculum.

References and Further Reading

Carey, J. (Ed.) (1995) *The Faber Book of Science*, London, Faber.This book contains the selected writings of scientists from Galileo to Richard Dawkins and is a mine of information and stories for science teachers.

Couvalis, G. (1997) *The Philosophy of Science: Science and Objectivity*, London, Sage.

Dawkins, R. (1976) *The Selfish Gene*, Oxford, Oxford University Press.

DfEE (1996) *Labour Market and Skill Trends*, Department for Education and Employment.

Koulaidis, V. and Ogborn, J. (1995) Science Teachers' Philosophical Assumptions: How Well Do We Understand Them? *International Journal of Science Education, 17*(3), pp 273–282.

Matthews, M. R. (1994) *Science Teaching: The Role of History and Philosophy of Science*, New York, Routledge.

Reiss, M. J. (1984) Courtship and Reproduction in the Three-spined Stickleback, *Journal of Biological Education, 18*(3), pp 197–200.

Roberts, M. B. V. (1986) *Biology for Life*, Walton-on-Thames, Nelson.

Solomon, J. (1991) *Exploring the Nature of Science: Key Stage 3*, Glasgow, Blackie.

Solomon, J., Duveen, J. and Scott, L. (1992) *Exploring the Nature of Science: Key Stage 4,* Hatfield, ASE.

Tinbergen, N. (1951) *The Study of Instinct*, Oxford, Oxford University Press.

Learning about Social and Ethical Applications of Science

Roger Lock and Mary Ratcliffe

We consider that learning about the social and ethical applications of science is an important part of pupils' entitlement in science education. In this chapter we examine some of the barriers to consideration of values, opinions and arguments in science lessons and provide practical guidance to assist teaching and learning.

Introduction

The class have just had assembly, where the headteacher has been expressing concern over the lack of support for the recycling project. She urges pupils to bring aluminium cans to the recycling point and not throw them in bins or, worse, on the ground. The class enter the science lab where the teacher is ready to start a lesson on the reactivity series. A pupil spies the different metals set out for an experiment and says, 'Miss, I think this recycling aluminium business is stupid, don't you? Doesn't it take energy and money to recycle things?' Before the teacher can reply, another pupil pipes in, 'Don't be silly, the school can get money from scrap metal. They want us to do the cleaners' work.' Faced with an involved discussion, the teacher urges pupils to their seats and starts the lesson in the way planned. She introduces an experiment in which pupils will put different metals into solutions of salts to appreciate that metals have differing reactivity. She expects pupils to be able to draw up a reactivity series and write equations for the reactions seen.

Why did the teacher not use the opportunity presented by the pupils' comments to start the lesson with a discussion about recycling metals?

We suspect that opportunities like this may not be taken up because of:

1) Perceived dominance of acquiring knowledge of abstract facts and concepts, encouraged by the assessment system.
2) Lack of confidence or ability in handling discussions where there may be no 'correct' answers but a range of value judgements.
3) Lack of clear teaching strategies to cope with controversial, social issues.
4) Views that social applications of science should not be part of the science curriculum.

What Do We Mean by Social and Ethical Applications of Science?

Social applications of science are those which impinge on our lives directly everyday and indirectly through political and economic decision-making. Science provides us with the evidence for what we *can* do, whether it be cloning, 'splitting' the atom or making new chemicals. Science is a process of rational enquiry which seeks to propose explanations for observations of natural phenomena. Ethics helps us to decide what we *should* do. Ethics is a process of rational enquiry by which we decide on issues of right (good) and wrong (bad) as applied to people and their actions (Fullick and Ratcliffe, 1996).

Development of Social and Ethical Issues in Science Curricula in England and Wales

Up to the early 1980s it was unusual for social and ethical issues to be considered in science lessons; only the occasional, committed enthusiast introduced such applications. ASE mooted a social context for science work in a consultative document (ASE, 1979). This influenced the nature of the new GCSE syllabuses that were developed in 1983. Physics was one of the first new syllabuses to be considered by the then Secretary of State for Education Sir Keith Joseph. The proposals argued that the syllabus should emphasise the wider social and economic implications of the subject. The rejection of the proposals by Sir Keith led the editor of the Times Educational Supplement to comment:

> *Where Sir Keith has gone farther out on a limb is in his total rejection of anything which suggests that the study of physics should include any consideration of the social and economic issues which arise from the application of scientific knowledge. Thus, while he insists that pupils must learn about the technological applications, he believes they must be rigorously steered away from the interesting questions of value, morality and expediency, of which (it is hoped) scientist have become increasingly aware.* (TES, 1983)

Although social and applied issues were included in the syllabuses for the new GCSE courses, the examinations assessed only fact and not abilities to weigh arguments and evidence.

A further bid for status for social and ethical issues in science was made in one of the early drafts of a Science National Curriculum. In the proposed attainment target 21, Science in Action, it was suggested that:

> *Pupils should develop a critical awareness of the ways that science is applied in their own lives and in industry and society, of its personal, social and economic implications, benefits and drawbacks.*

By proposing to devote a complete attainment target to such issues a clear signal could be given to pupils and teachers about the status of such work. However, by the time a statutory version of the curriculum had been produced, not only had the attainment target been deleted, but references to ethical issues were confined to the statements of attainment and the programme of study. The position with respect to genetic engineering is shown in the following extract from the Key Stage 4 programme of study:

> *Using sources which give a range of perspectives, they (pupils) should have the opportunity to consider the basic principles of genetic engineering, for example, in relation to drug and hormone production, as well as being aware of any ethical considerations that such production involves.* (DES, 1991)

Not only were the social, moral and ethical issues marginalised in terms of their status within the National Curriculum, but they were often included in a position which suggested that study of such issues was only appropriate for most able pupils.

This same statement of attainment illustrates the further progressive marginalisation of ethical issues. In the equivalent component of the *revised* 1995 National Curriculum it reads:

> *Pupils should be taught the basic principles of cloning, selective breeding and genetic engineering.*

The consideration of ethical issues has gone! The reality, however, is that it has been moved rather that deleted; moved to the beginning of the programme of study. In this section, which applies across all areas of science, it is made clear that pupils should be given opportunities to study the applications of science. It is explicit that pupils should:

> *Consider the power and limitations of science in addressing industrial, social and environmental issues and some of the ethical dilemmas involved.*

This version of the Science National Curriculum leaves it open for teachers to decide in which contexts the social and ethical applications are considered.

Why Should Social and Ethical Issues Be Addressed in Science Lessons?

For most people the period of compulsory education is the major lifetime opportunity for understanding the science that will impact on their lives and lifestyles. As adults we are expected to play a full and responsible role in society which includes applying the knowledge, understanding and the attitudes and opinions, gained from our study of school science, to our everyday life. However, there are some who consider that learning about social and ethical issues is the preserve of Religious Education teachers and English teachers, or that work on controversial science–society issues should be confined within Personal, Social and Health Education lessons. Such views are even shared by some science teachers. The view we develop here, is that science teachers have a special and unique contribution to make to learning about social and ethical issues. We do not, however, deny the right of other subjects to involve lessons on such topics. Indeed we think it can only be good for the profile of science that it is included in cross-curricular contexts – in this way the distinctive contributions that science and scientists make become evident.

Chapter 1.1 outlines the overlapping reasons for learning science. These should not be treated discretely. By exploring the social and ethical applications of science pupils may also acquire knowledge and will come to understand the methods of science.

The important first step is to include the learning about social and ethical science issues in work schemes as an integral part of science study. They should not be seen as an 'add on' at the end of a topic, as an extra for homework nor as the final element of material for fast workers, but as a central theme covered by *all* pupils. In this way the marginalisation, discussed in the previous section, will be avoided.

Having included such work, the unique contribution from science teachers becomes evident. We are the ones who have the conceptual knowledge that underpins the controversial issues. We have access to the data and information that informs such issues and the opportunity to see them in the broader science context. Our closeness to the knowledge base and the inevitable interaction of pupils with this in their learning, shows how lessons about social and ethical applications of science will also contribute to pupils' science knowledge.

Our training should also ensure that we bring a 'scientific approach' to lessons involving such work. As science teachers we can help pupils to distinguish between fact and opinion. We can encourage them to question the limits of accuracy of presented data and to check whether the interpretation offered is supported by the data. Such strategies help pupils to develop a respect for evidence and encourage the kind of open-mindedness to which scientists aspire. Working in such a way can develop a tolerance to uncertainty and an appreciation of the probability limits within which particular interpretations apply.

As science teachers we have an important role in helping pupils to understand an argument and to try to judge the validity of the 'expert' scientists' work. We should encourage them to independently investigate the literature and to carry out their own practical investigations to explore the data (Cross and Price, 1992). In addition, we should also be encouraging pupils to make up their own minds and to develop their own opinions and attitudes. We should try to ensure that such opinions are soundly based, that pupils are able to distinguish between fact and hearsay as well as able to critically evaluate the evidence. The exact *nature* of the pupil opinion should not be important, but gaining it through critical reflection and respect for evidence is (see Chapter 2.5).

We have shown how learning about social and ethical applications of science means that pupils don't just learn science and science practical skills, they also learn about the ways in which scientists work and think. Through this latter perspective pupils will come to see scientists in a different light. No longer the cold, hard, uncaring, unsympathetic and eccentric, balding male, but the warm considerate person concerned about the ethical dilemmas that his/her work produces. Pupils might come to see that scientists are not the 'boffins' that cause society's ills and problems, but the agents who are trying to alleviate them.

There is one further rationale for including social and ethical applications in our lessons and this relates to the falling proportion of our 16–19 year old population who choose to study science beyond the period when it is compulsory. It is often suggested that the humanistic side of science appeals to many pupils and in particular girls. By addressing such issues in science lessons it is possible that many more may be encouraged to study science longer.

Values in Science Education

Social and ethical applications of science require consideration of attitudes and values, which seem difficult areas for science teachers to engage in. Yet, in every science class in the country values are being transmitted.

Values are inherent in science. The ASE policy on values and science education considers that values which guide scientists' conduct include expectations:

- *to be thorough in all operations, including observation, calculation and reporting;*
- *to be intellectually honest, e.g. refraining from exaggeration, not plagiarising;*
- *to be open-minded, e.g. willing to look for and consider new evidence, facts and theories;*
- *to suspend judgement rather than make snap judgements;*
- *to be self-critical and to encourage others to criticise one's work.* (ASE, 1997)

These values of science can be mirrored in consideration of the social and ethical applications of science.

Planning for Teaching and Learning

The 'content' for social and ethical applications of science is readily available. Local and topical issues, applications of science relevant to the science topic are all appropriate. This section outlines useful methods for handling social and ethical issues.

In all these methods, particular views and values will be shown. It is important to be clear of the purpose of the activity. Bridges (1979) argues that there may be a number of functions for discussion of a controversial issue:

a) sharing individual perspectives – a sufficient goal in itself
b) reaching an understanding of the variety of available subjective responses
c) making a choice between differing values
d) finding a rational resolution of the controversy.

This list implies a hierarchy of purposes – rational resolution being perhaps the most difficult to attain.

For the chosen examples it may appear that people would not in practice give much, if any, consideration to scientific evidence in reaching an opinion. However, the intention in a science classroom is to show how scientific ideas and concepts interact with values and ideas from other disciplines.

We emphasise again that we see the goal of such activities as understanding the complexity and evidence base for viewpoints *not* the opinion arrived at itself.

1. Exploring 'What If?' Questions – Consequence Mapping

Consequence mapping is a simple technique which can be used with pupils of a wide age range. It consists of posing 'What If' questions and following through the consequences. It helps to consider two opposing 'What If' questions to get a balanced picture of what might happen. Fig 2.7A shows a simple consequence map.

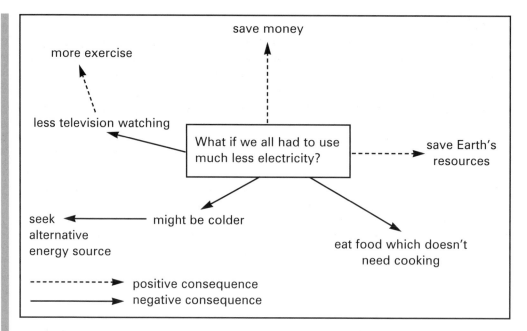

Fig 2.7A Simple consequence map

Examples of issues for consequence mapping:

- What if we all became vegetarians?
- What if pork was the only type of meat available? (This brings in a cultural and religious dimension.)

2. Focused Questions/Structured Debate

An easy way to introduce topical issues is to encourage debate around a focused question. This is used in many resources and, if the question is posed appropriately, prompts much discussion.

However, it is easy for discussions to become a sharing of views without clear evaluation of the arguments and evidence. Without a structure those most willing to express their views are heard, without all having an opportunity to debate the issue.

Strategies for allowing most pupils to become engaged with the issue include clear turn-taking or 'snowball' discussions – twos, then fours then eights, with a limited number of points for each group to make.

The teacher has to decide what role to adopt during the debate, particular if pupils' views clash with informed views of an adult. The teacher may disclose their own views explaining the reasons, act as a neutral chair or play devil's advocate (Ratcliffe, 1998).

Examples of focused questions:

- Should fluoride be added to the water supply?
- Should public money be used to finance exploration of other planets?

3. Role Play

A strategy which is useful for some issues is to act out the positions of the people involved. It allows pupils to empathise more closely with situations which they may come across later. It can be motivating for many pupils to engage with an issue in this way. However, role play has a number of pitfalls which can prevent good analysis of an issue. The purpose and 'science' in an issue can easily get lost as pupils get into role – the personal characteristics becoming more important than evidence. This allows pupils to see the feelings and values involved but can also affect their own views. This is particularly true if they have been put in an emotional position without considering their own reaction. Whenever role play is used for controversial and emotionally charged issues, de-briefing of roles at the end is important. Pupils need to talk through their feelings of being in role and their own views.

Example of issue for role play: Should all children be vaccinated against flu? (Roles: doctor, parent, children with different views towards vaccination.)

4. Goals, Rights and Duties

A strategy useful for ethical dilemmas as well as more general social issues is that of 'Goals, Rights and Duties' (Fullick and Ratcliffe, 1996). For each person or group of people affected by an issue, the goals, rights and duties are considered:

- Goal – what the person intends to accomplish through a particular action.
- Right – entitlement to particular kind of treatment no matter what the consequences.
- Duty – obligation to act or behave in a particular way.

Goals, rights and duties may be dependent on the culture and religion of the locality. Pupils are likely to find some conflict arises when considering the different people involved. This activity is not a way of providing a neat answer to a difficult issue but of showing the complexity of the issue. It allows pupils to see how different viewpoints on an issue may be *justifiably* reached.

Person	Goals	Rights	Duties
Life insurer	Make profit Only pay out valid claims	Knowledge of information affecting life span of insured	Treat those insured fairly
Insured person	Long & healthy life	To keep private irrelevant information	Disclosure of relevant information
Genetic Tester	Successful career	Maintain confidentiality to insured	Provide accurate test results

Fig 2.7B Goals, rights and duties in a life insurance company requiring the results of any genetic testing to be disclosed

Fig 2.7B shows an example of how pupils might consider the goals, rights and duties of people involved in genetic screening.

Example of issues for 'goals, rights and duties':

- Should a carrier of a genetic disease disclose his carrier status to his partner?
- Should pigs/mice/apes be used in medical research?

5. Structured Cost–Benefit Analysis

There are a number of different frameworks available for structured cost–benefit analysis of an issue (Baron and Brown, 1991; Fullick and Ratcliffe, 1996). At the heart of each is a consideration of the advantages and disadvantages of a particular course of action or solution to a social problem. At its simplest, this method consists of making a list under two headings – advantages and disadvantages. There are some other features which are important, however, including identification of different possible courses of action; evaluation of information and review of the decision-making process.

The use of a framework for considering which materials could be used for packaging convenience food is shown:

- Options – List or identify the possible alternative courses of action in considering the issue (e.g. plastic, tin-plated steel, aluminium).
- Criteria – Identify suitable criteria for comparing these alternative options (e.g. cost, strength, longevity, ability to be recycled).
- Information – Clarify the information known about possible options, with particular reference to the criteria.
- Survey – Evaluate the advantages and disadvantages of each option against the criteria (tabulate materials against cost, strength, etc.).
- Choice – Make a considered, informed response to the issue based on the analysis.
- Review – Evaluate the decision-making process and examine the different viewpoints reached.

As can perhaps be seen, a crucial element in this process is the adequacy of available information. In most situations we do not have all the information. Pupils can be asked whether there any crucial bits of information missing and how we proceed if there are. Structured evaluation of information and evidence is a skill worth developing.

Examples of cost–benefit analysis:

- Should an ozone-depleting pesticide be banned?
- Should private motor vehicles be banned from city roads?

With all these methods there are advantages and disadvantages. We encourage use of a variety. Those with an analytical framework, however, may be more helpful in relating social issues to the analytical nature of science.

About the Authors

Roger Lock is a native of Norfolk and a graduate of Aberdeen University. He taught in Kilmarnock, Birmingham and Leamington Spa. He has worked in the Universities of Leeds and Oxford and is currently a senior lecturer in education at the University of Birmingham.

Mary Ratcliffe has taught chemistry and science in comprehensives in Suffolk and Essex, including periods as head of department. She is currently a senior lecturer in education at the University of Southampton with research interests in pupils' learning science in a social context.

References and Further Reading

ASE (1979) *Alternatives for Science Education: a Consultative Document,* Hatfield, ASE.

ASE (1997) *Values and Science Education: Policy Statement*, Hatfield, ASE.

Baron, J. and Brown, R. V. (1991) *Teaching Decision-making to Adolescents,* New Jersey, Lawrence Erlbaum Associates Inc.

Bridges, D. (1979) *Education, Democracy and Discussion*, Windsor, NFER Publishing Company.

Cross, R. T. and Price, R. F. (1992) *Teaching Science for Social Responsibility*, Sydney, St. Louis Press.

Fullick, P.L. and Ratcliffe, M. (1996) *Teaching Ethical Aspects of Science,* Totton, Bassett Press.

Ratcliffe, M (1998) Discussing Socio-scientific Issues in Science Lessons – Pupils' Actions and the Teacher's Role, *School Science Review,* Vol 79, No 288, pp 55–59.

TES (1983) To the Barricades. *Times Educational Supplement*, March 18, p 16.

Useful resources for providing examples of contexts:

SATIS (Science and Technology in Society) materials available from ASE Booksales

SATIS 8–14 (1992)

SATIS 14–16 Books 1–12 (1986–1991)

SATIS Update '91 (1991)

SATIS 14–19 Atlas (1992)

SATIS 16–19 Units and Readers (1992)

SATIS 16–19 Earth and Environmental Sciences

SATIS (1997) *World of Science*, London, John Murray

Science and Environmental Education

Chris Oulton

For over twenty-five years it has been argued that environmental education should be a key part of the school curriculum and that science education has an important contribution to make to this process (Sterling 1992). Debate about the concept of sustainability following the conference on Environment and Development held in Rio de Janeiro has suggested new foci and directions for environmental education (Tilbury 1995) but many issues remain unresolved (Huckle and Sterling 1996). Despite a high degree of uncertainty about the nature and purpose of environmental education much guidance for teachers presents the topic as unproblematic. This can leave teachers struggling to find their own way through a bewildering mixture of contradictory advice, and with doubts about their own effectiveness. This chapter takes the problematic nature of environmental education as its starting point and aims to encourage teachers to work towards developing a personal theory of environmental education in their own context.

The Nature and Purpose of Environmental Education

One way to think about the nature and purpose of Environmental Education is to carry out the following activity. You can do this on your own, as a group of science teachers or as a staff development activity across your whole school.

Choose an environmental issue which you know something about. If there are a number of groups doing the exercise then they can each choose a different issue. Issues might include; energy consumption, rainforest destruction, urbanisation, pollution from cars, litter.

Now brainstorm any ideas you have about the nature of the problem you have chosen. For example, if I had chosen to work on pollution from cars I might have thought of:

- noise pollution
- oxides of nitrogen contributing to acidification
- connections to breathing problems for children and asthmatics.

Don't worry at this stage if you are uncertain about whether something you have thought of is correct. Environmental issues are full of uncertainties and many aspects of issues are contentious and open to debate.

When you have explored the nature of the problem, try to identify some possible solutions. In my case I might list:

- a better understanding of the chemistry of fuel burning

- improved public transport
- raising awareness and concern about the issue
- European legislation on emissions from cars.

Typically when we look across responses to different environmental issues we notice that they are:

- complex
- have local, regional and global aspects
- have social, political, cultural, economic as well as scientific dimensions.

In terms of solutions to environmental problems we might note the need to:

- raise awareness of the issue
- increase knowledge and understanding
- seek for new ways of working, e.g. collaboratively rather than competitively
- develop new technologies
- change attitudes
- change behaviours.

Looking across a series of environmental issues in this way it is difficult to avoid the conclusions that:

- our present way of life is unsustainable
- we do not yet know what a sustainable future would look like but we do have some ideas about what a less unsustainable one might be like
- formal education should contribute to life becoming less unsustainable but we need to be realistic about the potential for formal education to contribute compared to other influences such as the media.

Through doing this exercise you will have begun to develop for yourself an understanding of environmental education. At this stage it can be interesting to compare your ideas with 'official' definitions.

For example, the SCAA publication *Teaching Environmental Matters* states that:

> *Environmental education aims to:*
>
> - *provide all pupils with opportunities to acquire the knowledge, understanding and skills required to engage effectively with environmental issues, including those of sustainable development;*
> - *encourage pupils to examine and interpret the environment from a variety of perspectives – physical, geographical, biological, sociological, economic, political, technological, historical, aesthetic, ethical and spiritual;*
> - *arouse pupils' awareness and curiosity about the environment and encourage participation in resolving problems.* (SCAA, 1996, 2)

The ASE in its Policy on Environmental Education (ASE, 1997a) acknowledges that *'Environmental Education is essential to the well-being of all young people and the material of our society'* and accepts the purposes of environmental education as:

> *(a) about the environment through the development of*
>
> - *knowledge and understanding;*

- enquiry methods;
- *values, opinions and judgement.*

(b) for the environment, through the promotion of:

- *quality, sustainable life-styles and interactions with the environment;*
- *equality of access to resources and control of the environment;*
- *personal and public action to attain these ends.*

(c) in, or through the environment through the inclusion of:

- *regular first-hand experience of nearby localities;*
- *visits to a range of localities, including those further afield if appropriate;*
- *secondary sources of information about more distant environments.*

(ASE, 1997a)

One problem with definitions of environmental education such as these is that, whilst there is often a high degree of agreement between the different definitions there are also a number of important inconsistencies. For example, what is the significance of SCAA's use of the term 'sustainable development' and how does it relate to the ASE's use of the term 'quality sustainable lifestyles'? Sustainable development as a term is considered to be problematic (Sauve, 1996).

As a way of exploring some of these issues, you might try planning a science activity on an aspect of the issue you have chosen. As you develop the activity, keep asking yourself, 'How will this activity contribute to environmental education as outlined in the definitions above?'

Doing this as a group activity can be an effective way to begin to develop a shared understanding of the nature and purposes of environmental education and can be the first step in identifying elements of a school or department policy on environmental education. For ideas on developing a school policy see Baczala (1992).

The following section explores some of the issues which the exercise may raise.

Thinking about Practice

Science text books may sometimes suggest that pupils compare the range of species found on different trees by holding a white sheet under a branch, hitting the branch with a stick, collecting the organisms on the sheet, catching them, identifying them and then releasing them back into the wild.

Here I consider how three teachers might use, or chose not to use, this technique in their work with pupils. How each teacher thinks about this technique to promote environmental education may relate to:

- their views of what a less unsustainable future might be like
- their ideas about the kind of knowledge, skills and abilities needed to bring about a less unsustainable future
- the pedagogy which might facilitate these outcomes in schools.

For a discussion of how an individual teacher's view about environmental education is likely to be a combination of their environmental and their educational ideology see Fien (1993).

Teacher A believes that pupils need to understand ecological principles in order to *understand environmental problems* and thinks that this will lead them to *modify their behaviour* in some less environmentally damaging way. Teacher A therefore takes the pupils into the school field to try out the technique and to record the species found. Back in class they discuss what would happen to the invertebrates if the trees were cut down.

Teacher B agrees with everything that teacher A does. However, in addition, s/he believes that pupils should *explore real problems* and take action about those problems. Teacher B believes that pupils need to understand ecological, economic, social and political matters and also *develop their competence in action taking.* Therefore, teacher B carries out the ecological study with the pupils at the site of a proposed supermarket development. They share the outcomes of their survey with members of the public and ask for reactions to the fact that the supermarket development will destroy the habitat of the organisms they have found. The teacher goes on to encourage the pupils to send all of the information they have gathered to the local newspaper.

Teacher C believes that A and B's ideas are important but also believes that the central issues at stake in environmental education are the *ways in which humans think about and interact with other organisms in the environment.* Teacher C is concerned that the ecological technique used by both A and B *to collect* organisms is questionable as many of the organisms collected by this technique will be damaged or unable to return to their original habitat. C believes that this ecological technique carries the 'hidden' message that it is appropriate for humans to disrupt the environment of other organisms. This may lead pupils to develop an inappropriate attitude to species which humans feel they have the right to exploit to human ends, in this case human learning. S/he decides against using this technique with the class.

The choices that the three teachers make about what to do with their classes are underpinned by the values that they hold.

ASE policy on Values and Science Education states that:

> *All formal science education is imbued by values, even that which attempts to present scientific processes as uninfluenced by human characteristics*

and that

> *Teacher and learners should not shrink from tackling controversial issues in science.*
> (ASE, 1997b)

As we have already seen, ASE policy on environmental education indicates that teachers should promote the 'development of values, opinions and judgements' (ASE, 1997a). Of central concern here is which values should a school promote?

In some aspect of school life, theft of property for example, a school may feel that it is easy to *teach* and *enforce,* through punishment if necessary, a set of values which the school feels are consistent with those held by society. Similarly, in some aspects of environmental education, the school may feel it appropriate to teach and even enforce particular values. For example, most schools enforce rules on the dropping of litter. However, in relation to other issues, schools may feel it appropriate to *promote* certain activities, such as recycling, but would not, for example, punish pupils for failing to recycle an aluminium can.

In other aspects of environmental education, the school may feel inhibited in exploring an issue where the immediate needs of the community may be in conflict with the longer term needs of the environment – for example, teaching about the need to reduce our reliance on the motor car in a town in which the production of parts for motor cars is the main industry.

Jensen and Schnack (1997) to some extent resolve this dilemma by arguing that it is not the function of schools to solve the political problems of society nor to improve the world with the help of pupils' activities. Rather they suggest that schools should aim to improve pupils' 'action competence' generally. 'Action competence' is seen as a set of capabilities which equip individuals with the ability to act in whatever way they choose. In this sense, the success of a discussion in class about a controversial issue or an attempt to act in some way to improve the quality of the environment should be judged in terms of the educational development of the pupils, rather than a change in pupils' attitudes to the issue under discussion or the success of the environmental project *per se* (see Chapter 2.7).

If we accept this argument, we will need to be clearer about our educational objectives in relation to pupil learning outcomes. For example, applying the action competence approach in relation to controversial issues we might, amongst other things, aim to develop pupils:

Understanding:

- that most issues are complex and multi-faceted
- that other people will have different ideas to your own
- that attitudes and values can and should change and develop
- of the factors which can affect the way that humans think and act
- of how humans work co-operatively to make decisions.

Ability to:

- state their own ideas clearly
- find and retrieve appropriate information
- understand data presented in a number of forms
- identify bias in information
- understand the limitations of data
- negotiate with others to achieve a common goal.

Willingness to:

- listen to, respect and consider the ideas of others
- empathise with others
- be tolerant
- seek compromise
- take care not to offend others
- seek solutions to conflict.

What Next?

Although environmental education has been an international concern for over twenty five years, there is little evidence of significant impact of this work on world environmental problems. An essential first stage in bringing about change is recognising that change is necessary. The purpose of this chapter has been to highlight some of the apparent contradictions and challenges in our current statements about environmental education in the hope that this will stimulate a much wider debate about the direction that change may be need to take. I firmly believe that this debate should begin with practitioners in their own context.

About the Author

Chris Oulton is Head of Initial Teacher Education at University College Worcester. He was previously a member of the Centre for Research in Environmental Education Theory and Practice at the University of Bath. He is co-editor of the journal Environmental Education Research.

References and Further Reading

ASE (1997a) *Environmental Education: Policy Statement*, Hatfield, ASE.

ASE (1997b) Policy on Values and Science Education: Policy Statement, Hatfield, ASE.

Baczala, K. (1992) *Environmental Audit: towards a School Policy on Environmental Education*, Wolverhampton, National Association for Environmental Education.

CEE (1992) *Inset for Environmental Education 5–16: Introductory Activities*, Reading, Council for Environmental Education.

CEE (1992) *Inset for Environmental Education 5–16: Environmental Education for Science*, Reading, Council for Environmental Education.

CEE (1995) *Initial Teacher Education*, Reading, Council for Environmental Education.

Fien, J. (Ed)(1993) *Education for the Environment, Critical Curriculum Theorising and Environmental Education*, Geelong, Deakin University Press.

Huckle, J. and Sterling, S. (Eds) (1996) *Education for Sustainability*, London, Earthscan.

Jensen, B.B. and Schnack, K. (1997) The Action Competence Approach in Environmental Education. *Environmental Education Research*. 3, 2, pp 163–178.

Reiss, M. J. (1993) *Science Education for a Pluralist Society*, Chapter 5 'Teaching Controversial Issues in Science', Buckingham, Open University Press.

Sauve, L. (1996) Environmental Education and Sustainable Development: A Further Appraisal. *Canadian Journal of Environmental Education* 1, pp 7–34.

SCAA (1996) *Teaching Environmental Matters through the National Curriculum*, London, SCAA.

Sterling, S. (1992) *Coming of Age: a Short History of Environmental Education (to 1989)*, Walsall, National Association of Environmental Education.

Tilbury, D., (1995) Environmental Education for Sustainability: Defining the New Focus of Environmental Education in the 1990s. *Environmental Education Research*, Vol 1 No 2.

UNCED (1992) *Agenda 21*, Geneva, United Nations Conference on Environment and Development.

SECTION 3

Principles of Teaching and Learning Science

3.1 Planning for Teaching and Learning

Martin Baxter

It is always with the best of intentions that the worst work is done.

(Oscar Wilde)

Translating ASE policy on Learning and Teaching into practice is a most important aspect of our work as science teachers. There are ample examples in OFSTED inspection reports to illustrate what effective learning and teaching looks like in practice. However it can be a challenging and lonely job. Agreeing a policy within the science department, together with detailed schemes of work tailored to the needs of the pupils, provides security and promotes consistency. This chapter is about putting these in place and developing the professional skills of the science team so that, to paraphrase Oscar Wilde, *with the best of intentions the best work is done*.

Background

On the face of it, science teaching is very easy. All you need is a syllabus with the facts clearly organised, and if you present it in a logical order then the audience will understand it, especially if a bit of practical work or a demonstration is thrown in to illustrate the key points.

Well most of us have sat through lessons like this. My daughter complained bitterly about one university lecturer (thankfully not in the UK) who droned on for two hours each week. The students chatted to each other and the noise level was such that only the front row could hear. However they all stopped to listen whenever he said, 'You need to know this,' because they knew it would be in the test.

Fortunately such lessons in schools are rare because:

1) We have developed a better understanding of how children learn science thanks to people like Piaget (1926), Bruner (1987), and more recently Driver (1983) and Gardner (1991, 1993).
2) Young people, especially teenagers, are less tolerant of teaching which fails to meet their learning needs.
3) We recognise that teaching is not a mechanical process, but is as much an art as a science.

It is not easy to get the balance right. On the one hand we have to provide pupils with an entitlement to consistent teaching and on the other avoid curriculum over-prescription which leaves no room for individuality. More important though is that as teachers we have the important role of placing science content in the context of the audience. In practical terms this means finding out what pupils already know and understand, and building on it. Some teachers complain about over-prescription by the National Curriculum or the examination syllabus, but neither of these claim to be more than frameworks. If we let them, they can easily strangle inspired teaching. How the knowledge is organised and sequenced for pupils is the proper professional job of teachers who have to make judgements about the depth and breadth for any particular class.

Policy Perspective

The ASE policy on Learning and Teaching encapsulates what science teachers are striving to achieve:

> *By experiencing a variety of methods and approaches (which are transferable across the curriculum areas), learners will extend and adapt their knowledge, understanding, skills and attitudes. This ability to learn throughout life and adapt to new situations is essential in a world increasingly influenced by science and technology.*

> *Science should encourage individuals to define their attitudes and values in conjunction with the development and application of their knowledge, skills and understanding.* (ASE, 1997)

The most important phrases are at the beginning and end. Teaching and learning interact. Whilst it may be possible to agree a national core of knowledge, skills and understanding in science, it is only within a school, that we can place this in the context of local attitudes and values. It is here that the art of the teacher is at its most important. The cultural variables are challenging (see Chapter 1.5). It is also important not to exclude the effect of experience that pupils might have had prior to the lesson; a family row, a reprimand, a poor/good test result or an insensitive teacher. It is when we combine these characteristics in different ways for each pupil and then think how to meet their needs that we realise just how complex good teaching really is.

This description of effective teaching and learning can apply to many subjects of the school curriculum. However what is different is the context that science provides, and this is something which must be debated and agreed within the science team. Recent years have seen considerable media attention given to the question of how teaching can be made more effective. Some have looked for 'quick fixes' such as whole class teaching, organising classes on the basis of ability, concentrating on 'basic skills', or reducing class sizes. All carry with them a somewhat simplistic view of what happens between teachers and pupils. They perceive teaching as being about 'filling empty pots', rather than 'lighting fires'. The solutions to improving teaching lie with teachers. Hopkins *et al* (1997) provide not only a useful reference point on current strategies, but some exercises to provoke thinking within the science team.

Exemplification of Practice

If you do not know where you're going, you will probably end up somewhere else.

(Laurence J Peters, 1989)

Good Teaching – OFSTED Framework

There is nothing very mysterious about knowing what good science teaching looks like. The London Institute of Education carried out a study of over ninety secondary schools to examine academic effectiveness and drew together previous work on school effectiveness. On classroom teachers it reports:

> *While there is no prescription for good teaching, the benefits of a fairly struc-tured approach, of teacher enthusiasm, positive student–teacher relationships, clear planning and good order and control in the classroom for promoting students' academic achievement were evident from … our research and are in accord with the … teacher effectiveness literature. … the quality of teaching is a crucial component of departmental effectiveness. Important features are:*
>
> - *work focus of lesson (are most students on-task most of the time?);*
> - *strong academic emphasis;*
> - *clarity of goals for student learning;*
> - *student responsibility (independent learning is encouraged);*
> - *lessons generally challenge students of all ability levels;*
> - *teacher enthusiasm;*
> - *effective classroom control;*
> - *high teacher expectations for student performance and behaviour;*
> - *promptness starting and finishing lessons;*
> - *regular monitoring of student progress;*
> - *consistently applied marking policy;*
> - *homework given a high priority and homework policy consistently applied by all teachers;*
> - *teachers' knowledge of the content of the subject and the General Certificate of Secondary Education (GCSE) syllabus.* (Sammons *et al*, 1997)

Given this research evidence it is not surprising that an OFSTED inspector or other evaluator might look out for some of the following:

Knowledge

Does the teacher have a secure understanding of the subject to be taught?

Planning

Does the planning reflect the scheme of work?

Expectations

Are the expectations appropriate?

Organisation/Management

Is the organisation of pupils appropriate?

Special Education Needs (SEN)/Equal Opportunity (EO)

How are the needs of all pupils catered for?

Resources

Are resources appropriate?

Assessment

Does assessment inform teaching and record pupil progress?

Homework

How does homework consolidate or extend understanding?

Certainly a satisfactory lesson will contain all of the sections and good lessons will contain positive judgements in most. Keeping this up all day every day is very demanding, and yet if we were pupils we would not settle for a second rate lesson. So how can we make it easier for ourselves?

Developing a Policy for Teaching Science

> *Success is just a matter of luck. Ask any failure.*
>
> (Earl Wilson, 1989)

Before each match the New Zealand All Blacks rugby team do that spine-tingling Maori war dance. It is not just about bonding, it is about mutual support. Now think of your science preparation room at the start of the school day where you congregate before going out to perform your art. Do you feel mutual support ooze from your colleagues?

I hope that you do but in my experience it is rare. I find it strange that we have policies on pupil discipline, assessment and the curriculum, but not about the most important job that teachers do. The absence of an agreed policy, written or not, on the values that teachers in the team have agreed invariably leads to wide inconsistencies in the quality of teaching and frequently variations in the standards achieved by pupils.

A policy for teaching does not need to be a complicated or lengthy document, and it is a good discipline for it not to exceed one side of A4. However the process of developing an open debate can be rewarding because it provides an important opportunity for sharing practice.

A Science Teaching Policy typically has four sections:

Rationale

This encapsulates the values of the school which should be found in the aims. What is unique about the teaching of science in this school? How does science teaching justify curriculum time, expensive accommodation and equipment?

Purposes

These are the five or six objectives which put the rationale into practice and they should be measurable, e.g. 'Teachers must make the purpose of the lesson clear to pupils in order that they can understand the knowledge and skills to be learned.'

Broad Guidelines

These provide more detail about how the purposes are put into practice. So for the above example we might have 'Every lesson must have concise purposes which are written on the board for the pupils.'

Conclusion

This may relate the teaching policy to other policies such as Health and Safety and should indicate how often it will be reviewed.

Schemes of Work

> *Planning is an unnatural process. It is much more fun to do something. The nicest thing about not planning is that failure comes as a complete surprise rather than being preceded by a period of worry and depression.*
> (Anita Straker (Director of National Numeracy Project) in talk to primary headteachers, November 1997)

For many years schemes of work were synonymous with examination syllabuses, and this also tended to dominate the 11 to 14 curriculum. This led Her Majesty's Inspectors (HMI) to comment that:

> *The only guidance available was provided by the CSE and GCE science syllabuses. These describe the content of what the examiners expect but they are not intended as schemes of work and do not necessarily give the best teaching order of the material.* (DES, 1979)

Pupils were assumed to arrive at age 11 with no knowledge of science and little thought was given to the content and sequence of teaching. Following the Nuffield projects in the 1970s published science schemes proliferated, all claiming to have the answer. In truth the projects varied in quality or practicality although they had a profound influence on much of the current science curriculum. In most schools the schemes either became redundant or they created a dependency for the teacher which took insufficient account of the pupils. We have come a long way in twenty years but it takes good planning to gain the best from a scheme of work as the following example shows.

A Science Department's Planning

A review of the science curriculum from age 10 to 16 included discussions with primary teachers about the ideas in Key Stage 2 that pupils find most difficult. The teachers then examined the GCSE syllabus and identified all the key ideas that they knew most pupils could understand in Key Stage 3. The 11 to 16 science curriculum was mapped and divided into 10/12 lesson units. The science subject specialists traced the important key ideas indicating where consolidation or extension would be required. A variety of texts was purchased to support the scheme of work, and the librarian was asked to identify books and computer software to complement it.

This planning provided the department with a useful case to the headteacher to allocate time for the writing of units. They identified time when teachers could work in pairs to put more detail on each lesson unit including knowledge; skills; links to previous work and other subjects; assessment; text references and homework. When specialists had written a unit of work quality assurance was built in by a critical appraisal by a non-specialist who might have to teach it.

The Scheme of Work is the script or canvass for the teacher as the artist. The touchstone is *can any good teacher in your school pick up your scheme of work and prepare a lesson from it?* If not then perhaps it needs attention.

Essential Elements of a Scheme of Work

1) Does it reflect the ethos of the school?
2) Is there continuity? Has it been planned so that there is a consistent approach across a year group, between year groups, and between the parts or sections of the whole curriculum?
3) Does it provide, directly or indirectly, sufficient subject knowledge for all teachers to feel secure?
4) Is there progression? Do the ideas link together across and between year groups so that pupils and teachers can see how progress can be made?
5) Are the teaching and learning objectives (they may not be the same) identified for each section? In some schools these are specified for each 'core' lesson to ensure that all pupils receive their entitlement.
6) Does the foundation year take full account of the content and methods experienced by pupils in their previous school? (See Chapter 3.6.)

7) Are pupils being adequately prepared for the next phase or stage of their education? (See Chapter 1.4.)
8) Is there guidance for teachers in each section on how to promote literacy, numeracy, ICT, use resources such as video and key texts, and realise the potential of homework?
9) Does it feel as though it will 'turn pupils on to science', does it reflect their interests and the world in which they live?

Planning the Teaching and Learning

Quite normal children, adolescents and adults (as well as neurotic ones) experience learning as a conflict between a desire to hold on to the more or less satisfactory ways of the past and a need to meet the upsetting demands of the future.

(Goodwin Watson, 1984)

If the scheme of work is clearly set out then it is possible to concentrate on planning the lesson for a particular class of pupils who bring with them differences in, at least, learning styles, language competence and motivation.

We may all have a preferred style of learning. Honey and Mumford (1986) categorised learners as:

- *pragmatists* who like to get on with things; are impatient with reflective discussion; take the first opportunity to see if things work in practice; search out new ideas to apply
- *theorists* who like to think problems through in stages; like to analyse things; keen on basic principles, theories and thinking; link facts to theory
- *reflectors* who like to stand back and observe; value the collection and analysis of information; listen to others and like to be part of a broad picture
- *activists* who like to get involved in any new learning experience; enjoy the present; are open-minded and like brainstorming; get involved with together.

In practice pupils have a variety of learning styles although as we get older one or two tend to predominate. As adults we may have found that one style has given us success and this is reflected in our teaching style. The main point here is that the teaching itself may be a cause of underachievement, misunderstanding or demotivation for pupils if it is narrow and uses only one learning style.

Kolb (1984) developed the Honey and Mumford approach into a Learning Cycle which lends itself to the teaching of science. It can be conceived as four stages (Fig 3.1A).

There are several observations to be made about this model. First the cycle is continuous and we re-learn in the light of experience. Secondly the direction of learning is governed by personal goals. If these goals are unclear then learning is less efficient. This determines the third observation which is that learning styles are highly individualistic. This means that people will tend to learn more effectively within one or more stages of the learning cycle.

133

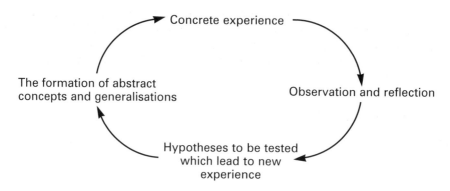

Fig 3.1A A learning cycle

For example in a lesson where pupils observe a demonstration of the van der Graaf generator and respond to questions from the teacher this approach will not meet the needs of all pupils. In practice most teachers also provide concrete activity, encourage pupils to reflect on their personal experience of static electricity, draw on the pupils' own ideas to develop abstract concepts about charge, and then require them to test these ideas in a new situation by charging polythene rods.

A lesson such as this visits each part of the cycle, and some parts more than once, which allows pupils to engage where they learn best. However the learning goals for the pupil must be made clear at the start of the lesson.

Existing conceptions of science are very resistant to change. Boys, girls, ethnic groups, SEN or highly-able pupils may all have quite different notions about static electricity which need to be brought into the public arena of the classroom. A good teacher who knows the class well will explore these through questions that draw out their ideas. Culture and language are closely linked and it is all too easy for the teacher to use technical words which amount to a foreign language for some pupils (see Chapter 3.3). Pupils need the opportunity to work out their ideas in the language that is easiest for them. In the same way mathematical ideas, calculations, algebra, graphs and charts can be a spur to some pupils and demotivating for others. Investigative Science provides a powerful tool for embracing all these issues and even within a lesson can provide pupils with personal challenge and the essential time for reflection and discussion.

To create three or four 60 to 70 minute lessons each day that take account of these ideas appears to be an awesome task. Yet many teachers do it successfully because they have a broad plan with a selection of alternatives to draw on as the lesson develops. Hopkins *et al* (1997) observe that effective teachers have a repertoire of lesson formats with idiosyncratic planning conducted as they go about their every day business.

> *Indeed it sometimes strikes us that final adjustments are still being made as the teacher enters the classroom and judges the mood of the class.*
> (Hopkins *et al*, 1997, p 48)

However for most of us having a common approach within the department is helpful, not the least because pupils get used to it over time. In practice many effective science teachers hand over much of the responsibility to the pupils and may adopt an experimental approach to their teaching (Hopkins *et al*, 1994). If pupils know what has to be learned and there are a variety of activities in the lesson, they will tap in at the stage where they feel secure and can safely take both the time and the risk to learn something new.

Using Teaching Time Effectively

> *If only I could stand at a street corner with a hat in my hand and beg people to throw their wasted time into it.* (Bernard Berenson, 1990)

Good lessons have a clear beginning, middle and end, such as described below.

Beginning

(10 minutes maximum)

- Outline the purpose of the lesson and what the pupils should have learned by the end in terms of knowledge and skills.
- Explain what the pupils are going to do (groups, individual, practical, book research, discussion, etc.) and how long each stage will take. Allowing pupils to talk about their ideas is important and it is here that we ensure that *pragmatists, theorists, reflectors* and *activists* all have the opportunity to enter the learning cycle.
- Assess what the pupils (as a group) already know by brainstorming ideas and gently challenging or asking questions about misconceptions.
- Identify what the homework will be about.

Middle

(30 to 45 minutes)
Pupils work according to the plan and the teacher visits individuals and groups to pose questions to check understanding and progress, clarify misunderstandings, move pupils on and generate pace. (I can hear you saying at this point that this is idealistic and not real. The fact is that we can observe teachers doing it. They insist on a way of working at the start of the lesson and provide an atmosphere in which pupils can feel they are achieving). Sensitive teachers who know the learning styles of individual pupils can intervene, support and challenge at the appropriate point in the lesson. Let us be honest, if pupils have not chosen to learn then we cannot force them. The art of the successful science teacher is to open that window on the world of science so that even the most reluctant learner is motivated to want to know a little more about it.

End

(10 minutes maximum)
Before the end of the lesson it is essential to bring pupils together to assess the progress against the learning objectives.

Indicating what will happen next lesson and what will the pupils need to do for themselves perhaps as homework, provides the continuity in learning and gives them a sense of their progress. My own view here is that praise for the whole class about some aspect of the lesson helps pupils to leave with a feeling that their achievement has been confirmed.

Evaluation of Learning Outcomes

If we achieve a sense of trust and partnership in the learning process where there are mutual goals, then evaluation is so much more productive because some of it can be done by the pupils themselves or with each other. So, *'How are you doing?', 'What do you think you did wrong?', 'How has this changed your ideas?', 'Can you explain this to me?'* are both diagnostic and remedial. What you want to know is, *'What progress are the pupils making, individually and as a class?'*

Through effective teaching you might be looking for evidence of:

- *Knowledge gain* – Are pupils increasing their knowledge and how quickly?
- *Understanding* – Are the gains similar for analysis, interpretation, evaluation and explanation of ideas?
- *Skills acquired* – Are there gains in practical, investigative, interpretation, prediction skills, and to what extent can pupils work independently or as a member of a team to share responsibility?

Final Thought

I started by suggesting that on the face of it teaching science is easy. In fact many science teachers make it look easy by combining subject knowledge, a repertoire of teaching models and sophisticated responses to circumstances, skills in managing young people, and the ability to reflect on their practice. Teaching science is a highly complex and professional task and I firmly believe that we should talk to each other and the general public in these terms.

About the Author

Martin Baxter is Inspector for Science and Senior Adviser (Standards) in Hillingdon and a member of the ASE 11–16 Committee. He has taught in primary, secondary and special schools, worked as an adviser and officer in four LEAs as well as in business. He has interests in curriculum planning, teaching, and school management about which he provides training in the UK and abroad.

References and Further Reading

Berenson, B. in Beer, M. (1990) *The Joy of Winning,* London, Mercury.

Bruner, J and Haste, H. (1987) *Making Sense: the Child's Construction of the World,* London, Methuen.

DES (1979) *Aspects of Secondary Education*, London, HMSO, pp 171.

Driver, R. (1983) *The Pupil as a Scientist?* Milton Keynes, OUP.

Gardner, H. (1991) *The Unschooled Mind and How Schools Should Teach*, London, Fontana.

Gardner, H. (1993) *Multiple Intelligence; Theory and Practice*, London, Fontana.

Hopkins, D. and West, M. (1994) Teacher Development and School Improvement. In Walling, D. (Ed) *Teachers as Leaders: Perspectives on the Professional Development of Teachers*, Bloomington, Indiana, Phi Delta Kappa.

Hopkins, D., West, M., Ainscow, M., Harris, A. and Beresford, J. (1997) *Creating the Conditions for Classroom Improvement*, London, David Fulton.

Honey, P. and Mumford, J. (1986) *The Manual of Learning Styles*, Maidenhead, Peter Honey.

Kolb, D. (1984) *Experiential Learning*, Englewood Cliffs, New Jersey, Prentice-Hall.

Piaget, J. (1926) *Language and Thought of the Child*, London, Routledge and Kegan Paul.

Peters, L. In Bone, D. and Griggs, R. (1989) *Quality at Work*, London, Kogan Page.

Sammons, P., Thomas, S. and Mortimore, P. (1997) *Forging Links: Effective Schools and Effective Departments*, London, Paul Chapman.

Watson, G. (1957) in Claxton, G. (Ed) (1984) *Live and Learn: an Introduction to the Psychology of Growth and Change in Everyday Life*, London, HEB.

Wilson, E. in Bone, D. and Griggs, R. (1989) *Quality at Work*, London, Kogan Page.

3.2 Assessment in the Classroom

Philip Hayes

Assessment strategies should be at the heart of teaching and learning. Learning is improved where there are clear assessment policies and effective use of formative assessment. Good use of summative assessment data can help long-term planning. This chapter outlines important assessment issues.

Purposes of Assessment

In order to be effective, the assessment processes used in the classroom or laboratory should directly affect the teaching and learning strategies used. In order to be really effective, assessment needs to serve a number of purposes:

1) *Assessment should provide information about the progress of pupils in relation to knowledge, skills and understanding* – from a curriculum viewpoint this generally refers to the syllabus or Programmes of Study in Science. This information is needed for a variety of audiences including the teacher, pupils and parents. However it will also be needed by the management of the department or school in order to evaluate overall effectiveness and value added in the subject.
2) *Assessment should identify where emphasis needs to be made in relation to the next stage of learning for a group of pupils,* and as such directly influences overall lesson planning.
3) *Assessment should identify specific learning issues for individual pupils and be the principal aid to target setting.* This will also be important for pupils with learning difficulties as an assessment of need as part of an Individual Education Plan.
4) *The assessment process should be a positive experience for pupils* providing them with information about their progress to date, celebrating their achievements, and helping them to identify ways to improve their work.

No one assessment instrument or strategy can serve these varied criteria. So effective assessment needs to employ a range of strategies. The degree of objective information needed by teachers has increased significantly in recent years.

Twenty years ago much of the assessment used by teachers was summative, i.e. it summarised progress against criteria which were mainly knowledge-based. In order to satisfy this particular focus the principal assessment instruments were tests in which pupils were marked according to how much they remembered about a topic covered. In the early 1980s the advent of Records of Achievement brought to the forefront formative assessment strategies which involved pupils more in assessing their own progress against specific criteria. With the introduction of the National

Curriculum the range of the aspects of learning which were assessed also expanded and in Science included investigational and process skills. This required a funda-mental change in the processes of assessment which placed the emphasis on pupil involvement rather than teacher testing. In the most effective classrooms this changed the way in which the curriculum was taught. It is apparent from the devel-opments of the last fifteen years that truly effective formative assessment strategies directly impinge upon the teaching strategies and classroom organisation used by teachers(To be really effective, pupils need to understand and be committed to the processes and outcome of assessment and not merely accept the results as a measurement of their progress identified by unknown criteria and a third party.)

Teachers are forming judgements about the progress of their pupils throughout all their lessons based on observations, knowledge of the subject and pupil response. However, in order to have objective and comparative data, all departments and classrooms need a co-ordinated Assessment policy which is a reflection of a whole school policy and which satisfies the statutory curriculum requirements. This means that an effective assessment policy will have a number of key features:

1) *A central record keeping system which links to whole school records for each pupil.* This may well be linked into a whole school computer administration system.
2) *Agreed criteria for the assessment of each aspect of the subject which have been shared and moderated across the department, so that they are applied consistently.* This may be relatively straightforward for those aspects of skills, knowledge and understanding defined by schemes of work, syllabuses or National Curriculum. However many departments also assess pupils' efforts as well as their attainment and this requires a similar degree of consistency. To achieve this, there should be well defined criteria for the award of any effort grades which have been agreed by all staff – not just within one curriculum area – but across the whole school. This means that a grade A for effort in one subject is similar to a grade A in another and thus the process may not only be more objective but also will provide a consistency for the pupil which will enable her, and her parents, to identify more effectively those lessons which require greater effort.
3) *All Schemes of Work should have outcomes defined in terms of the learning objectives to be achieved, and assessment strategies clearly identified against each outcome or group of outcomes.*
4) *The way in which the outcomes from day to day assessment are used by teachers to inform lesson planning should be clearly defined.* This means that if an assessment indicates that a pupil, or group of pupils is deficient in some aspect of knowledge or skills then this emphasis should be revisited through classwork, revision, investigational work or homework in order to support learning. The policy should indicate strategies which would enable teachers to reinforce or develop key learning aspects. For example, supposing a test on a recently completed topic indicates that a significant proportion of the pupils have failed to grasp a key concept. Rather than progress onto the next topic, as a natural development, homework could be set and marked which explores and reinforces the concept which has been misunderstood.

The ASE Assessment policy provides some additional guidelines to be borne in mind when constructing a departmental policy:

> *Assessment should:*
>
> - *take account of what is taught and learnt so that it can influence subsequent teaching and learning;*
> - *match the needs of the learner;*
> - *be flexible and responsive to changing needs;*
> - *involve a wide range of methods;*
> - *motivate and involve learners;*
> - *inform teachers, pupils and others about progress through measures of added value as well as attainment;*
> - *celebrate achievement.*
>
> *Schools should provide support for assessment by:*
>
> - *ensuring that assessment by teachers is as valid and reliable as possible;*
> - *ensuring that teachers receive appropriate training in assessment;*
> - *providing relevant information to those who have a right and need to know;*
> - *providing a whole institution approach encompassing the policies and actions of individual teachers and, where applicable, departments;*
> - *ensuring co-ordination across the curriculum.*
>
> (ASE, 1997)

Marking of Pupils' Work

Day-to-day marking of classwork, homework or projects is a key element in providing information about the progress of pupils. There are many ways of grading pupils' work. However a grade is merely a comparative mark and the main principle which marking should be trying to develop is to provide pupils with information about how they could improve their work and understanding. In order to be truly effective there should be a department or whole-school marking strategy which should aim to be formative as well as summative. Whilst grades on marked work are awarded against consistent criteria, the marking should include information which enables the pupil to improve their work next time. This provides a record for the pupil which constantly targets improvement. All pupils should be able to say how they should be able to do to improve their work in order to improve its quality.

Part of the hidden agenda in marking is the discussion which goes on between teacher and pupil about the work completed. In order to manage this effectively it may be necessary to identify different pupils each time work is returned and to discuss with them specific issue which will help them to improve their work – not forgetting that the key skills of literacy, numeracy and IT are as much the responsibility of the science teacher as of any other and therefore should be an element of the assessment of science.

Assessment Instruments

When devising any assessment instrument it is important to start with two questions: What am I actually trying to assess? Is this the best method of finding out? The instrument should be evaluated before use to see if it fulfils its purpose.

Tests are a major form of assessment used in most curriculum areas. If the focus of the test is simple, such as spelling, then devising the test instrument so that it actually assesses that which it is intended is relatively simple. However, in assessing progress at the end of a unit of work, or as part of end of year examinations then the test instrument is more complex and care must be taken that it is actually performing the intended task. Tests have limitations in assessment of higher-order skills and important processes, such as communication and analysis. Science has a very complex vocabulary and for many pupils – particularly those whose first language is not English – the vocabulary, context and examples used to illustrate questions may be unfamiliar to them. It is important to screen tests to ensure that the language or contexts do not form a barrier to the pupils which prevents them from displaying their scientific understanding.

Teacher assessment, through evaluation of projects, written work, homework and oral contributions, provides an important means of monitoring progress. Teacher assessment is most effective when:

- it uses clear assessment criteria which are agreed by all staff and communicated clearly to pupils
- pupils are involved in their own assessment
- evidence of pupil achievement is systematically collected and recorded
- good moderation strategies within departments and across schools are used to enhance reliability.

Assessment of Practical Work

The teaching and assessment of practical work and scientific process skills has become an important part of the science curriculum. This has been achieved in a variety of ways. Integrating process skills into day-to-day practical work is obviously the most effective way of doing this but for external examination assessment many departments run specific assessment projects directly drawn from knowledge or concepts identified in the syllabus. In order to do this it is important to remember that higher order *process* skills are complex and the degree of difficulty increases significantly if these are assessed through higher order *concepts*. If you are aiming to assess complex process skills then it is more effective to assess these through less complex concepts in order that the focus of the assessment is directed at the practical work.

Formative and Summative Assessment

It does not matter whether the assessment instruments are National Curriculum tests, external examinations, or class-based assessments the principles which underlie their construction and application to pupils appear to be common. However, some of these assessments perform a summative function in providing information about achievement at a particular reporting point. Others form part of formative assessment in assisting the improvement of learning in the short term. The difference between summative and formative is that the former gives information and data about progress whilst the latter is a way of using assessment information with pupils. Summative data can be used formatively with pupils. The outstanding feature about formative assessment is that it involves the pupil in identifying how to improve and thus enables targets to be set for improvement. (For a useful discussion of the use of formative and summative assessment, see Black (1993 and 1998).)

Formative procedures have a number of typical features which are intended to make the pupil a partner in the assessment process. In order to evaluate whether you are working with pupils in a formative way you need to ask yourself a series of questions:

1) Before assessing the pupils' work – be it a piece of written work, investigative work, or test – do they understand the criteria for assessment?
2) Do you provide feedback to the pupil through written comment, discussion or review which helps them to identify how any marks or grade have been awarded?
3) Does the pupil understand how he or she could improve her work and what steps to take to do so next time ? Are targets agreed to enable this to happen?

It is this partnership, understanding and commitment to improvement which is at the heart of formative assessment. In recent years this has been extended through action planning in courses such as the General National Vocational Qualifications which gives pupils even more responsibility for their own learning.

Target Setting

Reference has been made to target setting in learning throughout this chapter. There are two features of target setting which are current in schools:

The first is legislation in the 1997 Education Act which requires schools in England and Wales to set overall targets for improvement in the core subjects of the National Curriculum. This is done through Governing Bodies.

The second is the target setting referred to in this chapter concerning individual pupils. Individual target setting is only effective if there is a genuine commitment from all who are involved – teachers, pupils and parents.

In target setting, assessment information and data are used periodically to identify key issues which need to be addressed by the pupil in order to improve. This might be done at the individual subject level where the targets are agreed between the class teacher and the pupil. However, it could also be done at the whole school level where key targets are identified across a range of subjects. At the whole school stage there needs to be a high degree of co-ordination to ensure that the correct targets have been identified, communicated to pupils and teachers, and monitored. Whatever is the case successful target setting requires a number of key elements:

1) Comprehensive assessment information to enable targets to be identified.
2) A limited number of short-term and achievable targets agreed with the pupil.
3) Involvement of parents or guardians to support the pupil.

4) Provision within the teaching and curriculum to enable the targets to be achieved.
5) Monitoring and review after an agreed period to determine whether the targets have been achieved and what next needs to be done.

Benchmarking

This is a strategy of using assessment data which has been introduced by Government. In essence it refers to the process whereby schools of similar intake and social profile are compared in order to evaluate the degree of improvement achieved (see Chapter 4.2). Benchmarking takes basic data on issues such as free school meals in order to contextualise a school, so that performance in Key Stage tests or GCSE exams can be considered as a baseline for an individual school. This enables schools to evaluate their own performance against schools of similar intake. In turn this enables an individual school to consider the progress made by their pupils over time and is intended to provided a baseline for the calculation of value added progress.

Value Added

This is one of the areas of greatest growth in the development of assessment in recent years. Originally it sprang from the need for schools to give some context to the exam results required to be published in prospectuses and Annual Governors' Report. In recent years this has developed as an instrument for evaluating not only whole-school progress but also progress of individual departments.

The basis for Value Added stems from the growth in the use of baseline data by schools. This could be end of Key Stage tests or assessments such as the NFER CATS profile, which assesses pupils' development against Verbal, Non Verbal and Qualitative assessments and provides standardised scores which are age related for each pupil.

Using baseline and other data, such as end of Key Stage assessment results, departments can consider the progress made by individual pupils. In turn it can also be used to consider the progress made by a class, set or year group because gathering assessment data over time provides a longitudinal viewpoint of progress.

The sophistication of some of the baseline data now used in Secondary Schools means that it is possible to consider potential grades of pupils, using baseline data and thus evaluate how pupils have measured up to their potential when final results have been achieved. In primary schools baseline assessment and information such as reading scores on entry provide effective ways of considering progress made at the end of a Key Stage. Processes have also been developed whereby pupils' scores at GCSE can be used to predict their potential in Further Education and again used as a method to consider the progress made or overall effectiveness of a curriculum area. These methods tend to ascribe points to each GCSE score and use overall scores as a predictor of future potential grades. This is extremely useful in discussion with pupils as they progress through a course in terms of whether they are working to potential and the targets need for future success. Similarly they can be used by the management of an Institution to consider the effectiveness of a department (see Taylor Fitz-Gibbon, 1996, for a detailed discussion of value added monitoring systems).

The use of value added and baseline data is only really effective if it is considered through a whole-school approach. In this way the true potential of the information can be released. Data showing progress of an individual pupil across subjects can be used to discuss the teaching and learning strategies used in different subject areas. Why does this pupil do better in Science than Maths, if pupil data suggest there should be similar achievement in both? Why does this science class appear to be making poorer progress than a parallel group?

Baseline data are also useful for considering aspects of a departmental or school organisation, such the setting arrangements in place within a curriculum area. Individual pupil performance is the usual criteria for placing in a set. However, it should be remembered that within a year group pupils can be as much as 11 months apart in age. There is evidence that such age differences can have a significance effect on performance, due to the amount of time spent in formal schooling. The use of standardised assessments can enable schools and departments to consider the potential of pupils. Departments can compare performance in class and test scores to augment baseline data to see whether there is an anomaly between them. This can help them to consider placement in sets on wider criteria and thus help to release the true potential of pupils. For example, a pupil with a high non-verbal score may perform less well in school assessments and may be placed in a particular set. Careful consideration needs to be given to the reasons why such a pupil does not perform well in school assessments and whether the set placement is an accurate reflection of potential.

It is important to accept that modern education places a high degree of accountability on schools and teachers, both from the expectations of management as well as parents and politicians. Assessment data is a principal method of considering this accountability.

About the Author

Philip Hayes is a former LEA Senior Adviser for Curriculum and Assessment and an OFSTED inspector for primary and secondary schools. He was a member of ASE Assessment and Exams Committee and is currently a member of the ASE 11–16 Committee. At present, he is Head of a large 11–18 Comprehensive School.

References and Further Reading

ASE (1997) *Assessment: A Policy Statement*, Hatfield, ASE.

Black, P. (1993) Formative and Summative Assessment by Teachers. *Studies in Science Education* 21, pp 49–97.

Black, P. and William, D. (1998) Assessment and Classroom Learning. *Assessment in Education*, 5, 1.

NCVQ (now QCA) (1995) *Assessing Students' Work – GNVQ in Science,* London, NCVQ.

SCAA (now QCA) (1995) *Exemplification of Standards: Science Key Stage 3 Levels 1–3,* London, SCAA.

SCAA (now QCA) (1995) *Exemplification of Standards: Science Key Stage 3 Levels 4–8* London, SCAA.

QCA has a website which includes information on curriculum, assessment and their publications catalogue: http://www.open.gov.uk/qca/

Taylor Fitz-Gibbon, C. (1996) *Monitoring Education. Indicators, Quality and Effectiveness*, London, Cassell.

Dialogues in the Science Classroom: Learning from Interactions between Teachers and Pupils

Jerry Wellington

The focus of secondary education has largely been on science as a practical subject, often quite rightly. But for many pupils the greatest obstacle in learning science – and also the most important achievement – is to learn its language. One of the important features of science is the richness of the words and terms it uses. Almost all teaching and learning takes place using the medium of language, verbal and non-verbal. In this chapter I concentrate mainly on spoken language in the science classroom involving interactions between teachers and pupils. These interactions might involve questioning, explaining, shaping and controlling lessons, focusing discussion, word games, or demonstrating. I give examples of dialogues which illustrate some of the language games going on in science lessons. The stimulus for considering these dialogues comes from an earlier focus on 'critical incidents' (Nott and Wellington, 1995), i.e. events which happen in science lessons which raise important issues for teachers. The aim of the chapter is to increase awareness of the types of interaction which go on, to illustrate their complexity and to suggest some practical strategies for understanding and improving classroom dialogue.

The Policy Background

The debate about language in science education goes back a long way. For brevity, I start in the 1970s. Two of the fashionable authors of that era wrote:

> *Almost all of what we customarily call 'knowledge' is language, which means that the key to understanding a subject is to understand its language. A discipline is a way of knowing, and whatever is known is inseparable from the symbols (mostly words) in which the knowing is codified. What is biology (for example) other than words? If all the words that biologists use were subtracted from the language, there would be no biology. … This means, of course, that every teacher is a language teacher: teachers, quite literally, have little else to teach, but a way of talking and therefore seeing the world.*
> (Postman and Weingartner, 1971)

Four years later the Bullock Report was published which advocated that all teachers should see themselves as teachers of language. One specific suggestion was that science teachers should examine the dialogues which go on in the classroom so that they can become more skilful in 'orchestrating it' (Bullock Report 'A Language for Life', 1975, p 141). My aim in this chapter is exactly that: to examine some of this dialogue in the hope of improving it.

There is now a strong curricular justification for an increased emphasis on language in science teaching. The Science National Curriculum includes a 'Use of Language' section in its Common Requirements for Key stages 3 and 4. The Programmes of Study also include a section on Communication which states that pupils should be taught to: 'use appropriate scientific vocabulary to describe and explain the behaviour of living things, materials, and processes.'

Finally, there is a strong justification for a focus on language if formal science education is to be a major contributor to citizenship and the public understanding of science. Pupils should learn the language of science so that they can:

- read critically and actively
- develop an interest in reading about science
- develop competence in sceptically scrutinising claims and arguments made in the media based on 'scientific research' or 'scientific evidence'.

Frameworks for Looking at Classroom Talk

Transmission and Interpretation

Some of the most notable work in the area of thinking and learning through talk has been done by Douglas Barnes and his co-workers (1969, 1973, 1976). This work is not recent but it is still very relevant today. Barnes identified two different modes of classroom teaching; he termed these as 'transmission' and 'interpretation'. When knowledge is seen as some kind of commodity, owned by the teacher and displayed to learners only according to the teachers' decree, then the teacher seeks to *transmit knowledge, in a kind of restricted shopkeeper–customer relationship. When, however, knowledge is seen as something to be* shared, *to be* shaped by the act of learning itself, *then the teachers' task is to interpret* learning.

Barnes showed how teacher assumptions about language in learning could be placed at one point or another along a dimension, thus:

Transmission ←——————————→ **Interpretation**

The examples from classrooms in the next section show teachers using language at various points along this continuum.

Types of Language in Science Teaching

Barnes *et al* (1969) distinguished three types of language used by science teachers:

- *specialist language presented*: language unique to the subject which teachers recognise as a potential problem and therefore present and explain to pupils

- *specialist language not presented*: language special to the subject which is not delib-erately presented – because it has been explained before or teachers are unaware of using it
- *the language of secondary education*: language used by teachers which pupils would not normally hear, see, or use except in the world of the school.

This is an important classification. Fig 3.3A gives a summary of the categories, with examples from science.

The language of secondary education	Technical language/ specialist language
criterion	chlorophyll
... in terms of ...	amplitude
relatively	equilibrium
factors	mass
specifically	uniform
complex	force
proportional to	trachea

Fig 3.3A Types of language used by science teachers

Again, we will see many examples of these categories of language in the excerpts later.

Questioning

It is also useful to consider and classify the various types of question used by teach-ers during classroom dialogue. Some are closed questions having only one acceptable answer. Closed questions might ask for a name, a piece of information, or a specific line of reasoning (an argument). Others are open in that a number of different answers could be accepted. Open questions might ask for a pupil's line of reasoning, or an opinion or evaluation. Others, as we see later, are 'pseudo-ques-tions' which often involve pupils in a 'guess what's in my head' type of language game. Another type of question is used by teachers to shape, control and focus lessons. A lot of the questions used by teachers (both open and closed) can be called diagnostic questions, e.g. eliciting what they know; checking that pupils are on the right lines; finding out if any learning is happening.

'Moves' in Classroom Exchanges

Sinclair and Coulthard (1975) identified three parts or 'moves' to the typical class-room dialogue: initiation, response and follow-up. This has been confirmed by many other studies of classroom discourse since and is commonly know as the IRF frame-work. Its main features are that the teacher initiates and guides the exchange; speaking rights are unequally distributed; there is clear control by the teacher over what is said, by whom and when.

Examples of Classroom Dialogues: Good, Bad and Debatable

Critical Incidents and Classroom Dilemmas

I use one of our critical incidents here to lead into the look at dialogues in teaching and learning (Nott and Wellington, 1995). One which always seems to strike a chord is the incident where a teacher attempts to show that photosynthesis produces oxygen by exposing pond weed (elodea) in a test tube and hoping that enough oxygen is present to be tested positively. Things go wrong however. Some teachers react to this critical incident by saying they might 'rig' it, e.g. by exaggerating the conditions so that enough oxygen will be produced. Others simply cheat or conjure, e.g. by injecting oxygen in from a tank. Demonstrating in science has been called 'coercing material phenomena into being meaningful' or arranging events in the 'service of a theoretical conception' (Ogborn *et al*, p 78). Some teachers manipulate nature to serve theory, ethically and perhaps unethically. Others engage in what we call 'talking their way through it' (Nott and Wellington, 1995). They explain what might have gone wrong and discuss the perfect conditions which would have produced the desired result. Dialogues of this kind, although not always practically possible, do help pupils to learn about the nature of science and the obstinacy of nature.

The example below (from Delamont, 1976) shows a teacher (Mrs Linnaeus) dealing with two very different pupils, one with a cynical view of science 'experiments', the other with a view of how complex nature can be:

Michelle:	*Mrs Linnaeus, I don't see how that will prove it – it could be all sorts of other things we don't know anything about.*
Mrs L:	*(Comes down the lab. to Michelle's bench. Asks her to expand her question, explain what she doesn't see.)*
Michelle:	*Well you said if there was starch in the bare patches it would mean there was … it was because of the light, but it could be the chemicals in the foil, or something we know nothing about.*
Sharon:	*(butts in) Of course it'll prove it, we wouldn't be wasting our time doing the experiment if it didn't.*
Mrs L:	*I don't think that's a very good reason, Sharon… (she laughs…)*

The example illustrates Driver's (1983) insight into the impossible dilemma of teaching science both as an accepted body of knowledge and as a process of genuine enquiry (and the confidence tricks which some science teachers are tempted into when they attempt to marry the two).

This is a specific case of a more general dilemma which we face when teaching science and which shows itself in many of the examples here. On the one hand we are trying to elicit and generate pupils' *own* understanding of events and entities from their own thoughts and experiences; and on the other hand we have a curriculum to teach with an accepted body of knowledge and a lesson plan to follow. This dilemma necessitates a compromise between two often 'conflicting requirements' (Edwards and Mercer, 1987, p 143). This compromise is illustrated in many of the examples of classroom dialogue below. I have classified them, fairly arbitrarily, into four groups: learning the official language; questioning; explaining; focusing and shaping.

Learning the Official Language of Science

Many teacher–pupil (T–P) dialogues are intended by the teacher to initiate pupils into the language of science. Some of the word games which go on are fascinating.

Oral Cloze Procedure

At a very basic level some interactions are simply oral filling-in of blanks, i.e. cloze procedure by mouth. In this example the teacher (Elaine) is using the classic 'question–answer–evaluation' or IRF approach:

Elaine:	*Which of these things on the periodic table might be joined together to make hydrocarbons?*
Student:	*Hydrogen.*
Elaine:	*Hydrogen and [?]*
Student:	*Carbon.*
Elaine:	*Carbon, right. These are compounds of hydrogen and carbon.*

(Ogborn *et al*, 1996, p 5)

In another word game, the teacher (Alan) is trying to get pupils to link scientific words together so that they make sense when connected up into a sentence (text in SMALL CAPITALS corresponds to the word written on the board as well as spoken):

Alan:	*[Speaking aloud, making long pauses, as he writes on the whiteboard]. AS A SOUND [ ] BECOMES LOUDER, [ ] THE AMPLITUDE [ ] remind me what the amplitude does? [ ]*
Student:	*Gets higher.*
Alan:	*Higher or how could we? – what word would fit into that sentence? [ ]*
Student:	*Increases.*
Alan:	*It increases, good. So the amplitude [ ] INCREASES, good. Number 2 [ ] AS A SOUND BECOMES [ ] QUIETER [ ] SH SHHHH [ ] THE AMPLITUDE [ ] What does the amplitude do? The word that will fit into that sentence. DECREASES.*

[ ] = pause
(Ogborn *et al*, 1996, p.129)

Naming of parts

Some T–P interactions introduce the 'proper words' for entities such as the windpipe or the green stuff in plants:

Teacher:	*Now I don't know whether any of you could jump the gun a bit and tell me what actually is this green stuff which produces green colour...*
Pupil:	*Er......um......water.*

Teacher: *No..... Have you heard of chlorophyll?*
(Barnes *et al*, 1969, p.48)

Re-phrasing

Another teacher strategy involves re-shaping, directing and *re-phrasing* language, often *their* language:

Alan: *As the sound goes [speaking in a low pitch voice] lower, what happens?*

Student: *They get wider.*

Alan: *They get spread out. Now then, what measurement can we make on those waves? What can we actually – let me put it in a different way. You drew out a wave. OK? You said that the distance between a peak and a peak or between a trough and a trough had a certain name. Can anyone remember what that name is? Yes.*

Student: *[Inaudible] Wavelength.*

Alan: *The wavelength – the distance between two peaks or two troughs or any two corresponding points on the wavy lines. If the sound is going to get higher we've already said that the waves are going to get squashed, closer together, so what is actually happening to the wavelength? Is it increasing or decreasing?*

Student 1: *They're increasing.*

Student 2: *[Inaudible] decreasing.*

Alan: *The distance between two peaks?*

Student 1: *Decreasing.*

Alan: *OK. Good. I thought you knew the answer to that. So the wavelength is decreasing as the frequency or pitch is increasing.*

(Ogborn *et al*, 1996, p 128)

Notice at the end of this transcript how Student 1 changes his mind as a result of the little signal (the question) from Alan the teacher. Alan is trying to mould *their* language into an official version which he then gets them to write down into their books (the place for official, scientific language). This takes place not only with specialist words (the language of science) like wavelength and frequency but also with other official, higher currency but non-scientific words which are deemed to be more suitable (the language of secondary education).

Acquiring and Sharing the Official Vocabulary

Good teachers encourage pupils to adopt, use and share the official lingo. Here, a teacher guiding a pendulum investigation is trying to get pupils to use new jargon such as 'mass' and 'fixed point':

Teacher: *Now what did we say that they had to have Jonathan? A pendulum?*

Jonathan: *A weight at the bottom.*

Teacher: *Yes and yours has – OK? And yours is a washer.*

Jonathan:	*Mm.*
Teacher:	*Right. David what else does a pendulum have to have?*
David:	*A mass.*
Teacher:	*Jonathan's mentioned that.*
David:	*A string.*
Teacher:	*A string or a chain or some means of suspending the mass/ of hanging it down. Right/ and Antony what was the third thing it had to have?*
Anthony:	*Suspended.*
Teacher:	*Right./ From?*
Antony:	*A fixed point.*

(Edwards and Mercer, 1987, p 154)

Questioning

Pseudo-questions

Many of the questions teachers ask are not really questions but pseudo-questions. Peter Ustinov satirised these perfectly in a radio interview in which he caricatured a typical "dialogue" from his own schooldays:

Teacher:	*Who is the greatest composer?*
Pupil:	*Beethoven.*
Teacher:	*Wrong. Bach.*
Teacher:	*Name me one Russian composer.*
Pupil:	*Tchaikovsky.*
Teacher:	*Wrong. Rimsky-Korsakov.*

(printed in Edwards and Westgate, 1994, p 100)

With pseudo-questions, the teacher is playing a guess-what's-in-my-head game and may reject alternatives which are equally right or acceptable compared to the one he really wants! The activity is often done for perfectly good reasons and as part of the teacher's lesson plan. Pupils are usually very adept at guessing what the teacher really wants, perhaps from years of experience in learning the ground rules of the classroom.

Cued Elicitation

A slightly more complex process has been described as 'cued elicitation', as shown by this teacher in talking of Galileo's pulse in a lesson on the pendulum:

Teacher:	*Now he didn't have a watch/ but he had on him something that was a very good timekeeper that he could use to hand straight away. (Teacher looks invitingly at pupils) You've got it. I've got it. What is it?// What could we use to count beats? What have you got?// You can feel it here.*
Pupils:	*Pulse.*
Teacher:	*A pulse. Everybody see if you can find it.*

(Edwards and Mercer, 1987, p 142)

Here the teacher asks questions while, at the same time, using strong non-verbal tactics, e.g. gesturing, pointing, looking, pausing, beating her hand on the table.

Classroom questions are funny things and are of the type that would rarely be used in any other social context:

> *the teacher, who knows the answers, asks most of the questions, asks questions to which she already knows the answers, and, additionally, it appears, may ask questions while simultaneously doing her best to provide the answers via an alternative channel.*
> (Edwards and Mercer, 1987, p 143)

They suggest that we need to 'seek an understanding of the pedagogic function' of this sort of interaction – but this is easier said than done.

Explaining

Explaining anything in science is a complex business and this is well illustrated by the numerous examples in Ogborn *et al* (1996). Here, a Year 9 class are having an exchange with their teacher (Susan) following a class 'experiment' on detecting carbon dioxide in exhaled breath.

Susan:	*You can prove that the air you breathe out contains carbon dioxide. Obviously therefore more than you breathe in. Anyone like to have a guess how much carbon dioxide we breathe out [ ] in that air? If your air that you breathe out – the gas that you breathe out is a hundred per cent [writes 100% on whiteboard] of what you breathe out – anyone guess how much of that hundred per cent is carbon dioxide? [ ] Matthew?*
Matthew:	*Ninety per cent.*
Susan:	*Ninety per cent. Ricky?*
Ricky:	*Seventy per cent.*
Susan:	*Any more advances on seventy? Darren?*
Darren:	*Eighty.*
Susan:	*Eighty. More? Robert?*
Robert:	*Eighty-five.*
Susan:	*Eighty-five. Daniel?*
Daniel:	*Fifty.*
Susan:	*Fifty.*
Susan:	*You're all absolutely wrong. No way are you right. OK? It might surprise you – [ ] In actual fact you've forgotten one very important thing. There's something in this air outside that we hardly – we don't use at all. We take it in. [Gestures towards mouth]. We push it out. [Gestures away]. Don't use it at all. Don't touch it. Don't use it. Don't react with it at all. What gas is that, Daniel?*
Daniel:	*Nitrogen.*
Susan:	*Well done, OK. Nitrogen is in the air out here, around me, OK? And over seventy per cent of the atmosphere around us here is nitrogen. It goes in. [Gestures towards face]. It goes out.*

> *[Gestures towards face]. It doesn't play any role at all. It might surprise you to know that only [pause, writes on whiteboard] four per cent of the air that we breathe out is carbon dioxide. That's a very small amount. That indicator is a pretty good indicator.*

(Ogborn *et al*, 1996, pp 16–17)

The authors talk here of Susan having *orchestrated* the explanation. First she creates a *difference* of opinion by soliciting guesses, also creating a need or a reason for her to explain (and thereby a *motivation* to listen). Second, she brings in *entities*, such as respiration and the atmosphere. Then she goes on, with her speech and her gestures, to *transform* and *demonstrate* the process of breathing; the pupils are initiated into seeing breathing as an exchange or movement of gases.

Ogborn *et al* (1996, p 116–117) talk of different 'styles of explaining'. One style involves getting pupils to 'see it my way', e.g. a magnetic field, a cell under a microscope or the refraction of waves in a ripple tank. Another teaching style involves getting pupils to 'say it my way'. This is the style illustrated in some of the examples of 'Learning the Language' above. A third style, labelled 'Let's think it through together', involves the teacher in eliciting, collecting, re-shaping, and re-phrasing ideas from the class. Their fourth style, which suits some science teachers more than others, is 'the teller of tales' in which the teacher tells a story either from history, e.g. Fleming and penicillin or from current affairs, e.g. stories of people with cancer. This fourth style usually involves teacher monologue and so is not illustrated by an example here – it is important though because so much of science itself is a form of story-telling.

Their main point is that explaining often involves saying it, or seeing it, in a new way. This is why analogy and metaphor are so important in teaching science (see Chapter 3.4).

Focusing and Shaping in Interactions

Often, the questioning done by teachers is part of a general process of guiding or focusing a lesson so that it follows a path as part of a grand lesson plan. This plan may be a mystery to pupils, unless teachers declare it at the outset. The focusing or shaping strategy can leave little room for pupil questions.

This example illustrates the 'shaping' of a dialogue towards the predetermined ends of the teacher:

Teacher:	*What do you know about it so far.*
Pupil:	*You can have a skin on top of the water.*
Teacher:	*A kind of skin on top of the water, but remember it's not a skin like the skin on boiled milk, you can't scrape it up and take it off and leave it on the side of your plate – you can't do that with it. But it is a kind of skin and various insects can make use of it. Think of an insect that makes use of the skin – Michael?*
Pupil:	*Mosquito.*
Teacher:	*Good, a mosquito. How does a mosquito use this skin? Janet?*
Pupil:	*It lays its larva underneath it.*

Teacher:	*Well, yes, the eggs are laid in water and then what happens to the larva? What does the larva do? Well?*
Pupil:	*Hangs from the surface tension on top of the water.*
Teacher:	*Good, it hangs from the surface of the water. Why? Why can't it lie under the water altogether? Why does it need to hang from the surface?*
Pupil:	*It wouldn't be able to breathe.*
Teacher:	*Yes, it wouldn't be able to breathe. What it does is to put a breathing tube up into the air and breathes that way.......*

(from Edwards and Westgate, 1994, p 49)

Edwards and Westgate point out that this kind of dialogue is rather like a barrister questioning a witness, or a doctor asking diagnostic questions of a patient. Focusing is a technique which many science teachers use, often justifiably. However we need to be aware that this strategy restricts pupil participation only to statements judged to be 'relevant' by the teacher, which are then used to converge on pre-determined ideas (discussed in Barnes *et al*, 1969, p 124).

Discussion

The Complexity of Classroom Talk

What can we learn from these illustrations of T–P dialogues and the frameworks which can sometimes help to make sense of them?

Classroom dialogue is a complex business. All sorts of games are being played, often quite justifiably, and usually all parties are content to stick to the rules. The hidden ground rules (Edwards and Mercer, 1987) may sometimes prove too much for some pupils if:

- they are used to non-standard English or English is not their 'home' language
- their usual dialogue out-of-school uses the 'restricted' code rather than the 'elaborated' code of more formal, 'middle-class' English (Bernstein, 1961)
- they cannot operate with the language of secondary education
- they cannot learn and use the implicit ground rules of classroom talk.

The next section puts forward some suggestions for action.

Ideas and Suggestions

1) Be aware of language and how it is used in science teaching and learning (spoken language and written). The above extracts and the discussion may have helped to achieve this.
2) Have practical strategies and tools which will increase language awareness and help develop language skills, e.g. a Wordbank on the wall and in pupils' books; displaying pupils' writing on the wall; having a glossary of terms for pupils to consult; using news cuttings in lessons; and having writing displayed as it appears in newspapers and magazines.

3) In teaching, use analogy and metaphor, and 'collect' a range which can become part of your own repertoire. Listen and talk to other teachers.

4) When questioning, use a range of types of question – when the situation and the class permit.

5) In planning lessons, build in an accessible explanation of *what* you are doing, *why* you are doing it and the path that the lesson is likely to follow. Pupils follow and make sense of a lesson if its overall structure and purpose is made clear to them at the outset.

6) When practical work does not go according to plan 'talking your way through it' is an important activity (Nott and Wellington, 1995). You should not always be tempted to construct or 'rig' practical work which always gives the 'right answer'.

On a more general note, teachers, science departments and *curriculum developers* need to allocate more science teaching time to language and its development. Part of this time should be devoted to structured, well-disciplined pupil–pupil talk which can encourage their initiation into the language of science. It needs to be managed, monitored and controlled. The next section elaborates slightly on this.

Promoting Talking and Listening

We have seen that a great deal of science teaching involves little opportunity for pupil talk. As part of learning science, it is important for pupils to explore their own views in order to develop an independent way of thinking. To do this we must provide opportunities to practise the social skills of communicating and collaborating. Discussion based learning is not without its problems: pupils not used to this style of teaching may find it threatening; traditional laboratories are not conducive to discussion-based activities; careful structuring is required; a reconsideration of the respective roles of teacher and pupil is necessary. There are many strategies and activities which can be used to promote discussion and pupil talk:

- groups research a topic and present their findings to the rest of the class
- groups discuss their ideas and present a short talk or a poster
- individuals or groups plan an investigation and share ideas with the rest of the class
- the use of carousels, role play, simulation or drama
- individuals or groups interpret graphs or tables and present ideas
- small groups design a solution to a technological problem and share ideas with the class (Henderson, 1994; Henderson and Wellington, 1998).

The 1997 SCAA document 'Use of language: a common approach' also gives useful guidelines on developing oral language through speaking, listening and discussing and is well worth consulting.

In Conclusion

The ideas and findings of Barnes' work and the suggestions in the Bullock Report (1975) are still as important as ever for science education. For the pupil, the language barrier remains as real as ever in science and for many continues to be the main obstacle to their learning. There still remains a need for teachers to concentrate on the interpretation of language rather than just its delivery.

About the Author

Jerry Wellington taught science in Tower Hamlets, East London before joining the Division of Education at the University of Sheffield, where he is now a Reader. He has written and edited several books on science education and writes regularly for the Times Educational Supplement. Current research interests lie in the nature of science and the role of language in science education.

References

Barnes, D. (1973) *Language in the Classroom*, Milton Keynes, Open University Press.

Barnes, D. (1976) *From Communication to Curriculum*, Harmondsworth, Penguin.

Barnes, D., Britton, J. and Rosen, H. (1969) *Language, the Learner and the School*, Harmondsworth, Penguin.

Bernstein, B. (1961) Social Class and Linguistic Development. In Halsey, A., Floud, J. and Anderson, C. *Education, Economy and Society,* New York, Free Press.

Delamont, S. (1976) *Interaction in the Classroom*, London, Methuen.

DES: Bullock, A. (1975) *A Language for Life*, London, HMSO.

Driver, R. (1983) *The Pupil as Scientist?* Milton Keynes, Open University Press.

Edwards, D. and Mercer, N. (1987) *Common Knowledge*, reprinted in 1993, London, Routledge.

Edwards, A. and Westgate, D. (1994) *Investigating Classroom Talk*, London, Falmer Press.

Henderson, J. and Wellington, J. (1998) Lowering the Language Barrier in Learning and Teaching Science. *School Science Review*, Vol 79, No 288, pp 35–46.

Henderson, J. (1994) Teaching Sensitive Issues in Science: the Case of Sex Education. In Wellington, J. J. (Ed) *Secondary Science: Contemporary Issues and Practical Approaches*, London, Routledge.

Nott, M. and Wellington, J. (1995) Critical Incidents in the Science Classroom and the Nature of Science. *School Science Review*, Vol 76, No 276, pp 41–46.

Ogborn, J., Kress, G., Martins, I. and McGillicuddy, K. (1996) *Explaining Science in the Classroom*, Buckingham, Open University Press.

Osborne, J. (1996) Untying the Gordian Knot: Diminishing the Role of Practical Work. *Physics Education,* Vol 31, No 5, September 1996, pp 271–278.

Postman, N. and Weingartner, C. (1971) *Teaching as a Subversive Activity*, London, Penguin/Pitman Publishing.

Sinclair, J. and Coulthard, M. (1975) *Towards an Analysis of Discourse*, Oxford, Oxford University Press.

Sutton, C. (1992) *Words, Science and Learning*, Milton Keynes, Open University Press.

Wellington, J. J. (Ed) (1994) *Secondary Science: Contemporary Issues and Practical Approaches*, London, Routledge.

Wellington, J. (1998) (Ed.) *Practical Work in Science: Which Way Now?* London, Routledge.

Further Reading

1. An interesting account of *pupils'* questions is given in:
   Watts, M., Gould, G. and Alsop, S. (1997) Questions of Understanding: Categorising Pupils' Questions in Science. *School Science Review*, September 1997, Vol 79, No 286, pp 57–63.
2. Clive Sutton's work in this area is excellent, ranging from:
   Sutton, C. (1980) Science, Language and Meaning. *School Science Review*, Vol 62, No 218, pp 47–56
   to most recently:
   Sutton, C. (1992) *Words, Science and Learning*, Milton Keynes, Open University Press.
3. Clive Carre's book: *Language, Teaching and Learning: 4 Science* (1981), London, Ward Lock, is also well worth reading.
4. One of the classics of twentieth-century philosophy which discusses the way language is used is:
   Wittgenstein, L. (1958) *Philosophical Investigations*, Oxford, Blackwell.
   In the science field, another classic from the same era is:
   Savory, T. H. (1953) *The Language of Science*, London, Andre Deutsch.
5. Two excellent and influential pieces of research were carried out on pupils' understanding of non-technical words in science in the 1970s (words like 'pungent', 'significant', 'average', 'propagate', and 'valid'). They are still useful today.
   Cassels, J.R.T. and Johnstone, A.H. (1978) *Understanding of Non-technical Words in Science*, London, Chemical Society Education Division.
   Gardner, P.L. (1972) *Words in Science*, part of the Australian Science Education Project, Melbourne.
6. Some ideas on how news cuttings and other media can be used in science lessons is given in:
   Wellington, J. (1993) Using Newspapers in Science Education. *School Science Review*, Vol 74, No 268, pp 47–52.
   An example of an illustrated glossary of science words is published by:
   Questions Publishing, 27 Frederick Street, Birmingham, B1 3HH, and is entitled
       Science Dictionary, ISBN: 1 898149 84 4
   A *Wordbank*, in laminated poster form, of words required for Key Stages 3 and 4 can be obtained from ASE Booksales.

Acknowledgements

The author would like to thank Mick Nott for his contribution in providing ideas and discussion for this chapter.

3.4 Explaining with Models

John Gilbert

Theory and *model* play important roles in the language and understanding of science. This chapter explores the types and uses of models important in the conduct of science and in the learning and teaching of science. Practical advice is given about using models in teaching.

The Explanations of Science

Pupils and teachers ask each other questions to ensure that the former better understand the science that they are being taught. Definitive answers, given by teachers or textbooks, are *explanations* of phenomena. The particular characteristic of scientific explanations is that they refer to things which are believed to exist in the world-as-experienced. Five types of explanation are commonly used in science:

- *Intentional* explanation about the scope of a phenomenon or why it is important. For example, an explanation of how the velocity of an object changes with time is provided because such events are widespread and are important to humans.
- *Descriptive* explanation about how a phenomenon behaves. For example, the explanation of how the velocity of an object changes with time uses the idea of 'rate of change of velocity'.
- *Interpretative* explanation about the objects involved in a phenomena and how they are distributed in time and space. In the above example, the nature of the object and where it is at set intervals of time are given.
- *Causal* explanation about why a phenomenon behaves as it does. Newton's explanation of the movement of an object uses the concept of force.
- *Predictive* explanation about how the phenomenon might behave in different circumstances. Within the constraints of Newton's Laws (i.e. no friction), we can explain where a object will be at a fixed moment in time in the future.

A pupil is not just interested in any explanation, but in one which is *appropriate*. An appropriate explanation is one which meets the pupil's needs when the question is asked (e.g. so that a homework problem can be solved). In general, questions asked early on in a learning sequence are best answered by qualitative explanations, with quantitative explanations being introduced later. All appropriate explanations seem to invoke suitably simple models. For example, the explanations given above all depend on an idealised model of motion which assumes a symmetrical object and the absence of friction. (Gilbert *et al*, 1998a; Ogborn *et al*, 1996)

The Language of Models

Science has developed a specialist language, within which the words *theory* and *model* play important parts. A theory is a set of abstractions – assumptions which can be used to explain phenomena. Thus gas behaviour may be explained by using a theory consisting of Newton's Laws and the idea of dimensionless objects. A theory can be mapped onto the world-as-experienced through the agency of models. Thus the 'particulate model of matter' explains the behaviour of gases by imagining 'in the mind's eye' what happens as a consequence of dimensionless objects colliding with each other in accordance with Newton's Laws. A model is thus a simplified 'visualisable' intermediary between the idealised world of theory and the world-as-experienced, initially produced by scientists for a specific purpose. Models can be produced of:

- a set of ideas, e.g. a diagram showing how the Darwin–Wallace theory of natural selection applies in a particular case
- an object, e.g. a designer's model of an aeroplane, used to explore aerodynamics
- an event, e.g. to show the annual migration of a species of bird along the Middle East Corridor
- a process, e.g. of the industrial plant and sequence of reactions involved in the Haber method of making ammonia
- a system, e.g. of the circuitry in a computer (Gilbert,1997).

A model is produced by analogy. An analogy is the means by which a thing (the target) can be explained in terms of another thing (the source) which is more familiar to the modeller (Hesse, 1966). One thing is described as being 'like' the other. Those aspects of the source which seem similar to aspects of the target are selected to form a model. For example, Bohr's model of the atom is an analogy based on a simplified view of the planetary system, with the sun representing the nucleus and circular orbits of the planets representing the motions of electrons.

A model is produced by mental activity and can then subjected to a range of physical and social actions. Each of these conveys a different psychological/scientific status on it. Taking the case of Faraday's model of a 'magnetic field' (Nersessian, 1984, 1992) as an example, the range of possible statuses is as follows:

- A *mental* model is the product of personal cognitive activity by an individual, whether undertaken alone or in a group, e.g. Faraday must have imagined, in his 'mind's eye', a 'magnetic field'.
- An *expressed* model is the outcome when a mental model is placed in the public domain through gesture, speech, writing, or the use of some other symbolic form. Faraday's notebooks include sketches of magnetic fields.
- A *consensus* model is an expressed model which has gained social acceptance amongst the community of scientists. A 'draughtsman's version' of Faraday's notion of 'magnetic field' appeared in the academic papers that he published.
- An *historical* model is a consensus model which has been superseded at the 'cutting edge' of science. Faraday's ideas about the nature of magnetism superseded those of Oersted.
- A *teaching* model is one specifically produced to teach a difficult consensus or

historical model. Models which use pieces of string to represent Faraday's ' lines of magnetic force' have been used by teachers (Borges and Gilbert, in press).

Expressed, consensus, teaching, and historical models can be put forward in a variety of ways. These include:

- in the *material* mode (as an object), e.g. a child's model aeroplane.
- in a *symbolic* (or encrypted) mode (as written words or a mathematical equation), e.g. a written description of the billiard ball model of matter, the equation of the universal gas law.
- in a *visual* mode (as a graph or diagram), e.g. the distribution of input and output chemical species, as a function of position within the layout of the component parts of a production plant.
- in a *verbal* mode (as spoken words), e.g. a teacher's explanation of Bohr's model of the atom to a science class.
- and as mixtures of these modes, e.g. a taxonomy of plants in the form of a diagram with labels and illustrative drawings of ideal specimens.

The Significance of Models and Modelling

Models are important in both science and science education. They play a pivotal role.

Models in the Conduct of Science

Models are a mentally visualisable way of linking theory with experiment. They guide research by being simplified representations of an imagined reality which enable predictions to be formulated and tested by experiment. For example, 'gene splicing' is guided by the Watson–Crick model of DNA.

The presence of 'Experimental and Investigative Science', in the National Curriculum for England and Wales reflects the importance attached to introducing pupils to scientific methodology. The contributions of models and modelling are recognised. For example, the requirement for KS3 can be summarised as; 'The development and use of models of phenomena and of abstract ideas in the design, conduct, and evaluation of the outcomes of, experiments.'

Models in Communicating the Outcomes of Science

To be recognised as an authentic outcome of science, the product of a scientific enquiry has to appear in a refereed scientific journal. Most such articles contain models, which thus gain 'consensus' status. Inevitably, most if not all consensus models are superseded in time, but their contribution to science is often recognised by their retention in science curricula (and routine scientific enquiry) as 'historical' models.

Science curricula introduce pupils to many historical, and to some consensus, models of biology, chemistry, and physics respectively. For 11–13 year olds these are concerned with:

- General aspects of biology (models of classification, the cell, food chains); humans (models of nutrition, circulation, movement, reproduction, breathing, respiration, health); plants (models of nutrition and growth, reproduction, respiration); ideas to be used later in the study of Darwinian evolution (models of variation, inheritance, adaptation, competition).
- Model distinctions between: metals and non-metals; acids and bases; physical, chemical, and geological change. The particulate model of the nature of matter. Models of atoms and their combination.
- Models of electricity, magnetism, force and motion, light, sound, the solar system, energy.

Models in Learning Science

The 'cognitive science' approach to psychology is based on the idea that all learning involves the initial formation and subsequent further development of mental models. There is a deep division of opinion about the nature of mental models. On the one hand, they are regarded as sets of sentences held in the mind (Johnson-Laird, 1983). On the other hand, they are regarded as visualisations of objects held in the mind (Gentner and Stevens, 1983). Science, as a domain of enquiry, is specifically concerned with a world-as-experienced consisting of objects. Thus it is the latter (the 'mental visualisation') view which attracts the support of many scientists and science educators. A controversy rages over whether an individual has a given mental model as a pre-formed 'entity' in the mind at a given time or whether it is constructed from a 'tool kit' of 'model parts' when a particular problem has to be solved. The skills of mental visualisation are of great importance, especially in chemistry, where micro-level phenomena (e.g. molecular collisions) can only be directly experienced at the macro-level (observation of test-tube reactions) (Tuckey and Selvaratnam, 1993).

A major part of learning science involves forming mental representations of objects or models of objects, whether by direct observation, from two dimensional diagrams, or from verbal descriptions. There seems little doubt that individual pupils vary a great deal in their capacity both to form such mental representations and to respond to training to develop them (Raghaven and Glaser, 1995). Thus different pupils may well be able to learn from different modes of representation of models, e.g. from material models as opposed to mathematical models.

Models in Teaching Science

Consensus models are a major product of science. Science teaching thus involves developing an understanding in pupils of consensus models or, as is more likely in many fields of enquiry, of historical models. The obvious way to do this is by directly introducing and exploring the consequences of the use of particular models in providing explanations. However, pupils often find the formation of such an understanding very difficult. In such cases, teachers make use of 'teaching models', models developed especially to ease the path of understanding towards that of the consensus or historical model under consideration (Treagust *et al*, 1992). Individual teachers develop a repertoire of such teaching models, which they sometimes share with others through articles in School Science Review and elsewhere (Gilbert, 1993). When pupils face difficulties of understanding on their own, they seem to develop their own teaching models, which have been shown to be very effective (Cosgrove,1995).

Teaching through Models

Realising the potential of models in science education involves explaining to pupils:

- consensus and historical models
- what models are and how they contribute to scientific methodology
- how to form and test their own models.

Explaining Particular Models

There are often several available models associated with a given topic. For example, Justi and Gilbert (in press, a) identified eight models which have played a major role in the study of chemical kinetics. How might a series of historical models in a science topic be used in science education? What should not happen, but which often does, is that a 'hybrid' model composed of elements of several discrete models, is constructed and taught. Such an approach renders the topic ahistorical, so that it has no relation to the past, present,or future, of science *per se* (Justi and Gilbert, in press, b).

A useful approach is to identify and teach a model, from the historical series in a topic, which provides an explanation appropriate to the demands of the curriculum and the learning needs of the pupils. A progression to later models in the series can take place as pupils' experience and knowledge of the topic widens and deepens. Criteria for the selection of a model from a range are that it should:

- be, or have been, important in the development of the field of enquiry in which it is set – Bohr's model of the atom in 1913 was a breakthrough in the explanation of electron-related phenomena
- be physically simple, if only so that it is more readily memorised by pupils – being based on the structure of the solar system, Bohr's model is readily understood and remembered by many pupils
- provide an explanation of a phenomenon which meets the needs of the pupils at the time, i.e. it should be appropriate – Bohr's model provides the basis for a very convincing explanation of the spectrum of hydrogen, a topic found in many curricula
- preferably be able to provide explanations of a range of phenomena, and not only that one under immediate consideration – Bohr's model, in addition to explaining spectra, also formed the basis of the Lewis–Kossel explanation of chemical bonding, which was put forward in 1914.

Particular care is needed in the selection or development of a teaching model, because misunderstanding can result from the inclusion of aspects in it which do not map onto the consensus or historical model to be explained, or the omission of aspects that have to be explained. A valuable teaching model is one:

- which relates to a consensus/historical model which forms an significant part of the curriculum. The Krebs Cycle, the Born–Haber Cycle, and Special Relativity, are at the heart of much advanced biology, chemistry, physics, respectively. Teaching models may be needed for each of them
- for a consensus/historical model which pupils find difficult to understand. Pupils do find the structure of the double helix model of DNA difficult to understand, so teaching models are often needed. On the other hand, the introduction of unnecessary teaching models, for topics where pupils have no problems of understanding, may confuse them, e.g. a 'football stadium' teaching model for the Bohr model
- for which the source is familiar and acceptable to the pupils. Teachers must be alert to the range of personal experiences which pupils may have had, which will govern the range of sources which can be drawn on. Particular attention is needed to the gendered evaluation of a particular source (e.g. some females dislike 'sports' analogies, some males dislike 'relationship' analogies), and to religious views (e.g. Orthodox Jews dislike reference to pigs)
- which has a number of elements roughly equivalent to those in the consensus/historical model to be explained. The 'planets' teaching model for the Bohr atom has the correct number, for that is where it was derived from in the first place. Pupils can find an 'excess' or 'deficiency' of elements disconcerting
- bears a high degree of similarity to the consensus/historical model to be explained. Pupils will thus be readily able to perceive its relevance.

When a consensus/historical model is being directly introduced to a class, the target to be explained is the phenomenon under consideration. Where a teaching model is being used, the initial target is the consensus/historical model. Good practice suggests that in both cases the teacher should:

- identify the main elements and relations within the model
- identify the main elements in the source from which the model was developed
- establish the analogy between the source and the model
- use the model to interpret the target
- identify those aspects of the target which cannot be interpreted by use of the chosen model
- evaluate the scope and limitations of the chosen model in providing the relevant explanation of the target at an appropriate level.

If this approach is adopted, pupils will not be led to believe that the model is 'real', i.e. that it is a faithful copy of the target. Where a teaching model is used, it is essential that the topic be persisted with until pupils have achieved an understanding of the consensus/ historical model involved and are not just left with an appreciation of the teaching model. This latter is, in curriculum terms, worthless.

Explaining about Models

The development of both an understanding of consensus/historical models and the capacity to form and test models will only be fully achieved if pupils have an appreciation of what a model *is*. An enquiry by Grosslight *et al* (1991) in the U.S.A.

showed that most of a representative sample of science pupils in the age range 12–17 years had not developed a perspective that would be accepted by scientists. The great majority were at 'Level 1', believing that models are either toys or copies of reality which may be incomplete because the producer of them wishes it to be so. A few were at 'Level 2', where models were thought of as consciously produced for a specific purpose, with some aspects of the world-as-experienced omitted, suppressed, or enhanced. Almost none, and only then the older pupils, were at 'Level 3', where models were seen as being constructed to service and develop theory, rather than being a copy of the world-as-experienced. At 'Level 3' (the accepted view of scientists), the modeller was seen to play an active role in the modelling process, manipulating and testing for specific purpose. There is every reason to believe that similar results would be obtained in the UK, although higher Levels might perhaps be achieved at lower ages because of the greater attention paid to science in UK schools.

Little effort has been made to overtly and systematically develop a 'Level 3' appreciation of the nature of models in pupils. Where this has been attempted the evidence is that rapid progress can be made (Raghaven and Glaser, 1995). It does seem that the following general classroom measures will encourage the development of the notion of 'model' by pupils:

- an examination of the scope and limitations of all consensus/ historical models that are learnt
- encouragement of pupils to become overtly aware of their own mental models and of how these are formed
- opportunities to produce expressed models in a wide variety of media, e.g. as diagrams, written descriptions, in material form
- opportunities to test expressed model through the design and conduct of experiments.

Such measures are likely to be most effective when embedded within a systematic approach to the history and philosophy of science within the curriculum (see Matthews, 1984 and Chapter 2.6).

Explaining How to Model

The most effective way of explaining to pupils how to form models is within the context of them doing so as they conduct investigations (see Chapter 2.4). The core elements of success will be associated with what Simon and Jones (1992) termed open work', i.e. where the definition of the problem to be investigated, the design and conduct of the enquiry, and the drawing of conclusions, are all driven by the pupil, with the teacher acting in an 'expert consultant' role.

About the Author

John Gilbert is currently Professor of Education at the University of Reading, where he convenes the 'Models in Science and Technology: Research in Education' (MISTRE) international research group. A chemist by academic background, he worked on 'alternative conceptions' before moving on to the study of models in science, technology, and education.

References and Further Reading

Borges, A. and Gilbert, J. K. (in press). Models of Magnetism. *International Journal of Science Education.*

Cosgrove, M. (1995) A Study of Science-in-the-making as Pupils Generate an Analogy. *International Journal of Science Education*, No 17, pp 295–310.

Gilbert, J. K. (Ed.) (1993) *Models and Modelling in Science Education*, Hatfield, ASE.

Gilbert, J. K. (Ed.) (1997) *Exploring Models and Modelling in Science and Technology Education*, Reading, University of Reading, New Bulmershe Papers.

Gilbert, J. K., Boulter, C. and Rutherford, M. (1998) Models in Explanations, Part 1 Horses for Courses. *International Journal for Science Education*, Vol 1, No 20, pp 83–97.

Gentner, D. and Stevens, A. (1983) *Mental Models,* Hillsdale, Erlbaum.

Grosslight, L., Under, C., Jay, E. and Smith, C. (1991) Understanding Models and their Use in Science: Conceptions of Middle and High School Pupils and Experts, *Journal of Research in Science Teaching,* No 29, pp 799–822.

Hesse, M. (1966) *Models and Analogies in Science*, London, Sheen and Ward.

Johnson-Laird, P. (1983) *Mental Models,* Cambridge, Cambridge University Press.

Justi, R. and Gilbert, J. (in press, a) History and Philosophy of Science through Models: the Case of Chemical Kinetics. *Science and Education.*

Justi, R. and Gilbert, J. (in press, b) A Cause of Ahistorical Science Teaching: the Use of Hybrid Models. *Science and Education.*

Matthews, M. (1994) *Science Teaching: the Role of History and Philosophy of Science*, New York, Routledge.

Nersessian, N. (1984). *Faraday to Einstein: Constructing Meaning in Scientific Theories*, Dordrecht, Kluwer.

Nersessian, N. (1992). Constructing and Instructing: the Role of 'Abstraction Techniques' in Creating and Learning Physics. In Duschl, R. and Hamilton, R. (Eds) *Philosophy of Science, Cognitive Psychology and Educational Theory and Practice,* New York, State University of New York Press, pp 48–68.

Ogborn, J., Kress, G., Martins, I. and McGillicuddy, K. (1996) *Explaining Science in the Classroom,* Buckingham, Open University Press.

Raghaven, K. and Glaser, R. (1995) Model-based Analysis and Reasoning in Science: the MARS Curriculum. *Science Education*, No 79, pp 37–62.

Simon, S. and Jones, A. (1992) *Open Work in Science*, London, Centre for Educational Studies, King's College.

Treagust, D., Duit, R., Joslin, P. and Lindauer, I. (1992) Science Teachers' Use of Analogies: Observations from Classroom Practice. *International Journal of Science Education*, No 14, pp 413–422.

Tuckey, H. and Selvaratnam, M. (1993) Studies Involving Three-dimensional Visualisation Skills in Chemistry: a Review. *Studies in Science Education*, No 21, pp 99–121.

3.5 Differentiation

Stuart Naylor and Brenda Keogh

This chapter attempts to describe differentiation from the teacher's perspective. It stresses the importance of pupil involvement and points out the limitations of an approach based on close matching. A range of alternative strategies is suggested, along with more general factors which contribute to successful differentiation. The importance of keeping expectations to a realistic level is emphasised.

Background

Dickinson and Wright (1993) describe differentiation as 'intervening to make a difference'. They recognise that differences between pupils – such as in their learning capabilities, their prior experience, their preferred learning style and their motivation – make it inevitable that there will be differences in their learning. They suggest that the aim of differentiation is to maximise the potential of each pupil by intervening in the most suitable way.

However maximising the potential of each pupil is easier to describe than to achieve. If differentiation was easy or straightforward then teachers would not be so concerned about it today. The lack of confidence which many teachers feel about how they differentiate is evidence of what a complex challenge it represents. In most classrooms it will not be possible for teachers to plan to meet the learning needs of every individual pupil. It is therefore important for teachers to be realistic in their expectations of what they hope to achieve in order to avoid the disappointment of repeated failure.

Making Sense of Differentiation

Viewing Differentiation as Part of Everyday Teaching

Differentiation is sometimes seen as what we do for pupils who are not typical, such as those with identified learning difficulties. These pupils may be viewed as 'special', requiring a different sort of provision from the rest of the class. The drawback with this view is that differentiation becomes an extra burden on the teacher, something that would not be necessary without those pupils. In reality the research evidence (e.g. Simpson, 1997) shows that differentiation is a concern for all of the pupils, and that it is more helpful to aim to provide a suitable curriculum for all. Russell *et al* (1994) put it bluntly:

> *differentiated practice represents a view of what 'good science teaching' might*
> *be – the provision of appropriate teaching/learning experiences for all pupils,*
> *not just those at the extremes.*
> (Russell *et al*, 1994, p 8)

Viewing the Purpose of Differentiation as Differentiated Learning

The purpose of differentiation is to make a difference to the pupils' learning. Sometimes this might require setting different activities for different pupils, but much of the time this may not be necessary. The issue is whether all of the pupils are learning and how much they are learning, not whether the teacher has used a particular approach to differentiation.

Teachers should also recognise that their influence on pupils' learning may be limited. However much we like to think that we are completely in charge in the classroom, this is rarely the case. It is possible to plan the details of the curriculum in advance of the lesson, but it is not possible to plan learning in similar detail. Learning depends on many other factors, such as pupil involvement and motivation, so even if the teacher has planned for differentiated teaching there is no guarantee that differentiated learning will result.

Pupils who are willing partners in learning are more effective learners. If they understand the value of assessment, help to ensure that the teacher has relevant information about their progress and discuss some of the details of their curriculum then they will also enable the teacher to be more effective in providing for differentiated learning. Not all pupils are willing to share this responsibility, and there are no simple solutions to the problems of pupils being alienated by the school culture, indifferent to the opportunities provided or disruptive in the classroom. However our experience is that most pupils are able and willing to share the process of making judgements about their own learning and how it can be enhanced. Giving pupils greater responsibility in their learning frequently leads to greater involvement, increased motivation and better differentiation in learning.

Recognising the Limitations of an Approach Based on Close Matching

Matching the level of difficulty of an activity to the pupil's capability is usually called differentiation by task. This is something that many teachers aim for, but it is difficult. It is difficult always to get enough relevant information about each pupil's capabilities, and there are practical difficulties in managing the process of matching in a large class. In science there are problems in identifying how progression in understanding of specific scientific concepts develops, and defining the level of difficulty of activities in advance may not be possible. The way that the pupils' existing ideas affect their learning in science is an added complication.

Simpson (1997) found that even teachers identified as being good at differentiation had difficulties in allocating tasks which were appropriate to the pupils' attainment levels. Setting appropriate tasks for the most able pupils has been identified in numerous HMI reports as a particular problem for teachers. Perhaps this is not surprising, since the only evidence that pupils are not being sufficiently challenged may be that they are consistently successful!

In recent years the job of a teacher has become even more demanding. Changes to national curricula and assessment arrangements, inspection processes, large class sizes and a reduction in the support available from advisers combine to make the job more difficult. An emphasis on whole-class teaching is increasingly evident in central government policy. It therefore seems unlikely that teachers will be more effective at matching tasks to individual pupil capabilities in the future than they have been in the past.

So although differentiation by task, based on an analysis of individual learning needs, is an important aim it is not always achievable. Alternatives to differentiation by task are necessary if teachers are to feel confident in their approach. Some of these alternatives are set out in the next section.

Strategies for Differentiation

What many teachers would value is a set of strategies which enables them to build some degree of differentiation into their teaching without having to work even harder than they do already. Fortunately we know that many teachers already use a wide range of relevant differentiation strategies, though these are often used intuitively. The challenge for teachers is to become more aware of what strategies are already in use, to make more conscious decisions about when to differentiate and which strategies they intend to use, and to make differentiation more explicit in their planning.

Sometimes it is claimed that differentiation can be either by task or by outcome. This is unhelpful. Differentiation does not just occur at the planning stage (differentiation by task) or by the end of the activity (differentiation by outcome) – it also goes on during the activity. When pupils are working on an activity their responses will provide important information about the suitability of the task. It is generally possible to adjust the task at that point, making it more challenging for some pupils or more accessible for others.

Summaries of the range of strategies which may be useful are provided by several authors, including Stradling and Saunders (1993), NCC (1993), NIAS (1995) and Naylor and Keogh (1995). These lists emphasise the crucial role of the teacher in interacting with the pupils while they are working.

The kinds of strategies that we have found helpful include the following:

Using a Range of Learning Styles

Sometimes it may be possible for different pupils to cover the same content in different ways, such as using a structured workcard, designing a practical investigation, using a computer simulation or using a textbook for research. Each learning style may be more suited to some pupils than to others. Using a range of learning styles will ensure that no pupils are continually disadvantaged by always using teaching approaches which do not suit them (see Chapter 3.1).

Taking the Pupils' Ideas into Account

This does not mean planning a different investigation or activity for every pupil!

Obviously teachers need to follow a scheme of work and to plan their lessons in advance of finding out the pupils' ideas. However it may be possible to provide an opportunity for pupils to contribute their ideas and then to set up investigations where the purpose is to test out their ideas. In this way the pupils will all be working in the same general area and may well be carrying out similar investigations but with different purposes in mind.

Adjusting the Level of Scientific Skills Required

The level of demand can be influenced by the scientific concepts and the scientific skills involved in an activity. Even if the pupils are working on exactly the same content, the nature of any investigation or experiment can vary for different pupils. Investigations can be made more demanding by involving more factors, building on more extensive background knowledge, using more sophisticated techniques, requiring more careful observation or handling more data.

Adjusting the Level of Linguistic Skills Required

Sometimes differentiation is best achieved by adjusting the level of demand in the oral or written language used. The complexity of the text structure, the use of scientific vocabulary, the use of pictorial representation and the use of everyday illustrations will make a difference to how accessible the activity is (see Chapters 3.3 and 4.4).

Adjusting the Level of Mathematical Skills Required

Adjusting the level of mathematical demand in an activity can also provide an effective means of differentiation. The degree of precision in measurement, the level of quantification in observation or analysis of observations, the use of units or symbols and the scale of any numbers involved can make a difference to how accessible or challenging pupils will find the activity.

Varying the Amount and Nature of Teacher Intervention

Pupils vary in the amount and type of support that they need to be successful in scientific activities. Sensitive teachers will take this into account. They will try to offer early support to the pupils who are slow starters, to provide extra guidance to those who lack confidence and carefully monitor those who are easily distracted. Clearly teacher intervention is more likely to be appropriate when the teacher knows the pupils well.

Varying the Distribution of Teacher Time

The teacher's time is the most important learning resource available to the pupils. It seems surprising that teachers usually carefully plan the distribution of physical resources (mirrors, magnifying glasses, etc.) but may not make any attempt to plan how their time is distributed. It will be helpful to consider whether to target individuals or groups at certain times and whether all pupils get a reasonable share of teacher attention. Attention from other adults, such as support teachers and parents, is also part of this equation and needs careful planning to be effective.

Varying the Degree of Independence Expected

In general the greater the responsibility the pupils are expected to take, the more demanding the activity will be. Science investigations provide many opportunities for pupils to act independently as learners, such as defining the problem, using a range of information sources and evaluating the procedure. Further suggestions for providing opportunities for independence can be found in Jarman, Keogh and Naylor (1994).

Using Suitable Questions

Questioning is probably the most useful form of teacher intervention. Questions can help to identify pupils' existing ideas, map out possibilities for investigations, identify individual learning needs and offer additional challenges. Many teachers are very skilful at targeting particular questions to individual pupils, attempting to match the level of difficulty of the question with the pupil's likely ability to answer successfully. Preparing a range of possible questions in advance can help teachers to intervene more successfully. Harlen (1996) provides useful guidance on questioning styles (see also Chapter 3.3).

Varying the Response Expected

When teachers know pupils reasonably well they tend to differentiate in their expectations of how pupils might respond to a challenge. Whether it is the answer to a question, a plan for an investigation, a piece of text-based research or a set of observations, teachers expect some pupils to produce higher quality work than others. This is evident when teachers are managing discussion to ensure that every pupil's contribution is valued.

Varying the Pace or Sequence of Learning

Pupils can undertake the same set of activities but complete them at different speeds, with or without support from the teacher. Alternatively they may follow a different sequence of activities through a topic. NIAS (1995) provides excellent examples of differentiated pathways through a scheme of work.

Varying the Method of Presentation or Recording

Sometimes the same activities may be presented in different ways to the pupils, e.g. as a problem to solve, as a question or as a procedure to follow. It may be possible to offer a choice of how the pupils engage in an activity so that their preferences can be taken into account. When they engage in an activity they may be able to analyse, record or present information in a variety of ways. The level of detail, accuracy or quantification involved will influence the level of demand.

Providing Suitable Resources

A range of resources can provide additional support or challenge for some pupils. Sometimes pupils may be offered a choice of whether or not they want additional support or challenge. Suitable resources include workcards, reference texts, audio tapes and computer-based material. The only realistic strategy is to adopt a systematic long term approach to generating, obtaining, trading and sharing suitable resources.

An Illustration from Practice

Differentiating by taking pupils' ideas into account may be viewed as difficult to manage in practice. Increasing numbers of teachers are finding that the use of concept cartoons is a successful differentiation strategy (Keogh and Naylor, 1997).

Fig 3.5A Starting points for differentiation (from Keogh, B. and Naylor, S. (1997) Starting Points for Science, Millgate House Publishers)

Fig 3.5A shows what appears to be a simple everyday situation involving a snowman melting. However using the concept cartoon as a basis for discussion and debate reveals that pupils disagree about what will happen. Research evidence confirms that pupils are likely to hold a range of views about heat transfer. This process of finding out the pupils' ideas creates a context and a purpose for them to investigate the situation. Although their investigations may appear similar, they will be matched to their existing ideas – some pupils will be trying to prove that the coat speeds up melting, some that it slows down melting and some that it makes no difference! Pupils who have a better understanding of the situation introduce other relevant factors, such as the ambient temperature, the colour of the coat and whether it has a reflective surface. Although they are investigating the same situation they go about this in a more sophisticated way and take account of a greater variety of factors.

Actively involving pupils and enabling them to contribute their ideas in this way ensures that there is a close connection between their ideas and their investigations. Their ideas are taken into account without the problems of classroom management becoming impossibly complex.

Making Differentiation More Likely

Having a list of strategies is useful. It can help teachers to feel more confident in the approaches that they are already using, broaden the range of approaches available to them and make planning more effective. Only some of these strategies will normally be used at any one time. Teachers therefore need to use their professional judgement to decide which are most likely to be suitable on any particular occasion and to recognise this in their planning and teaching.

Other more general factors are also important in creating a climate in which differentiation is more likely to be successful. They include:

- actively involving pupils in their own learning, so that differentiation is a process negotiated with them rather than something done to them
- involving pupils in the assessment process, so that they realise the value of assessment and work with the teacher to maximise the usefulness of the information available
- creating a questioning climate, so that pupils see the value of questions as starting points for learning and make good use of opportunities to ask their own productive questions
- establishing routines that maximise the pupils' independence as learners, so enabling the teacher to spend more time on monitoring, supporting, challenging and extending their learning rather than simply organising them
- creating a flexible learning environment, so that pupils can be involved in decisions about grouping, timing, sequencing and resourcing and support the teacher's attempt to provide a differentiated learning environment
- creating a supportive classroom climate, so that pupils feel that they are valued individually and that differentiation is a person-centred rather than a curriculum-centred process
- working towards a whole-school approach, so that there is continuity in the approach used as pupils move from one teacher to the next.

These factors describe the classroom climate and the nature of the learning environment. Although they do not require additional resources, they may require significant changes in the ways that some schools and teachers work if differentiation is to be successful.

About the Authors

Brenda Keogh and Stuart Naylor are Lecturers in Science Education at Manchester Metropolitan University, Brenda in the Crewe School of Education and Stuart in the Didsbury School of Education. They both have extensive experience in teacher education, as well as experience in primary and secondary schools as teachers, advisory teachers and technicians. They were members of the ASE Working Party on Continuity and Progression.

References and Further Reading

British Journal of Special Education, (1992), Special issue on differentiation, 19 (1).

Dickinson, C. and Wright, J. (1993) *Differentiation: A Practical Handbook of Classroom Strategies*, Coventry, National Council for Educational Technology.

Harlen, W. (1996). *The Teaching of Science in Primary Schools* (2nd Edition), London, David Fulton.

Jarman, R., Keogh, B. and Naylor, S. (1994) *I've Done This Before: Continuity and Progression in School Science*, Hatfield, ASE.

Keogh, B. and Naylor, S., (1997) *Starting Points for Science*, Sandbach, Millgate House Publishers.

NCC (1993) *Teaching Science at Key Stages 1 and 2*, York, National Curriculum Council.

Naylor, S. and Keogh, B. (1995) Making Differentiation Manageable, *School Science Review*, Vol 77, No 279, pp 106–110.

NIAS (1995) *The Differentiation Book*, Northants, Northamptonshire Inspection and Advisory Service.

Russell, T., Qualter, A., McGuigan, L. and Hughes, A. (1994). *Evaluation of the Implementation of Science in the National Curriculum at Key Stages 1, 2 and 3. Volume 3: Differentiation*, London, School Curriculum and Assessment Authority.

Simpson, M. (1997) Developing Differentiation Practices: Meeting the Needs of Pupils and Teachers, *The Curriculum Journal*, Vol 1, No 8, pp 85–104.

Stradling, R. and Saunders, L. (1993). Differentiation in Practice: Responding to the Needs of All Pupils. *Educational Research*, No 35, pp 127–137.

Visser, J. (1992) *Differentiation: Making It Work*, Stafford, National Association for Special Educational Needs.

3.6 Progression and Continuity

Hilary Asoko and Ann Squires

Learning and teaching are bound together. A teacher's sense of achievement comes from a recognition that pupils are learning. Pupils' progress is influenced by many factors. Well-informed, effective teaching, within a structure of curricular continuity, is one of the most important.

Introduction

The words progression and continuity are frequently used, often in the same breath and sometimes as if they were interchangeable. It is important, therefore, to clarify the meaning of these terms and to recognise that they are distinct, although inter-related.

Progression relates to the pupil's learning. It describes the personal journey an individual pupil makes in moving through the educational system.

Continuity, on the other hand, is a characteristic of the curriculum and its implementation by the teacher. It operates in the broadest sense and also at the level of the finest detail. It refers to design, both in long-term planning and in lesson planning and it refers to a teacher's informed and sensitive interactions with pupils as a lesson proceeds.

The term 'progression' is sometimes used to describe the ways in which a curriculum is structured and sequenced. Thus people talk about building progression into schemes of work or classroom practice. In essence this relates to challenge rather than to learning. It means first giving pupils things they can easily achieve, to build confidence, and then increasing the demand of the task or reducing the support provided. This interpretation of 'progression' is an aspect of continuity. Here 'progression' is used exclusively in relation to pupils' learning.

The link between progression and continuity is strong, but not so strong that our best attempts at continuity can *guarantee* progression. Teachers often feel disappointed in themselves and in their pupils. However planning and teaching with a commitment to continuity, both in structure and in detail, is the most effective way to support a pupil's progression and it provides the best chance of achieving successful and satisfying outcomes.

Imagine the start of the school year, with a new class. To the pupils this is another stage on their journey through education. The teacher may be different in many ways, both personal and professional, from the teacher they had last year. The work may make new demands. The pupils will have to adapt and some may find it difficult. The teacher is faced with the task of getting to know the pupils and translating long term plans into work appropriate for them. Records may provide information about what they 'did' last year and some indication of the strengths and weaknesses of individuals. The teacher has past experience to draw on. When the pupils move on at the end of the year, they should have 'made progress' as a result of the teaching. This means there is a sense of direction to the work. To a large extent this direction is determined by National Curricula and examination syllabuses, translated into whole school and departmental plans. However plans are made in the ideal world. In reality, however good they are, they need to be adjusted and adapted to suit particular circumstances and requirements. Individual teachers, with their own ideas, values and opinions, adapt and implement plans in relation to individual pupils. If this is not done skilfully some pupils will feel disorientated and confused. They may become disillusioned with the subject. Learning will become a chore and teaching an uphill struggle. If it is done well, pupils will feel confident and interested and prepared to tackle new work. Continuity will be maintained and progression supported.

A Pupil's Progression in Science

Progression in learning science describes the personal journey an individual pupil makes from first experiencing aspects of the physical world towards an understanding of it in scientific terms: an appreciation of the methods, ideas and significance of science. This journey may involve stops and starts, small steps and sudden leaps, wrong turnings and difficulties to overcome. For the pupil the journey is something of a mystery tour. It is the teacher, who knows where things are leading, who is able to plan an appropriate route and provide help of the right kind, at the right time.

Progression in learning science can take many forms. Within a given context it might involve shifts from being aware that something happens to being able to make it happen or from observation, description and comparison to explanation.

For example:

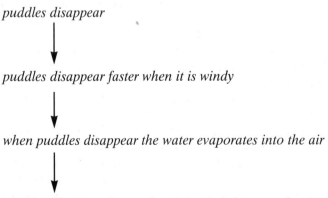

puddles disappear

puddles disappear faster when it is windy

when puddles disappear the water evaporates into the air

puddles disappear faster when it is windy because the air above them does not become saturated with water vapour

Pupils may progress from explanations couched in everyday language to the intelligent use of scientific language. They can come to expect explanations to be supported by evidence and to subject the evidence to rigorous scrutiny. Qualitative descriptions and comparisons may lead to quantitative measurements; explorations give way to investigations and experiments. Ideas used in single contexts become linked to other ideas or are used in wider contexts so that apparently different events are seen as explainable by a single set of ideas (see Chapter 2.1). Ideas about evaporation, for example, can be used to explain washing drying, hardening of nail varnish and parts of the water cycle as well as puddles disappearing.

Some steps on the journey are especially difficult. These are the ones which involve the learner in abandoning well-tried and trusted ideas. Whilst some of these ideas can be challenged by physical evidence, it is often the evidence, not the idea, which is disbelieved. Pupils who believe that heavy objects fall faster than lighter ones will not necessarily be convinced by a demonstration. They are likely to see what they expect – that the heaviest object lands first, or they will try hard to find fault with the test in order to hang on to the idea. Here the teacher must challenge the thinking and provide a new perspective from which to view the evidence.

The learner's progression is the cumulative effect of different kinds of learning event, large and small. Some will involve language learning or the development of practical know-how; some will involve extending ideas already held into new contexts or making connections between ideas; some will involve abandoning existing ideas and constructing new ways of accounting for familiar events and phenomena.

Just as a pupil's long-term progression is made up of particular learning steps, the teacher's long-term provision of curricular continuity is made up of particular elements of support for learning. The teacher's role is to recognise the many different kinds of learning step and identify and provide the necessary support.

Building Background Knowledge

Much of pupils' early development in science involves taking notice of and discussing an ever broader range of experiences. A pupil needs confidence to cope with new ideas and experiences. This confidence comes from having a background of familiar things to draw on and the language to talk about them. In a strange context where pupils lack knowledge and experience, they are not in a position to use capabilities which they could easily use elsewhere.

Teaching may therefore involve drawing attention to significant familiar experiences and stimulating discussion of them so that explanations have meaning. For example, learning about the rotation of the earth as an explanation for day and night is more meaningful to someone who is aware that the sun is not always in the same place in the sky and that darkness is an absence of light.

Some areas of science learning are long-term tasks which both require and develop a broad background knowledge. When studying materials, for example, pupils may be well aware of broad categories such as plastic, metal, fabric or wood. However, knowledge and recognition of specific metals or fabrics, or discussion of their properties or origins, demands background knowledge accumulated as a result of exposure to many experiences and pieces of information. The teacher's role is to seize opportunities to develop such knowledge whatever the topic in hand.

Modest Steps in Understanding

A pupil may recognise some examples of metals and know that metals conduct electricity and other materials do not. Here the teacher can open up new possibilities, perhaps that some metals may conduct better than others, or that the length of a wire may have an effect. An existing idea can thus be refined by small steps.

Major Leaps in Understanding

Major leaps in understanding often allow a shift from description of observed events to explanation in terms of abstract ideas and models. Beginning to think about materials in terms of their constituent particles is a leap in understanding. It is a new insight which, once available, can be tried out in a range of contexts. Pupils who have begun to think about particles in the context of sugar dissolving in water might be challenged to consider whether similar ideas might be used to think about puddles drying in the sun. Once such a major leap has been taken, the idea can be refined and developed by thinking about how particles move in relation to one another, or about the different particles in different materials. The teacher's role is to introduce the idea clearly, at the right time and in the right context. In the longer term opportunities must then be provided to use, reinforce and develop the idea. It is also important for the teacher to know when to stop and to ensure that pupils don't feel that they have lost contact with what they already know.

Constructing Frameworks of Understanding

Science ideas about the world form a coherent framework. Young pupils may not have developed the bigger ideas which apply across many contexts. As understanding develops and ideas become more sophisticated, they also become wider in their application and pupils come to recognise that the ideas used in one context may be equally well applied in another. Ideas about personal energy, for example, are the start of a progression towards a concept of energy which embraces physical, chemical and biological contexts. The teacher's role is in drawing attention to the wider application of ideas. Relating different contexts, either within science or between science and everyday life, may involve recognising and resolving conflicting ideas.

Relating Ideas to Evidence

Just as pupils learn to distinguish between events and accounts of events, they need to distinguish between their experiences and the ideas they construct to describe and explain these. Progression in learning involves pupils becoming aware of the need to think explicitly about their experiences, to put ideas to the test and to recognise the value of evidence, both positive and negative.

Although pupils can find out what happens in a given situation, the teacher needs to appreciate that the ideas which explain what happens may need to be introduced explicitly. For example, pupils can discover that objects travel further on smooth surfaces than on rough ones. However the ideas about frictional forces which explain this are not self-evident from the activity.

Awareness of Learning

Satisfaction and confidence in learning depend upon an interest both in our own ideas and those of others. We sometimes only know what we think when we hear what we have to say about it. Ideas may only show themselves as inadequate when we start to spell them out to someone else. It is often a discussion of differing views which leads a pupil towards better understanding. Articulating and considering ideas is essential. It is the teacher's role to stimulate interest in the ideas of science as well as its practical experiences, so helping pupils to become aware both of what, and how, they learn.

Curricular Continuity

A teacher may foster curricular continuity in different contexts:

- in terms of planning for and interacting with the pupils they teach
- in contributing to decision making about planning and teaching within school
- in local and inter-school developments
- in formulating national policy.

All of these will eventually impact on individual pupils.

In curriculum planning we need to keep in focus the variety and complexity of the pupil's task. What will make learning easier and what are the barriers which make the task more difficult or even impossible?

The role of the teacher is vital, as guide and mediator between science and the learner. The teacher has made the journey already and guided others through it. The teacher has the professional knowledge and skills to plan experiences and to relate in appropriate ways to pupils as they work.

Planning and Adapting

The logic of the subject may suggest a particular curricular sequence of concepts. Spirals may be built in to ensure revisiting and extending of ideas. In an ideal world we could plan activities which would result, reliably, in smooth progress and desired learning. But planning, particularly for the long term, tends to make assumptions that everyone will start from the same place, bring the same skills and experience, be subject to the same influences and, therefore, respond in the same way. Pupils, though, are individuals and the interactions and interventions of teaching must be responsive to them (see Chapters 1.5 and 3.5).

Nevertheless, planning can be informed by past experience and by research evidence. Plans can be adapted to take account of the ideas and experiences, both helpful and otherwise, which pupils are likely to bring to their science learning. National curricula provide guidance on what should be taught, but teachers need to decide how to structure teaching so that pupils' progression is supported. A knowledge of research into children's learning can be helpful here (see Chapter 2.1).

Expectations

Research shows the wide range of preconceptions which pupils can hold (e.g. Driver, Squires *et al*, 1994). It is important to guard against low expectations which may arise from a misinterpretation of this research. Many of the studies have been concerned with thinking and behaviour *in the absence of instruction*. Effective teaching does make a difference. Research can say something about where to begin and the problems which may be encountered but it cannot say what the goals should be. Sometimes the teacher will meet constraints which are unlikely to respond to teaching at that time. It is essential to distinguish such cases from other constraints, such as lack of background knowledge, which can be addressed by appropriate provision.

A Sense of Direction and Purpose

Science tries to understand the physical world through its 'big ideas'; its ways of investigating and seeking evidence and its commitment to developing ideas in relation to the evidence.

The big ideas of science are where a pupil's journey is leading; they provide a sense of direction even for the earliest work. A teacher who knows that a long term aim for pupils is an understanding of motion in terms of outside forces acting on things will, even from an early stage, encourage pupils to notice the surfaces and surroundings of objects. This doesn't mean imposing explanations on the pupil who is not yet receptive, nor does it mean watering down the incomprehensible. It simply means knowing where things are leading and preparing the way.

However, the ideas and skills of science are not ends in themselves; science makes its contribution to society and the lives of individuals. A teacher who shows an enthusiasm for science and its role in society can help pupils to appreciate this.

Record-keeping, Review and Liaison

Successful review and liaison depend upon effective communication of information about pupils' progress, both between pupil and teacher and between teachers. Teachers have to find effective ways for pupils to make explicit their developing understandings and abilities so that their progression can be followed. This will involve discussions with individuals during learning as well as formal assessment procedures. It may include pupils' self-assessment, particularly as pupils develop an interest in their own learning (see Chapter 3.2).

Some of the most valuable communications are those informal discussions between colleagues, both within and between schools, about pupils or teaching. More formal written communications document pupils' progress or curriculum plans. Meetings at which curriculum planning and implementation are discussed provide opportunities for practicalities to be decided. They can also allow the sharing of views on issues such as science learning or the aims of science education and help to promote shared goals and a common approach.

What Information is Useful?

Preparing and referring to recorded information is very time-consuming. Providers and users of information should share views as to what it is important. Communications need to be sharply focused, yet detailed enough to avoid misunderstandings.

Information communicated in an abbreviated form may have little use or be open to misinterpretation. References to having 'done air pressure' or to having 'reached level 4' give no indication of the experiences pupils have had or of the deep-seated ideas they may hold.

Joint Initiatives

SCAA indicate that joint activities with a specific focus on curriculum and/or assessment can benefit pupils in the following ways:

- *developing a better sense of the continuous nature of learning from primary through secondary school;*
- *having their previous experiences and achievements recognised and valued;*
- *experiencing appropriately challenging work which builds on skills, knowledge and understanding acquired in previous key stages;*
- *having similarities and connections with prior learning made explicit.*
(SCAA, 1996, p 13)

Although this advice is given in relation to continuity between primary and secondary school, it applies equally to other transitions.

Transfer of Records between Schools

As pupils transfer from primary to secondary school, particular efforts are needed to maintain continuity of curriculum and to monitor pupils' progression. The ideal arrangement is when the staff of two schools view continuity as a shared enterprise. The statutory transfer of records will take place in the richness of direct collaboration. Even without the advantage of such a close relationship, primary and secondary schools find benefit in supplementing the statutory transfer of information and SCAA gives guidance on this and other aspects of transfer (SCAA, 1996).

About the Authors

Hilary Asoko taught in schools for many years before becoming a lecturer in Science Education at the University of Leeds. She is involved in the initial and in-service training of teachers and is a member of the Learning in Science Research Group.

Ann Squires co-ordinated the Leeds Middle Years Curriculum Project and the Leeds National Curriculum Science Support Project, later editing materials from the latter for publication as *Making Sense of Secondary Science*.

References and Further Reading

Jarman, R., Keogh, B. and Naylor, S. (1995) *'I've done this before' Continuity and Progression in School Science*, Hatfield, ASE.

SCAA (1996) *Promoting Continuity between Key Stage 2 and Key Stage 3*, London, SCAA.

Lee, B., Harris, S. and Dickson, P. (1995) *Continuity and Progression 5–16: Developments in Schools*, NFER.

Driver, R., Leach, J., Scott, P. and Wood-Robinson, C. (1994): Progression in Students' Understanding of Science Concepts: Implications for Curriculum Planning. *Studies in Science Education,* No 24, pp 75–100.

Driver, R., Squires, A., Rushworth, P. and Wood-Robinson, V. (1994) *Making Sense of Secondary Science*, London, Routledge.

3.7 Safety in Science Education

Peter Borrows

Science in schools is safe but schools must nevertheless comply with legislation. The key to safety is risk assessment, usually by comparing proposed activities with model risk assessments in nationally available publications. Studying documented accidents and incidents can lead to an understanding of the causes of accidents and strategies to avoid them. Teaching safely is not the same as teaching safety and schools need to consider how science education can contribute to preparing youngsters for hazards in the home and in the world of work.

The Legal Framework for Safety

Science in schools is very safe (ASE, 1996a, pp 22–23). Fewer than 1% of the serious accidents involving pupils happen in science laboratories. Nevertheless, teachers and technicians must obey the law on health and safety matters. A few extremely serious accidents do occur, resulting in injury to pupils, technicians and teachers and sometimes subsequent legal action.

The main legislation governing health and safety is the Health and Safety at Work, etc. Act 1974 (HSW Act). Under the umbrella of this Act, governments have introduced many regulations, e.g. the COSHH Regulations, the Management of Health and Safety at Work Regulations, the First Aid Regulations, the Electricity at Work Regulations, etc. If an accident took place, an inspector from the Health and Safety Executive (HSE) could interview staff involved, under caution, and might then prosecute in the criminal courts for a breach of the Act or one of its Regulations. Since the Act was passed in 1974, as a result of laboratory accidents three science teachers in schools or colleges have been prosecuted, one school has been prosecuted and no technicians have been prosecuted.

If no prosecution takes place, it is still possible for an injured party (or parents, on behalf of a pupil) to sue for damages in the civil courts. Such cases are almost invariably settled out of court. ASE membership provides some protection, covering the cost of lawyers in both civil and criminal cases, and any damages awarded in the civil courts.

It cannot be emphasised too strongly that the main purpose of the HSW Act is to protect *employees*, i.e. teachers, technicians, cleaners, caretakers, etc. If pupils are also protected, that is a bonus, not the primary purpose of the legislation. In 1991/2, statistics from the HSE show that 4676 pupils were seriously injured in schools, 0.9% of them in science lessons. In the same period some 3289 school staff were seriously injured. As the number of staff must be very much less than the number of pupils it is a matter of some concern that so many accidents involve staff. The law requires staff to take care for themselves and for each other. Teachers must be alert to possible dangers facing technicians preparing or clearing up their lessons. Technicians must warn teachers if they consider the planned activity to be unsafe.

Risk assessment is required by several Regulations. It is the responsibility of the *employer* to carry out risk assessment before hazardous chemicals or micro-organisms are used, or before any hazardous activity takes place. The employer is the person or body with whom you have a contract of employment. For most teachers and technicians that will be the education authority, but in some cases it will be the governing body or the proprietor. Although risk assessment is the employer's responsibility the *task* of carrying out risk assessment can be delegated to employees. However, *responsibility* can NOT be delegated – the employer must check that the employee is carrying out any delegated task competently and in accordance with policy.

Sometimes, safety is blamed for a decline in exciting science. This accusation is unfair and is sometimes used as an excuse for unexciting teaching. A number of myths have grown up in recent years about bans on particular chemicals or procedures. In fact, at a national level, virtually nothing is banned (see ASE, 1996b, pp 19–22). It would be perfectly in order for a particular employer to issue a local Code of Practice, banning certain activities. Teachers would then be obliged to co-operate with their employer by observing such bans. However such bans are quite rare and teachers generally can carry out much the same experiments as they did 25 years ago, subject only to the requirement that they are done safely. This may mean adopting more stringent safety precautions than they did in the past, for example using more dilute solutions, safety screens, eye protection or fume cupboards but with very rare exceptions the activities themselves should still be possible.

Managing Safety in Science

Risk Assessment

The key to managing safety in school science – and, indeed, elsewhere – is risk assessment. In practice, science teachers have been carrying out risk assessment since long before the phrase was invented.

A *hazard* is anything with the potential to cause harm. Hazards will therefore include many chemicals, electricity at high voltages and such activities as carrying a tray of microscopes up and down stairs. In the particular case of chemicals, the hazard is an intrinsic property of the chemical.

Risk is the probability that harm will actually be caused by the hazard. There are two elements to risk:

- How likely is it that something will go wrong?
- How serious would it be if something did go wrong?

Risk assessment involves answering these two questions and then deciding what control measures, if any, are necessary to reduce the risk.

Risk assessment is the employer's responsibility and it must be carried out before a hazardous activity is undertaken. This might seem a daunting task given the large number of schools and the relative freedom for teachers within those schools to plan how they will teach the National Curriculum. Soon after the COSHH Regulations were implemented, education employers were given guidance (HSC, 1989) about how this might be achieved:

> *In order to help those undertaking these responsibilities, a number of general assessments have already been developed for most of the substances and experiments found in school science. Examples are included in the second edition of the Association for Science Education's (ASE's) Topics in Safety and the Hazcards produced jointly by the Consortium of Local Education Authorities for the Provision of Science Services (CLEAPSS) and the Scottish Schools Equipment Research Centre (SSERC) ...*
>
> *For science subjects, employers have the choice of*
>
> *(a) adopting and if necessary adapting to particular circumstances such well researched and established general assessments for school science work ....*

This approach was made more formal by inclusion in the Approved Code of Practice accompanying the Management of Health and Safety at Work Regulations:

> *Employers who control a number of similar workplaces containing similar activities may produce a basic 'model' risk assessment reflecting the core hazards and risks associated with these activities. 'Model' assessments may also be developed by trade associations, employers' bodies or other organisations concerned with a particular activity. Such 'model' assessments may be applied by employers or managers at each workplace, but only if they:*
>
> *(a) satisfy themselves that the 'model' assessment is broadly appropriate to their type of work; and*
> *(b) adapt the 'model' to the detail of their own actual work situations, including any extension necessary to cover hazards and risks not referred to in the 'model'.*

Note that 'model', 'general' and 'generic' risk assessments mean the same thing – the terminology has changed over the years. Most education employers have followed this advice and adopted a number of standard safety texts as the basis for their model risk assessments (see Further Reading). Here it will be assumed that this is the approach to be followed but if employers have adopted a different procedure then teachers and technicians are obliged to co-operate with it. Some employers, particularly small independent schools, do not make their procedure for risk assessment clear, or they attempt to pass the responsibility to the head of department. If they have not been given clear guidance, staff in such schools are advised to follow the procedures suggested here, but their employer still has legal responsibility and staff should inform their employer in writing that that is what they are doing.

There are two aspects to risk assessment – a thinking process, followed by record-keeping to show that that thinking has taken place.

Thinking Process

A science department should systematically review all its courses, identifying all the significant hazards. If staff are unsure whether there is a recognised hazard, they should be able to find guidance in the various standard publications. Once the hazard has been identified consulting the model risk assessments (i.e. the standard publications) will identify whether the activity is generally considered acceptable and whether any control measures need to be adopted. The science department then needs to consider whether the model assessment can be used as it stands or whether some adaptation is necessary to meet the particular circumstances of that school, or, indeed, particular classes in the school. For example, an individual teacher will need to know whether there are pupils with asthma or allergies in a particular class as this may need to be taken into account in some activities. The presence of pupils with Special Educational Needs in a class may necessitate some modification of the model risk assessment. For example, pupils with visual impairment may work rather more closely to test tubes of chemicals than other pupils. They may therefore need face shields when other pupils are wearing goggles. It is quite likely that pupils will pick up hot tripods from time to time, but the consequences are usually not very serious, so we tend not to do very much about this hazard, apart from the usual verbal warning. However, if you have a seriously disturbed pupil who might use the tripod as a branding iron then the risk assessment from this hazard will be very different. If tripods are in use such a pupil might require close personal supervision, or, if this is not possible, removal from the laboratory. Alternatively, the activity could be removed from the curriculum, although it is difficult to see why the education of most of the pupils should suffer because of the behaviour of one.

Record Keeping

The Regulations require that the 'significant findings' of risk assessment should be recorded. The Approved Code of Practice states that there is no prescribed way of recording risk assessment. Throughout industry and in higher education it is usual to record risk assessments on special forms. Such forms may have their place in schools when recording risk assessments for grounds maintenance staff using pesticides, or cleaning staff using bleaches, etc. However they are not well suited to the complex range of activities which take place in school science (Tawney, 1992). There is, in any case, little point in copying out information that is already available in the standard safety texts, but, if this is what the employer requires, staff must co-operate.

In most schools it is possible to identify a document (or documents) which define what a teacher is expected to teach on a day-by-day basis. Sometimes, this will be a school's do-it-yourself scheme of work or lesson plans, sometimes an examination syllabus and in some schools it may be the teachers' or technicians' guide for a commercially published course. Whatever it is that a teacher reads in order to find out what they are meant to teach next, that is the best place to put important safety information. Risk assessment forms, neatly tucked away in a filing cabinet, will not be read by a busy teacher; the outline of what s/he is to teach next *will* be read and at a time when the lesson is being planned. Inspectors from the HSE will be much more impressed by a well-thumbed document that shows signs of adaptation and alteration over time than a pristine risk assessment form that nobody ever reads.

Sometimes, a school will want to carry out activities for which it cannot find a model risk assessment or for which the model is inappropriate. For example, a middle school may have no fume cupboard but may wish to carry out an activity for which the model assessment states a fume cupboard should be used. The activity may still be possible, for example by working on a sufficiently small scale to do it in the open laboratory, or it may be possible to contain the fumes in some way. Or an A-level project may require the use of some novel chemicals or microorganisms not normally used in schools and thus not mentioned in the model assessments. In such circumstances a Special Risk Assessment is required and again the employer should have defined how this is to be obtained. For the great majority of education employers the answer will be to consult CLEAPSS, or, in Scotland, SSERC.

Once a scheme is in place in a department, there must be a strict understanding that no deviation from it can be allowed, without going through a further risk assessment procedure. New ideas can be welcomed, but they must first be checked against model risk assessments, or, if necessary, a special risk assessment obtained.

When considering risk assessment it is all too easy to focus on what happens in the teaching laboratory and forget what happens in the prep. room. In some cases the model risk assessments *do* give guidance to technicians, for instance in preparing solutions or dealing with spills but they don't cover everything. A department should think systematically about all the types of activity technicians are involved in and assess the risks involved, in line with any guidance issued by their employer.

Departmental Safety Policies

By law, employers must have a safety policy. There is no legal requirement that a science department should have a safety policy but many education employers require it and staff must co-operate with their employer on safety matters. Even if the employer does not require a safety policy, heads of science may still find it a useful management tool. In effect, a safety policy says, 'This is the way we do things here: this is our procedure for risk assessment, this is how we deal with various sorts of emergencies, these are our rules for pupils and for staff (including security), these are the people who have got particular safety functions in the department and these are our arrangements for training members of the department in safety matters.'

Guidance on possible content has been published (ASE, 1989). Discussion of safety policies also forms an important feature of the *Managing Safety for Heads of Science* course run both by ASE INSET Services and by CLEAPSS. Checklists are available for testing out the adequacy of departmental policies (Borrows, 1995).

Merely having a written policy is not sufficient. It needs to be put into practice and the head of department needs to check from time to time that this is the case. There is no easy way of doing this. Formal and informal lesson observations will play a part, as will regular discussions at departmental meetings. Talking to technicians and pupils may elicit useful information, as will looking at pupils' books, teachers' lesson plans and requisition sheets, the radioactive sources log book and other documentation. Perhaps the most effective strategy is to have a Safety Week where everybody observes others teaching, and where everybody (teachers, technicians and pupils) is encouraged to jot down any safety points they notice on yellow Post-it™ notes, for analysis and discussion at a subsequent departmental meeting.

Teaching Safety

Teaching safely is not the same as teaching safety. The HSE has expressed concerns at the high proportion of accidents happening to young people in their first job, on work experience or on youth training schemes. Teachers have been good at protecting children from the hazards but not very good at getting them to think about the risks: too much 'Follow these safety rules', not enough thinking about the underlying reasons for the rules. Partly as a result of this concern the 1995 version of the Science National Curriculum has a section on health and safety in the programme of study for all key stages. Ideas for teaching aspects of safety through science are available (CLEAPSS, 1997; SATIS, 1997; Borrows *et al*, 1998).

Learning from Accidents

A small number of practical activities have given rise to nearly all the serious accidents and legal actions (ASE, 1996a, pp 27–29). It is worth noting that most of these accidents occur during teacher demonstrations; pupils are then badly injured because they have been too closely crowded around the demonstration bench. Science teachers need training in safe ways of carrying out high risk activities.

Hydrogen Explosions

Over the years, there have been a number of explosions involving hydrogen, of which the following example, the first prosecution of a science teacher under the HSW Act, is typical (see ASE, 1996b p a1 and p c7). It resulted from an explosion when the teacher was passing hydrogen over hot copper oxide, intending to burn off the excess hydrogen at a jet. The teacher lit the jet before all the air had been flushed out. The apparatus exploded, showering pupils and teacher with broken glass. No eye protection was being worn and no safety screens were in place, although both were readily available and the LEA had issued instructions that they were to be used during such demonstrations. A similar explosion a few weeks later did *not* result in prosecution – there were no injuries, because safety screens and goggles had been used. The HSE has repeatedly said that they are not interested in stopping exciting practical science – only in making sure it is conducted safely.

Alkali Metals

Another teacher was prosecuted when he involved pupils in a demonstration in which sodium was burnt in chlorine and then in bromine in gas jars. He then added water to the bromine gas jar, intending to show its acidity. An explosion took place, showering pupils and teacher with broken glass, bromine, etc. The teacher was prosecuted for not co-operating with his employer on a safety matter. The employer had provided CLEAPSS *Hazcards* and the CLEAPSS *Laboratory Handbook* which referred to the need for eye protection, safety screens and fume cupboards – none of which were being used (see also ASE, 1996b, p c32).

Fireworks

One teacher was prosecuted for getting pupils to make gunpowder as an end of term treat (see ASE, 1996b, p a1). The mixture blew up, injuring two pupils. In this case, the HSE prosecution was based on the fact that the teacher had failed to exercise his general duty of care. The LEA did not have a specific rule about making gunpowder, but the HSE argued that it was self-evidently so dangerous that it was unreasonable to expect the employer to have a rule about not making it.

In another incident, pupils were making sparklers as part of an open day demonstration (see ASE, 1996b, p a7–8). They were dipping wooden splints, coated in glue, into a mixture of magnesium powder and potassium chlorate. At some point during the evening the mixture exploded, seriously injuring the pupils. In this case, the HSE prosecuted the school, arguing that although on paper there were reasonable safety policies and procedures for risk assessment, in practice these were not being implemented and the implementation not being monitored. The school decided to plead guilty and so the HSE case was not challenged. The teacher himself might have been prosecuted but prior to interviewing him, the HSE inspector had failed to caution him.

Ethanol

Although there were no prosecutions, the 1980s saw a number of accidents, resulting in major burn injuries, caused by ethanol (methylated spirit) fires (see ASE, 1996b, p c2a). Mostly, these involved the fuel in model steam engines, which is why solid fuel tablets are recommended these days. Other accidents have involved the extraction of chlorophyll from leaves: it is far safer to obtain hot water from an electric kettle or thermostatically controlled water bath, than using a Bunsen burner.

Chlorine

There are frequent reports of pupils being rushed to hospital following incidents with chlorine (see ASE, 1996b, p c27–28). Fortunately, most are not serious, but in one case a school was sued for damages after a pupil collapsed and had to be put onto a life support machine. The teacher made chlorine in a one litre beaker, and got pupils queuing up to smell it, giving no warning about the dangers and no instruction in a safe technique. The odour of chlorine can be sniffed safely, on a very small scale, but pupils need to be taught how to do it, need to practice the technique with safe gases and need to be closely supervised. Many teachers, especially non-chemists, may need training themselves in the safe technique.

High-voltage Transmission Line

Several teachers have nearly killed themselves when carrying out this old Nuffield demonstration (see ASE, 1996b, p d19). Usually, a step-up transformer is used to convert 12 V to 240 V, which is then passed down a pair of wires stretched for a couple of metres along the bench, before being stepped down again. Teachers, seeking to adjust the length of the wire through which the current is flowing, inadvertently grab hold of crocodile clips, live at about 240 V, and cannot let go. The HSE issued a warning about this demonstration in the 1980s, and suggested some safe ways in which it could be carried out (ASE, 1988). Some years later, the HSE came close to prosecuting an LEA and the head of science and headteacher of the school concerned when a young teacher was injured when carrying out this demonstration. The LEA would have been prosecuted as the employer (with an obligation to take care for the safety of their employees) and the headteacher and head of science would have been prosecuted as the local managers, charged with the task of implementing their employer's safety policies.

About the Author

Peter Borrows spent over 20 years teaching science in London schools, ending up as senior teacher at Pimlico School. He then spent 11 years as science adviser in Waltham Forest, before becoming director of the CLEAPSS School Science Service in 1995.

References and Further Reading

ASE (1988) *Topics in Safety* 2nd edition, Hatfield, ASE, pp 18–23.

ASE (1996a) *Safeguards in the School Laboratory* 10th edition, Hatfield, ASE.

ASE (1996b) *Safety Reprints*, Hatfield, ASE [Up-dated 1998].

Borrows, P. (1995) How Safe is Your Science Department. A Checklist for Managers. *School Science Review,* Vol 76, No 277, pp 19–23. Reprinted in ASE (1996b, pp b11–b15).

Borrows, P., Vincent, R., and Cochrane, A. (1998) Teaching Safety: Using Mole Calculations to Teach Aspects of Safety in Post-16 Chemistry. *School Science Review,* Vol 79, No 288, pp 67–70.

CLEAPSS (1997) *Student Safety Sheets*, Uxbridg4, CLEAPSS.

HSC (1989) *COSHH: Guidance for Schools*, London, HMSO, pp 2–3.

SATIS (1997) *The World of Science*, London, John Murray.

Tawney, D. (1992) Assessment of Risk and School Science. *School Science Review,* Vol 74, No 267, pp 7–14. Reprinted in ASE (1996b, pp b20–b27).

Vincent, R. and Borrows, P. (1992), Science Department Safety Policies. *School Science Review,* Vol 73, No 264, pp 9–13. Reprinted in ASE (1996b, pp b6–b10).

Some or all of the following books are usually adopted by education employers as the basis for their model risk assessments.

ASE (1988) *Topics in Safety.* 2nd edition, 1988 (3rd edition in preparation 1999). Hatfield, ASE.

ASE (1996a) *Safeguards in the School Laboratory*, 10th edition, Hatfield, ASE.

ASE (1996b) *Safety Reprints*, Hatfield, ASE (Updated 1998).

CLEAPSS (1995) *Hazcards,* Uxbridge, CLEAPSS School Science Service.

CLEAPSS (1997) *Laboratory Handbook,* Uxbridge, CLEAPSS School Science Service.

DES (1985) *Microbiology: an HMI Guide for Schools and FE*, London, HMSO. (This useful booklet is now out of print and is unlikely to be re-printed.)

DfEE (1996) *Safety in Science Education*, London, HMSO.

SSERC (1997) *Hazardous Chemicals Manual*, Edinburgh, SSERC. (This replaces the previous edition published by Oliver and Boyd in 1979 and is available at a considerably reduced price to SSERC and CLEAPSS members via their respective organisations.)

For those carrying out risk assessment for project work, the following gives useful advice:

SSERC (1991) *Preparing COSHH Risk Assessments for Project Work in Schools*, Edinburgh, SSERC.

Most CLEAPSS and SSERC publications are only available to those working in member schools.

Useful Addresses

Consortium of Local Education Authorities for the Provision of Science Services (CLEAPSS), Brunel University, Uxbridge, UB8 3PH. Tel: 01895 251496. Fax: 01895 814372.

Scottish Schools Equipment Research Centre (SSERC), St Mary's Building, 23 Holyrood Road, Edinburgh, EH8 8AE. Tel: 0131 558 8180. Fax: 0131 558 8191.

3.8 The Use of Information and Communication Technology

Roger Frost

This chapter considers the ways that computers can help science teaching. It discusses their role as investigating tools and lists the benefits that can come from using them. In addition to examples of activities, it offers advice on choosing resources, using software, data logging and the Internet.

Do We Have to Use ICT?

The National Curriculum in England and Wales sets out the requirement to use ICT quite succinctly: it asks that information technology be used appropriately in science courses. ICT could be seen as another issue to add to teaching, but it is more helpful to look at how it can *improve* learners' appreciation of science. Information and communication technology is a diverse range of technologies, with each year bringing in something new. In recent years we've seen the growth of multimedia, the Internet, the portable computer, the talking word processor – each offering something unique and of interest to education. It is perhaps just as well that the national curriculum keeps the options open, and the requirements deliberately vague. Another reason, for this very open invitation to use ICT, is that schools differ greatly in their ICT resources. If you have convenient and easy access to technology there is a great deal that you can do to enhance the quality of your work. Without this, progress will be slow. Either way, if there's little guidance on how much you should use ICT, there is agreement on one thing: the requirements and the opportunities to use ICT should be built into schemes of work. The sections that follow present some of ways that ICT makes the effort and the expense worthwhile.

How Does ICT Help Those Learning Science?

One aspect of a science curriculum concerns the processes of being a scientist. The key words are very familiar – hypothesising, measuring, modelling, analysing are part of a set of '-ing' words that make up investigating science. ICT can help in these processes and it can conveniently be looked upon as a 'tool to help a scientist'.

Scientists – and in this context learner scientists – can gain a stimulus to their work using CD-ROM or the Internet. They can research the work of others, pick up facts and pictures from reference sources – such as CD-ROM or online ency-clopaedia. They can explore database files to look for information and patterns. The Internet also allows them to work with others by asking questions or pooling results. It may help to look at CD-ROM and the Internet as comparable resources – the future Internet might be like a CD-ROM covering every subject. A CD-ROM may be more limited but it's a useful technology offering multimedia that the Internet is still learning to deliver.

Scientists express their ideas and explain them to others using models (see Chapter 3.4). They can use spreadsheets, modelling software and pre-built models. What we call 'science software' – with its models and simulations might be useful here. Data logging software is extraordinarily helpful to scientists in making measurements in experiments. It also provides useful feedback. The software can calculate changes, gradients and areas. It does this with such ease that we can go further with our current science experiments and teaching. For example, instead of investigating the question, 'Does a wool jumper keep you warmer?', where we know the answer anyway, we can use the technology to answer more useful questions such as, 'How much warmer would you be?' or, 'Would a sweatshirt be as good?'.

Scientists handle data by setting it into a table, sorting it and drawing graphs. For this they can use a spreadsheet program. If they have a large amount of data they might use a database program instead. Putting their data into a database program encourages scientists to think carefully about how they collect their data. They can look for patterns in their data by sorting it, drawing graphs and presenting it appro-priately. They can also do the same on other people's databases which today can happen over the Internet. For example, they might do a school survey to try to see what factors (e.g. age, wearing glasses, hand-size) affect reaction time but find that they need a larger data set to produce useful results. It is here that the Internet, which facilitates pooling of results finds a key role.

At many points scientists need to plan, write up and present their work. They can use a presentation program or word processor to produce work of publishing quality. They can put the work on the Internet or an Intranet (meaning the school network) to gain a very public audience for this. Indeed if the trend toward doing school work on a screen continues every child's exercise book will one day be stored on computers! Maybe there is something in this. Ultimately students need to revise and reinforce what they have done. Revision packages can tailor the work to the syllabus they cover and they can offer help with their particular weaknesses. They can act as diagnostic tools too.

Learner scientists have additional needs in that they need to learn efficiently. Integrated learning systems, like a lot of multimedia software, make claims to being electronic teachers. These claims encourage scepticism, but there are no doubt things that computer software can do. For example, it can give learners drill in learning symbols and formulae, or practising calculations. It can also be 'adaptive' and offer appropriate tasks according to a learner's responses. Software can offer a rich experience through film clips, animation and interaction. The most open verdict would be that if there is software that achieves our aims better than we can, we should use it. As it happens, software design is still a developing art. Furthermore, if science education was so simple that we could just leave learners to peck at a keyboard, this book would be much thinner.

What Are the Benefits of Using Computers?

The computer can be a calculator, typewriter, graphing machine, telephone (e-mail), and even a teacher. It is not a homogenous artefact and so the differing tasks it performs will generate different benefits. Classroom practice and a number of research reports, tell of the benefits of using software. Unlike measuring the time saved by drawing a graph on the computer, measuring educational benefits is hard, as the classroom is not a closed system with easily predictable outcomes. People measuring these things have different aims. Some researchers have looked at the retention of facts and some at improvements in science skills. And to confound these studies some reports say that learners need to reach a threshold level of computer experience to show benefits. Many agree that, just like using an oscilloscope or a tray of marbles, the way that the teacher uses the tool is crucial. So if the teacher uses data logging to develop graphical interpretation then we should find that the pupils will become better at this. On the other hand, the teacher may see some other purpose for data logging and achieve a different outcome. In short, the research repeatedly shows that teacher's aims and approach are supremely important.

The often cited benefit of using ICT is the boost to learner's motivation, enjoyment, and commitment to work. It may not do this all the time, or it may work until the novelty wears off but it can indeed stimulate pupils and positively affect their attitude to science.

Software can support individualised learning by offering differentiated work. It can provide an engaging focus, and be an aid to concentration. Computer work can be open ended and consider more complex and challenging situations than normal. Unique 'What if?' situations can be considered with a computer model. These allow learners to take decisions, try out different things and take risks. Software can actually make difficult ideas more understandable and thus help those with less ability.

The use of productivity tools, partly by removing time-wasting procedures, can lead to higher quality work. When learners are relieved of say drawing graphs or taking readings, they can find themselves in more challenging situations.

Integrated learning systems have been associated with developing basic skills. There are reports, at least in maths, of improved attitudes to and increased responsibility for learning, high attention levels and attendance. Industrial training seems to make use of computer-based instruction and this is also seen as a way of ensuring a consistent delivery to students. Such training can be made accessible through networked systems. Students work at their pace and courses can start anytime. As a result, studies talk about reduced course times, better retention, less failure and more motivation. There may be cost savings due to less demand on teacher and laboratory time.

The many opportunities to use computers and the rich set of benefits that can arise must lead to another question – given that there is so much to do which of these are useful, and which are extremely valuable? Inevitably, we answer the question when we start to plan and integrate ICT into our work. What we choose to do is tempered not just by our aims, but by resources and skills. The shortest answer is that the benefits come from using computers in situations where conventional teaching cannot do justice.

How Does ICT Help Teachers?

If any aspect of ICT use has grown remarkably, it is teachers using technology for administrative work. While some will argue that computers were put into schools for pupils' use, others will argue you cannot teach what you do not know. In short, the use of computers for re-skilling the teaching population can be seen as efficient staff development.

Using a computer, staff can not only prepare worksheets using a word processor, they can embellish them with ready-made diagrams and apparatus available as clip-art. For those with a school network (Intranet), this work can be stored to make a filling cabinet of resources that can be unusually accessible. There are packages that allow teachers to create on-screen presentations much like overhead transparencies. An example of this is a head teacher who gives a weekly lecture and then puts the electronic overheads on the network for learners to read later.

There are also packages to prepare tutorials – with built-in assessment. Special exam tools, with banks of questions and answers, help to assess pupils. Using them teachers can quickly assemble tests and examinations. In addition producing a mark scheme or a list of syllabus items covered is a very easy task.

A range of reporting and profiling systems are available to monitor or report on students' progress. A module in a popular administration package allows teachers to map their topics and tests against curriculum levels. It can then very quickly do a curriculum audit or summary of pupil achievement. Increasingly, teachers will find packages that make light work of pre- and post-course profiling, and integrate these with computer-based 'courseware'.

It might seem that here are many new packages to learn but ICT tools will become more versatile. For example, you can find a word processor that works as a presentation program, desktop publisher, multimedia and Internet page-making tool. Furthermore, some packages also integrate spreadsheet and database features.

Having easy access to the Internet from the computer you use most can dramatically affect its usefulness – in communication and access to information. In the most connected schools, e-mail has come to replace internal memos and circulars and make dealing with trivial requests quick and painless. It is not all good, as the easy flow of communication between staff, pupils and parents can in itself create new problems – piles of mail to deal with, and some of it time wasting. The positive side of using the Internet to communicate is that it adds people to your resources. There are science teachers' staff rooms on the Internet where you may ask a question and gain a kindly answer. It is comparable to belonging to as many working parties and groups as you have time for, only in this Internet world you can pop into a meeting and pop out again when you wish.

The Internet can also provide information – books, software, worksheets, exam facts, safety facts and up-to-date information. Given the infrastructure (for example, a national science teachers' centre) that allows teachers and publishers to contribute their material there are rich pickings to be had. The benefits of professionals using the Internet and computers are that they enable us to do things more efficiently, do them better and continue to improve them.

There is always a caveat as at first everything takes longer – especially when you use trial and error to do things. It is worth seeking training that appreciates your starting point and goals.

Practical Advice and Exemplars

Data Logging

Data logging typically involves using the computer to record readings taken from sensors. If any one ICT tool is seriously on task for enhancing the teaching of science then data logging may be that. This statement is more than a gut feeling as articles in journals add to a growing body of research data showing the benefits to pupils (see for example School Science Review, December 1997). When pupils use computer sensors to take readings in experiments they see graphs appear in real time, can do more investigations and access unique data analysis tools. Consequently pupils observe, question and go much further with their work, though outcomes depend upon the teacher's approach. For example, if your aim is to develop an investigative approach to science this technology will be a useful ally.

With the twenty or more different types of sensor available, the scope for using sensors is as limitless as there are experiments to do. You can measure force, conductivity and magnetic fields but it is more common to find schools using a few core activities. Some ideas follow, but they are in no way prescriptions as each school will have different resources and find its own core of activities. Here remember that 'resources' means sensors, computers, time and trained staff. A number of secondary schools have the resources to run whole-class experiments and this has become a benchmark. Secondary schools without should at least try demonstrations, or get a class to analyse data in a computer suite.

A few examples of using sensors:

- Use temperature sensors to study cooling curves or insulation, e.g. heat loss from the building.
- Use a light sensor to study the rate of the reaction where a precipitate forms.
- Use light and temperature sensors as simple meters to compare habitats.
- Use a data logger to measure light, temperature and oxygen readings in an aquarium, pond, or greenhouse.
- Use light gates to measure speed, time and acceleration.
- Use a position sensor to monitor the movement of a pendulum.
- Use sensors to study current–voltage relationships.

Tips:

- Get a large screen you can use for demonstrations and discussion.
- Think about the progression though using sensors and build data logging activities all through a science course.
- Treat the more esoteric sensors as luxuries to get when you are up to speed. After a demonstration set, a class set of basic sensors (a couple of temperature sensors and light gates) is a useful next target.

- Modern data-logging software tends not to need a modern computer. A class set of older discarded computers can be put to good use.
- When windfalls arise, the portable computers, from laptops to hand-held devices, should be very seriously considered in preference to, say, a set of desktops.

Internet

It helps to separate Internet uses into those that help teachers and those which help learners. We mentioned teachers' uses earlier, and many of these can be realised with a single computer. The purposes and activities of using the Internet with learners depend on the kind of access you have (e.g. permanent or dial-up), and where it is kept. Learners can, for example:

- collaborate with peers in other schools – share data, reports or thoughts
- research and deal with real data – from say, companies or environmental campaigns
- obtain live news or data – about say, bush fires in Australia, an eclipse or disaster in another part of the world
- access learning materials and journals not available in school
- take part in research projects or field trips when they can't be physically present
- talk to scientists and ask questions
- publish their work.

Some schools will invest heavily in the technology and use this unique method of making every kind of learning resource you need accessible from a screen. Some will prefer to toe-dip and access it occasionally. Either way some tips follow:

- While connecting to the Internet for information seems like the whole point of the system, you risk wasting time. Preview, bookmark and check places before your lesson – this rehearsed approach is less exciting but has a better guarantee attached. Be prepared in case a site is unavailable – have other sites or other work in reserve.
- Rather than search the Internet openly, explore the Web with a purpose in mind and find a school curriculum focused area as a starting place for your searches.
- For some activities, one computer will not be enough. For a large class, a large monitor will help, but exceptional skill is needed to hold all pupils' attention.
- If the material you access will not date, store it on your computer rather than accessing it fresh from the Web every time. Note too that links on the Internet can date, so last year's worksheet may be out of date this.
- Use school Internet places to find project partners. Discuss your expectations with your partner school: establish when the project will start and finish, what the aims are, when you will receive a reply; when you will respond. Match the abilities of your group to the partner group.

Science Software

Another way that a computer helps in teaching is in 'delivering' the content. There are many examples of genuinely interactive software, engaging learners in useful tasks. For example:

- There are software databases of food that allow us to work out exactly what nutrients we eat. There are also databases of the chemical elements, plants and animals that are ready for analysis. For physics work, there are databases of film of moving objects that allow us to do analysis – of, say, a crashing vehicle – that we could not do normally.
- There are models for teaching many aspects of science. For example, genetics software allows us to 'speed up time' and examine more about heredity than we could normally. Other examples include experimenting with moving molecules, populations, polluting ponds, dissecting frogs or dismantling nuclear reactors.
- There are revision, test and exam practice titles that purport not to teach, but to revise work. These seem to be finding favour.

We all have ideas about what makes a good lesson and could easily list them. We intuitively fit the work to the curriculum, the audience and the time slot. We choose activities and experiments that 'work' and satisfy. We can apply these ideas to deciding whether software enriches and supports learning.

In choosing software resources it can save money to find out what others think before buying. It helps to get a couple of independent opinions rather than scanning catalogues in the hope of a great discovery. The following questions help in assessing software:

- Does it fit the curriculum? Does it support our learning goals?
- Does it fit the learners? Is the depth of treatment right for the audience? Does it suit the ability range within a class?
- Does it fit the time slot? For example: does it suit a five-minute demonstration, pupils taking short turns, or whole lesson use in a computer room?
- Does it fit the hardware? If the software is on CD-ROM, can it be used with a network of computers? Does it need demonstrating on a large screen?
- Does it enhance science education? Can it do things better than we can normally? Does it encourage problem solving, investigating, modelling, classifying, sorting, questioning, pattern finding, data exploring, researching, group work, out of class work?
- Does it fit the teacher? Is it easy to get started or does the effort put in to use it produce a pay-off? Does the manual say how you're supposed to teach with it? Is it possible to customise the software to suit your approach?

Finding Out More and Keeping in Touch

New software and new technology are changing fast and you need a regular update. The need to keep in touch has to be balanced against ability to do so, but as a minimum, someone within the school should carry the responsibility. They might also be given the resources, such as the time to visit trade shows, go on courses or use the Internet to keep in touch. In particular, they might note the following sources:

- ASE School Science Review, TES newspaper, Interactive, Educational Computing and Technology magazines carry reviews.

- ASE Annual Meeting is an excellent, even the best, opportunity to get to see software. A visit to this and/or the annual BETT Show can achieve a great deal in a day. Both events take place in January.
- If you use a published 'science scheme' look for an ICT section which can make it easier to plan ICT into your work.
- BECTA (formerly NCET) and the Virtual Teachers Centre publish information and case studies about computers and science as well as advice on meeting the curriculum imperatives. Their Internet site has reviews of hundreds of independently evaluated CD-ROMs. The TES newspaper site has an archive of reviews you can search.
- Science teacher's areas on the Internet such as the ASE will guide you to current hot spots and curriculum projects.
- Some software publishers offer details and sometimes working demonstrations over the Internet. Science teachers' discussion groups are starting to appear where people post questions about resources on a notice board.

About the Author

Roger Frost is a freelance writer and runs training on the use of computers in science. He can be contacted at ICT in Science, 7 Sutton Place, Hackney, London E9 6EH. Tel/Fax: 0181 986 3526. e-mail: RogerFrost@csi.com. Web: ourworld.compuserve.com/homepages/RogerFrost

References and Further Reading

Web Sites

ASE: http:// www.ase.org.uk
BECTA, Milburn Hill Road, Science Park, Coventry CV4 7JJ. Telephone: 01203 416994 Fax: 01203 411418. Internet: http://www.becta.org.uk
BT CampusWorld: http://www.campus.bt.co.uk/
Research Machines Internet for Learning: http://www.eduweb.co.uk/
Roger Frost: http://ourworld.compuserve.com/homepages/RogerFrost/
ScI-Journal – for students to publish their investigations: http://www.soton.ac.uk/~plf/ScI-Journal/
TES newspaper: http://www.tes.co.uk

Paper Materials

Enhancing Science with IT. A pack with classroom materials for secondary schools. Available on paper or over the Internet from BECTA: http:// www.becta.org.uk
What Works. Booklet summarising research on the benefits of ICT. From BECTA: http:// www.becta.org.uk
Frost, R. (1997) *The IT in Secondary Science Book – a Compendium of Ideas and a Topic by Topic Planning Guide to the Science Curriculum.* From ASE Booksales.

Frost, R. (1997) Data Logging and Control – Ideas for Using Computer Sensors with Pupils aged 11–18. From ASE Booksales.

Frost, R. (1998) *Software for Teaching Science – a Critical Catalogue of Software for Teaching Science*. From ASE Booksales.

Frost, R. (1998) *Data Logging in Practice – a Practical Guide to Using Sensors in the Secondary School.* From ASE Booksales.

School Science Review (1997), Themed issue on IT, Vol 78, No 287.

SECTION 4

Management and Development

Introduction: The Professional Development of Teachers

Mary Ratcliffe

Teacher Development

Effective teaching and learning cannot happen without good teachers of science. The principles and methods of initial teacher education (ITE) and continuing professional development (CPD) are therefore very important.

There are important elements which go towards good science teaching (see Chapter 1.2), yet these elements combine in ways which are difficult to describe.

An atomistic view of teacher development may take an approach which identifies each separate element of teacher knowledge and skill and then seeks to tackle each separately with teachers in training. This atomistic approach has similarities with a strict competency model. Competences underpin the Standards for qualified teacher status (QTS) and the National Curriculum for Initial Teacher Training (ITT) in operation through the Teacher Training Agency (TTA) in England and Wales.

An holistic view of teacher development sees the sum of these elements as greater than the separate parts. Trainee teachers develop knowledge and skills in context, integrating the variety of different experiences as they develop a good understanding and ability of teaching. An holistic view, in assessing teachers' progess, perhaps relies on professional judgement, on knowing quality teaching when you see it and on a standard of entry to the profession based on expert agreed judgement.

Furlong and Maynard (1995) characterise learning to teach as:

the development of an appropriate body of practical professional knowledge with which student teachers can come to frame actual teaching situations. This body of knowledge is made up of both a stock of concrete experiences as well as more abstract concepts.

They argue that teachers' knowledge falls into four domains – knowledge of pupils, knowledge of strategies, knowledge of content and knowledge of context.

But teachers' practice does not depend on knowledge from a cluster of discrete domains; rather, it depends on the complex interaction and interplay between these domains. Effective practice, rather like a complex, three dimensional jigsaw puzzle, is only achieved when all the pieces are in place, when there is a sense of 'balance'.

Learning to teach science is thus a complex business and is assisted by activities which allow student teachers to integrate their experience of these four domains.

Initial Teacher Education

In recognising the complex interplay of these knowledge domains, it is still sensible to try to articulate the skills and attributes of beginning teachers. This then provides a basis for further development.

Principles of provision in ITE should be closely linked to achieving the purposes of science education (Chapter 1.1) and high-quality learning in science (Chapter 1.2).

Good initial teacher education should allow new entrants to the profession to:

- be reflective, enthusiastic, flexible, thoughtful and skilled practitioners able to show good pedagogical content knowledge in their teaching
- support pupil learning in science through using 'fitness for purpose' in identifying appropriate learning activities and assessment methods
- progress in their professional development with the support of more experienced colleagues.

ASE, in responding to TTA consultation on the shape of an ITT National Curriculum in Science, argued for the use of key themes in which student teachers can integrate the domains of professional knowledge. These themes can guide the developing expertise of student teachers in supporting pupils' learning and in using appropriate teaching and assessment methods (ASE, 1997a).

Five areas of pupils' development, related to the purposes of science education, are important:

- *The nature of scientific ideas* – generation and evaluation of evidence, science as a human and team endeavour.
- *Systematic enquiry in science* – including conceptual and procedural knowledge, development of practical skills.
- *Science in everyday life* – development of science ideas in context.
- *Communication of scientific ideas* – development of skills of literacy and numeracy in relation to scientific ideas.
- *Health and safety* – understanding and demonstration of safe practice.

Themes for developing student teachers' experience in assisting these areas of pupils' learning include:

a) An understanding of the nature of science including: the role of theories; evidence generation and evidence evaluation; the human context of scientific development.
b) An understanding of the practical processes and skills of science including observation, manipulation, etc.
c) An understanding of how pupils learn in science and an appreciation of the nature of misconceptions in scientific ideas.
d) The use of models in explaining scientific ideas.
e) An understanding of the industrial and community context of science.
f) An understanding and demonstration of good health and safety practices in science.

g) An understanding of the links between science and other subjects, particularly mathematics, technology, information technology and English.

h) Thinking and working scientifically and enthusiastically using appropriate language – i.e. *a synthesis of all the above.*

Each of these themes are discussed in chapters in this book.

Standards for QTS identify what beginning teachers must achieve from a course of initial teacher training in order to enter the profession (DfEE, 1998). These Standards are grouped under headings of:

A) Knowledge and Understanding
B) Planning, Teaching and Class Management
C) Monitoring, Assessment, Recording, Reporting and Accountability
D) Other Professional Requirements.

The Standards are detailed – specifying skills, knowledge and attributes which need to be demonstrated before a student teacher can be awarded qualified teacher status.

National Curricula in ITT for the core subjects of English, Mathematics and Science and for ICT support and add further detail to these requirements (DfEE, 1998). They specify:

A) Pedagogical knowledge and understanding required by trainees to secure pupils' progress.
B) Effective teaching and assessment methods which trainees must be taught and be able to use.
C) Trainees' knowledge and understanding of the subject.

Interesting issues are raised by the prospect of a National Curriculum in initial teacher education. In particular, the TTA consultation prompted a debate on the nature of subject knowledge needed for teaching science at any particular level. Clearly we cannot teach science without a sound understanding of the subject but this needs to be integrated with other knowledge. However, there seems no consensus on what constitutes a sound understanding of science. Proxy measures such as a GCSE grade 'C' or a PhD in physics give some idea of previous experience and depth of engagement with key ideas of science. We probably come to best realise the extent and use of our subject knowledge when we engage in explaining and teaching. This is as true for people teaching from a background of degree level study in the subject as for those teaching from a lower base. We learn a lot from our own teaching. Use and development of subject knowledge in context seem important principles for ITE and CPD.

Continuing Professional Development

Teacher development should be seen as a continuum. Whatever length of time we have been teaching we continue to learn. ASE:

> *firmly believes that all teachers of science should be entitled to high quality continuing professional development from initial teacher education onwards throughout their career.* (ASE, 1997)

This entitlement also brings with it an obligation for teachers to maintain and improve their professional skills and understanding.

There are obviously many ways in which to engage with professional development opportunities. The management issues outlined in section 4, provide opportunities and challenges in professional development. However, professional development should be coherent and systematic, matching school and individual requirements.

A CPD framework should:

- allow progression from initial training through induction as an NQT to ongoing professional experience
- be meaningful to all who use it – the teacher, mentor, senior management
- be realistic enough to have achievable goals
- be flexible enough to respond to the individual's particular circumstances and ensure that the needs of both the teacher and employer are being met
- be rigorous enough to provide evidence of achievement
- be part of a reflective process to enable individuals to identify their own levels of expertise and further development
- encourage a support system involving an experienced mentor to assist in target setting and monitoring.

One framework for CPD is being piloted by secondary science teachers through an ASE initiative. The potential of the framework lies in giving a structure for needs analysis and identified CPD activities, supported by a more experienced professional as mentor. The ASE framework proposes a number of domains – all being important in professional development. Just as initial teacher education requires a synthesis of different elements, the areas in a CPD framework should not be seen as discrete but overlapping. The framework is to guide and assist coverage of interrelated elements of teacher development and includes the following areas:

- *Pedagogical content knowledge* – examination of the teaching of particular parts of the science curriculum including translation of one's own subject knowledge into suitable classroom activities. This is an overarching area which brings together all the others listed.
- *Subject knowledge* – development of secure understanding in the sciences taught; awareness of recent advances.
- *Practical teaching skills* – development of teaching skills which are felt to be underdeveloped or under-used by the individual. It also includes development in appropriate assessment and evaluation techniques.
- *Theoretical understanding of teaching and learning science* – reflection on the basis for the classroom practice of oneself and of others – How do pupils learn? Why do I teach this way?
- *Knowledge of external changes affecting the teaching of science* – development of knowledge relating to the context of science teaching, e.g. awareness of curriculum policy developments at national level; links with industries; regional and national initiatives in curriculum development.
- *Development of personal skills and attitudes towards science and science teaching* – development of any changing responsibilities, management tasks, extra-curricular activities, etc.

The use of a framework like this may assist teachers in systematic evaluation and development of professional practice. Teachers and managers may find it useful in identifying appropriate CPD activities both within and outside the school. Evidence can be collected of achievement in each area and impact on classroom practice and pupils' learning.

This developmental framework is intended to be a tool to assist ongoing professional development *whatever stage a teacher's career is at*. The TTA take a different approach – setting Standards for different key points of a teacher's career:

- Entry Standards (DfEE, 1998).
- Standards for Special Educational Needs Co-ordinators.
- Standards for Subject Leader (see Chapter 4.1).
- Standards for Headteacher (National Professional Qualification for Headteacher).

This model of teacher development perhaps assumes a particular career path for most teachers.

Mentors

We are all assisted in our professional development by the support and guidance of a more experienced professional – a mentor. Teachers in training rely on the guidance of the class teacher and head of science for constructive criticism of their developing expertise. Equally, more experienced teachers benefit from the critical guidance of a supportive mentor. Effective mentoring is not easy and may challenge the most expert of teachers. Expert teachers often have intuitive responses to classroom situations:

> *They are acting effortlessly, fluidly, and in a sense this is arational, because it is not easily described as deductive or analytic behaviour.* (Berliner, 1994)

It can be a difficult business to unpick practice, particularly one's own, and explain how the teacher's activities contributed (or not) to effective learning. However, it can be a rewarding learning experience for the mentor as well as the person being guided. Monk and Dillon (1995) provide activities to support the mentoring of inexperienced secondary science teachers. Partnership between schools and Higher Education Institutions can be effective in together providing good support for professional development both in ITE and CPD. Indeed, the ASE believes

> *…that initial science teacher education courses are best provided by partnerships between schools and higher education institutions, with each side of the partnership adopting the role(s) it is best placed to provide.'* (ASE, 1997c)

References

ASE (1997a) National Curriculum for Initial Teacher Training in Science – Response to Consultation June 1997, Hatfield, ASE.

ASE (1997b) *Continuing Professional Development: Policy Statement*, Hatfield, ASE.

ASE (1997c) *Initial Teacher Education: Policy Statement*, Hatfield, ASE.

Berliner, D. (1994) Teacher Expertise. In Moon, B. and Shelton Mayes, A. (Eds) *Teaching and Learning in the Secondary School*, London, Routledge/Open University Press, pp 107–113.

DfEE (1998) *Circular 4/98, Teaching: High Status, High Standards, Requirements for Courses of Initial Teacher Training*.

Furlong, J. and Maynard, T. (1995) *Mentoring Student Teachers*, London, Routledge.

Monk, M. and Dillon, J. (1995) *Learning to Teach Science: Activities for Student Teachers and Mentors*, London, Falmer Press.

Departmental Management

Mike Evans

There are two main elements to management. The first is to ensure that objectives are met and the second is to seek improvement. A significant part of management is to do with managing people and getting the best from them. Encouraging openness within a science department, participation from everyone and planning ahead using clear targets helps all staff work together. Teams do not work together naturally and it is important to pay attention to team building. Good management is not a secret garden and there are sets of national standards which identify the roles and responsibilities of managers. These standards can provide a framework for continuing professional development.

What is Management?

Increasingly heads of department are expected to manage a department well and provide leadership. What is the role and scope of management? What do good managers do? The management charter initiative (MCI), which is the operating arm of the National Forum for Management, a registered charity, was originally set up by Government to outline good management. It has since produced National Standards for Management in the form of National Vocational Qualifications (NVQ) (MCI, 1997). These standards define the role and scope of managers across all walks of life. More recently, the Teacher Training Agency has produced its own draft set of standards targeted specifically at 'subject leaders' in schools – National Standards for Subject Leaders (TTA, 1998). These stress the leadership aspect of management. Both sets of standards outline clearly what is expected in the role albeit in different ways. Both are designed to guide professional development. Both define the purpose of leadership and management:

> *... to achieve the organisation's objectives and continuously improve performance...* (MCI)

> *... to provide professional leadership for a subject to secure high quality teaching and effective use of resources and ensure improved standards...* (TTA)

These definitions recognise the significance not only of managing but also the need to seek improvement.

Managing People

Leadership

Leaders provide a sense of purpose and direction to work, but in doing so they need to be consultative. A head of science needs to listen to the views of members of the department. A good leader makes sure that the team achieves tasks, works well together, is motivated and that individuals are developed within their role. A popular view of the leadership role is represented in Fig 4.1A.

Fig 4.1A The leadership role

The job of a leader is to satisfy all three areas.

The task may be to teach Key Stage 3 science and enable pupils to achieve high standards. This requires clear schemes of work, careful decisions about who teaches which year group or set and the allocation of appropriate resources, and monitoring progress.

Group needs are satisfied by building the teachers into an effective team, ensuring all understand the objectives in the scheme of work, all complete work on time, and there is a good team spirit.

Individual needs can be addresses by teaching, counselling, motivating, giving feedback and recognition. For instance a teacher may need help with how to teach a particular aspect of energy. Conflict may arise between a technician and a teacher over the provision of equipment in a lesson. Giving positive feedback to individuals on jobs well done is one key way of motivating staff, building self esteem.

When teachers were asked what are the qualities of a good leader they suggested that effective leaders were people who are:

enthusiastic	good communicators
good listeners	confident
thinkers	decision makers
teachers	advisers
counsellors	effective delegators
responsible	loyal to the team
inspirational	setters of high standards

purposeful	flexible
analytical	prepared to admit mistakes
able to deal with conflict	

Above all a sense of humour was valued – being human it seems is still important!

OFSTED (1997) recognise the significance of leadership by identifying *'leadership which is strong but consultative'* as one of the key characteristics of well managed subject departments.

Team Building

Leadership qualities are important when building teams. Teams do not naturally work together, they need to be developed:

- teams need to have clear aims and objectives
- teams need to go through a developmental process in order to perform
- team members need clear roles and responsibilities
- team members need motivating
- work needs monitoring and evaluating
- individuals need development where weaknesses affect team performance.

Setting Objectives

In order for a team to perform they need clear objectives which are understandable to all. In a science department teachers may have to respond to objectives in a scheme of work, objectives in development plan or specific objectives relating to outcomes from appraisal.

It is common to think of objectives as **SMART**. Objectives should be:

Specific
Measurable
Achievable
Relevant
Time Related

In one science department the head of science noticed that even though all members of the department were following the Key Stage 3 scheme of work, different groups were taught differently. Pupils had very different outcomes written in their books. Discussion amongst staff revealed that the root cause was the way in which the scheme of work expressed learning objectives. Some were vague, some used language of 'know ...' or 'understand ...'. It was soon realised that when expressed in this way they were open to misinterpretation. For instance 'understand how the eye works' led to a range of different outcomes related to different depths of treatment. The department discussed how they could make their objectives more specific and measurable. They turned to the level descriptions in the national curriculum for science and noted typical performance was expressed more in terms of pupil outcomes, e.g. describe..., explain..., use models to... This was felt to be more specific and measurable, so objectives were rewritten in these terms, e.g. name parts of the eye..., explain objects are seen because light is reflected and enters the eye...

Clarity of objectives is of great significance when guiding the work of teams and you should not underestimate the potential for misinterpretation. Others do not see the world in the way you do. Each of us brings different experiences to any situation which colours the way in which we interpret what we are asked to do. When setting objectives ask yourself are they SMART. Check them out with others. How do they interpret them?

The Development Process and Responsibilities

Whenever people are brought together to form a team or even when an existing team is set a new task it tends to go through a four-stage development process which was described by Tuckman.

Forming

During this stage team members are involved with clarifying objectives, seeing how they fit in, exploring opinions and views of others and their leader and sizing up the situation.

Storming

In this stage conflict develops, members tend to argue, are assertive, the task is resisted, members go off task.

Norming

Here conflict is resolved, views and trust develop, co-operation develops, with people speaking and listening to each other.

Performing

People work together, have a shared understanding, roles are flexible, solutions are found and ideas implemented.

It is important for a head of science to realise that this happens. For example when a department is asked to develop a greater use of information technology the conflict which may arise is part of a natural development. Allowing members to go through the process is beneficial. The team leader needs to help a team through the stages so that they do reach the stage of performing.

Forming

The leader needs to be clear about purpose, checking for understanding, inviting views, valuing opinion and addressing misunderstanding.

Storming

The leader needs to be supportive, allow views to be expressed, clarify views, remind members of the task, and begin to resolve conflict. In some cases it might be helpful to ask particularly awkward members how they might achieve the goal, and remind them that the goal itself is not negotiable.

Norming

The leader needs to encourage individuals to express their confusions, help resolve these and encourage any signs of co-operation by setting pairs or groups tasks.

Performing

The leader needs to provide space for the team to perform; stand back and delegate. Then monitor and evaluate.

Once the way forward has been agreed then specific roles and responsibilities can be allocated.

Following a whole-school initiative on improving the use of information technology to support the curriculum, the science department agreed what had to be done. It created a development plan which allocated tasks to different individuals. Specific measurable targets and deadlines were set and resources allocated, including time to individuals. One member of the department was responsible for ensuring that computers in the department were networked, another for identifying uses of the internet to support data-handling skills in specific topics and another on developing the use of data logging to increase the efficiency of teaching some aspects of science.

Many teachers' roles are tightly defined in job descriptions, e.g. Head of Physics. There is no reason, however, why areas of responsibility cannot change from year to year in a planned way. Increasingly science departments are being more flexible in their use of job descriptions. Whilst staff may have a section which remains constant there are many examples where specific responsibilities are given for a period. This works best when these responsibilities are clearly linked to a departmental development plan.

Motivating Team Members

People respond in different ways to their work. Research has indicated that there is no one way of motivating staff, but it is important that a leader is aware of what motivates staff.

Motivational factors are likely to include:

- achieving success
- recognition of achievement from others
- respect of other teachers
- opportunities for advancement
- taking responsibility
- supervision
- the teaching of science itself and finding better ways of doing it
- salary and status.

Following a negative OFSTED report a newly appointed head of science was charged with 'motivating the science staff' by the headteacher. Discussions quickly revealed that science staff had never been told whether or not they had done a good job, even though an appraisal system was in place. The new head of science made an effort to ensure that all teachers received positive feedback about their work. For example, 'Those set of books were marked well... you did particularly well with...' or, 'Thank you for ordering that equipment, I was pleased you managed it on time'. In these small ways motivation quickly improved and staff were more prepared to receive feedback about how they might improve performance.

Staff Development – Identifying Training Needs

Knowing the strengths and weaknesses of individual team members is important and needed to plan for staff development. One effective method of identifying training needs for the team is through the completion of a competency matrix (see Fig 4.1B). The work of a science team can be broken down into a set of competencies needed for the department to perform and to meet objectives in its development plan. These competencies may be divided into:

- *Subject competencies*, e.g. to teach GCSE Physics, to teach Experimental and Investigative science, to assess Knowledge and Understanding in science.
- *Technical competencies*, e.g. to use a database, to use a spreadsheet, to complete risk assessments.
- *Team role competencies*, e.g. to monitor marking, to monitor safety, to observe and give feedback on teaching.

Once necessary competencies are identified they can be matched against individuals to obtain a picture of the level of competence throughout the department. There may be some competencies which are needed by all team members, whereas other competencies may only be needed by one or two members.

Fig 4.1B Science department competency grid

After completing a new development plan, a science department meeting was held where the competencies needed to implement the plan were identified. All members of the department contributed. A matrix was then drawn up and each member was invited to put a dot in the grid where they felt they were competent and leave a blank where they felt they needed training. These were returned to the head of department for collation. Far from being threatening, because the process was open and involved all members of the department in identifying the competencies, teachers were positive and felt a sense of ownership.

214

Staff Development – Giving Feedback

At some stage a head of science will have to provide feedback to a member of the team who is perhaps not performing as well as they might. Other members of department may support student teachers and newly qualified teachers (NQTs).

For feedback to be effective it should:

- be planned
- be given in a supportive manner
- end with positive agreed action.

When planning feedback to individuals consider:

1) Are you clear about the purpose of your feedback? What do you want to happen as a result? Is it realistic? What support can you offer?
2) Are you well prepared? Do you have evidence or specific examples to support your view? Have others been asked? Do they support your view?
3) Have you chosen a venue where you can talk in confidence and will not be disturbed? Have you set aside sufficient time to give feedback and allow for discussion?

When giving feedback:

1) Start with a positive, move to the negative and end by agreeing positive action. A good way of starting is to ask how things are going. Staff will often be aware of problems and can do much of your work for you. If this happens pick out and reinforce what is done well, then move to the problem areas and ask them how things might be improved.
2) Aim for a friendly and supportive atmosphere.
3) When discussing problem areas be descriptive, explain what the problem is and be specific rather than general. Be prepared to quote examples.
4) Explore ways forward and agree what needs to be done. Aim to end on a positive note.

Agreeing positive action.

1) Agree what each of you will do next.
2) Write down some clear goals and the dates by which the agreed actions will be achieved.

An NQT was having difficulty managing the behaviour of a particular science group. After the head of science discussed the problems with the NQT, it was agreed that she would 'help out' in the lesson so that she could observe the way in which the NQT dealt with the behaviour. The head of science noted that he tended talk over pupils rather than waiting for them all to be quiet. She also noted that one individual was particularly problematic. This individual was removed and a strategy was agreed to ensure that pupils were silent before instructions were given. Review dates were set. Over a period the behaviour of pupils started to improve.

Running Meetings

Departmental meetings can be important team-building events. They need to be conducted efficiently. Any meeting should result in the productive use of everyone's time. The checklist can help the chair of the meeting to make sure things run smoothly.

Chair's Checklist for Meetings

1) Make sure the purpose is clear.
2) Create a written agenda.
3) Declare a start and finish time for the meeting.
4) Include a manageable number of topics for discussion.
5) Allocate time to each topic.
6) Encourage participation of all present.
7) Summarise after each topic. Agree actions, staff who are responsible and deadlines.
8) Provide a written summary which focuses on the agreed actions (e.g. minutes).

The use of time is important to everyone:

- Don't use a meeting for just passing on information that could be communicated in another way, e.g. a notice board.
- Don't hold a meeting because of 'habit'.
- Don't invite anyone who is not necessary.
- Don't run overtime.

- Do use a meeting for sharing opinions and making reaching decisions.
- Do make sure everyone participates.
- Do use the meeting as a professional development opportunity.
- Do evaluate meetings and try to improve them.

One head of science regularly shared responsibility around, not only for taking the minutes but also for chairing the meeting. Whilst novel at first this was seen by staff as a positive development opportunity. Not only did staff begin to appreciate the difficulties of chairing a meeting for themselves but as a result they began to modify their behaviour when not in the chair, improving efficiency. Meetings became increasingly productive. All staff were stakeholders and felt responsibility.
Teachers were not only able to cite the experience on their CV when applying for other jobs but were also able to use the insight to discuss the role of management at interview.

Managing Resources

Resources which need effective deployment and management include teachers, technicians, equipment and secondary resources (texts, CD-ROM, etc.).

Deployment of Staff

All members of staff, including yourself have strengths and weaknesses. Knowing these is important so that the best use can be made of particular talents. The competency matrix is one means of capturing these (Fig 4.1B). Are staff strengths known and drawn upon?

Financial Planning and Deployment of Learning Resources

The efficient use of resources is important and they should be evaluated carefully. Do new resources really provide value for money? The evaluation of texts is explored in Chapter 4.4.

Obtaining sufficient funds to operate a science department is vital. The ways in which funds are allocated to science departments vary significantly from school to school. Some apply a formula based on the number of pupils; some only provide what is asked for in a bid and in some schools the size of the budget is decided by negotiation. Whichever method applies, being clear about why the department needs a particular funding allowance; how it is linked to the development plan and how it will contribute to raised standards will bring about a more positive response.

How much money should a department receive? There is no clear answer to this and much will depend on circumstance. Some headteachers' organisations provide guidance on formulae that can be applied and periodically the Royal Society (1997) publishes its view on science resources for 11–16 year olds.

Preparing an annual budget based on the needs of the department is an important tool for a manager. It can:

- make clear which financial areas you are responsible for
- help you plan your resources effectively
- help you think strategically
- enable you to plan for replacement of major equipment
- help you negotiate levels of funding
- give early warnings about potential problems
- help manage change effectively by costing proposals (i.e. development plan).

The items which should be considered for inclusion in an annual budget are:

- consumables – chemicals, glassware, other equipment
- replacement equipment (breakages and through wear and tear)
- new equipment as a planned change or to equip new areas of curriculum
- stationery; photocopier bill
- text books
- video, IT software and hardware
- maintenance, e.g. microscopes, safety equipment/checks
- replacement costs of furniture/fittings
- staff INSET; reference books for staff
- visits/field studies.

These can be costed under the budget headings of capital costs (new and replacement equipment), materials costs (chemicals, consumable, breakages), INSET, overheads (postage, maintenance, photocopying).

Seeking Improvement – Development Planning

Continually seeking improvement is a key feature of leadership and management. A development plan is the formalised statement of the improvements the department is seeking and the steps that are needed to achieve them.

It is good practice for development plans to:

- focus on the school and department aims
- arise from an audit which may include analysis of test and exam results, departmental review or OFSTED inspection
- identify priorities
- map out progress in brief over a longer period (three years) and provide more detail in the form of an action plan for the current year
- be costed and tied to INSET needs
- address the categories of Curriculum, Staff development, Resources and Accommodation
- be constructed with the involvement of the whole department.

A Framework for a development plan is provided here. Fig 4.1C shows an outline three-year plan. Here there is space for specific targets. Fig 4.1D shows a more detailed action plan for the current year.

Category	Year 1	Year 2	Year 3
Curriculum			
Resources			
Staff			
Accommodation			

Fig 4.1C Three-year development plan

Target	Action plan	Deadline	Personnel involved Responsibilities	Resources/ time required	Success Criteria	Evaluation Procedures

Fig 4.1D Action plan for the current year

In one school a series of targets was identified following a departmental review which included a detailed analysis of examination results. The categories in the three year framework helped prioritise the targets. Improvements were sought in the standards of Experimental and Investigative science and physical processes at both KS3 and KS4. In order to achieve this it was realised that some staff training and particular resources were needed and the schemes of work needed improving at KS3. Thus the priorities for the first year were identified as training for all staff in investigative science, training of two staff for physics and better planning for investigative science in schemes of work. The purchase of extra resources was also identified as a priority for the current year but the review of the physical processes aspects of the schemes of work were left to the forthcoming year, following the training of the two staff members.

Summary

A large part of management is about dealing with people. Creating a climate which is open, honest and self evaluating helps people work together. We can be critical of the work of the department, in our desire to seek improvement, but we need to search for solutions together. In this way the department acts as a team. If you are interested in developing your role as a manager further then the two helpful frameworks mentioned earlier are available (MCI, 1997; TTA, 1998). These set out clearly the competencies and knowledge and understanding which are expected.

About the Author

Mike Evans has taught in a number of schools and has been a Head of Department. He is an OFSTED Trained Registered Inspector, contributes to ASE Inset Services' management courses and currently works for Southampton City Council as a Science Inspector.

References and Further Reading

Boutall, T. (1994) *The Good Managers Checklist,* Management Charter Initiative.

MCI (1997) *Management Standards Level 4,* Management Charter Initiative, Russell Square House, 10–12 Russell Square, London WCIB 5BZ.

OFSTED (1997) *Subject Management in Secondary Schools – Aspects of Good Practice*, a report from the Office of Her Majesty's Chief Inspector of Schools Reference 93/97/NS, OFSTED Publications Centre, PO BOX 6927, London E3 3NZ.

Royal Society (1997) *Science Teaching Resources; 11–16 Year Olds. A Report by a Working Group of the Education Committee of the Royal Society,* October 1997, The Royal Society, 6 Carlton House Terrace, London SW1Y 5AG.

TTA (1998) *National Standards for Subjects*: National Standards Pack, Teacher Training Agency.

Tuckman, B.W. Development Sequences in Small Groups, pp 384–99. In Torrington, Wightman and Johns (1985) *Management Methods,* Institute of Personnel Management.

4.2 Inspection and the Evaluation Cycle

David Oakley

Accountability has been the theme of much of the education legislation over the last ten years. Schools have been swamped by external imperatives, including inspection and national performance tables. A culture of measurement of attainment in order to raise standards has been generated by the school improvement and effectiveness movement. OFSTED inspection is the way which government has decided will most effectively guarantee schools' commitment to raising standards in England and Wales. The purpose of inspection is 'to identify strengths and weaknesses so that schools may improve the quality of education that they provide and raise the educational standards achieved by their pupils.' The inspection process is heavily focused on classroom practice. Documentation supporting the work of the school is analysed and judged in terms of its effectiveness in raising standards or maintaining high standards. Staff, particularly senior staff and co-ordinators, are interviewed about their roles. Parents are canvassed on their view of the school by questionnaire and at a meeting. After inspection, the feedback and report are intended to give direction to the school's strategy for planning, review and improvement by an evaluation that is rigorous and identifies key issues for action. This chapter outlines perspectives before, during and after an inspection. It is useful to visualise the process as an evaluation cycle:

- Pre-inspection – what have we achieved so far and where are we going?
- Inspection – external evaluation snapshot, where we are now?
- Post-inspection – what has been achieved and what do we need to do next?

Although the *context* for discussion is the practice in England and Wales, the *principles* of planning and evaluation apply across the UK.

Background and National Perspective

Until September 1993 external evaluation of schools in England and Wales was largely the province of HMI. As there was only ever a maximum number of 500 HMI to cover all areas of curriculum and management, their visits for survey purposes or as part of general inspections were on a very long cycle – 20 to 50 years! Local Education Authority advisers worked with schools in a variety of ways, including subject reviews, but these visits were seldom in the inspection mode. The rationale for advisers' visits to schools varied and criteria were rarely shared with schools. This changed in 1993 with the establishment of OFSTED and the recruitment of thousands of inspectors. LEA advisers metamorphosed into inspectors and the OFSTED culture became a fact of life.

OFSTED Inspection, School Monitoring and Self-evaluation

The function of OFSTED inspection is threefold:

- To provide information to parents. (OFSTED was set up as part of the first plank of the Parents' Charter.)
- To provide data for the national picture.
- To raise standards and help schools to improve.

Schools share with OFSTED the third aim. Strategies to enable departments and schools to monitor and evaluate themselves are an essential part of the repertoire of an effective school/department. The purpose of monitoring is to provide information about practice. It is the gathering of information and evidence, followed by the sifting, sorting, classifying, analysing and generally making sense of the information and evidence collected. Evaluation is about identifying strengths and weaknesses, finding out if stable systems need to change or whether changes have been effective, drawing conclusions, making value judgements and proposing improvements. The endorsement of successful strategies is not precluded! The process provides a firm basis for accountability and confirms that intentions have been translated into action. OFSTED criteria provide a suitable agenda on which schools can base their own criteria and superimpose their own priorities. The criteria for teaching, for example, are fundamental to any examination of the quality of teaching taking place. Any external monitoring is very orientated towards these criteria. Accountability is on the political agenda for the foreseeable future.

From February 1998 schools have had data about their performance from OFSTED statistics which compare a school's performance in the national curriculum tests with the national average and against those of similar schools. Schools are grouped on the basis of the proportion of pupils eligible for free school meals as an index of disadvantage. QCA provide these benchmark figures. Schools are also rated against others with similar intakes under the headings 'Standards Achieved by Pupils' and 'Quality of Education'. The ratings are reached by taking assessments from the reports prepared during OFSTED inspections. Schools are given one of four grades, ranging from 'very good' to 'substantial improvement required'.

Measuring Attainment – Where Are We Now?

Any strategy for improvement must be a continuous one, but as schools come up for re-inspection the need to check out how well they are on target is particularly vital. The key features looked at by inspectors are performance indicators – the measurable outcomes of pupils' attainment and progress.

Collection and management of data is a relatively new responsibility for primary co-ordinators, but they need:

- Baseline information.
- KS1 teacher assessment.
- KS2 test results and teacher assessment for science.

- Any optional QCA interim tests results.

The task is also a very important aspect of the role of the secondary head of department, though this could be delegated. Essential data for secondary schools are:

- KS2 results of the intake.
- KS3 data.
- GCSE, vocational qualifications and other certificated results at age 16.
- GCE AS/A levels, vocational qualifications.

Middle schools may have to deal with mid key stage transfer and adopt their own strategies for assessing their intake and output. Introduction of mid-KS2 optional tests may be applicable.

The data needs to be collected on an annual basis and displayed in a graphical or tabular form that conveys the pattern of attainment of the pupils in the subject. Computer software enables data to be manipulated in seemingly infinite ways. It is important not to be seduced by the technology; the audience must always be the focus. Is the school communicating with parents, LEA inspectors, OFSTED inspectors or the local press? Is a bar chart, pie chart, 3-D histogram or line graph appropriate? Trends are vitally important in the analysis of data. The three-year rolling average of results is probably the most important data to be communicated. This technique irons out the fluctuations in annual performance. It is important to set annual targets that are realistic and take into account previous performance. A commentary should summarise the analysis of the data, explaining trends and deviations and should be accompanied by analysis of strategies adopted as a consequence of previous analysis and evaluation.

Comparisons can be made by adding other sets of information, e.g. KS2 data on entry with the data on GCSE results or relative performance of boys and girls. This is particularly useful in value added analyses (see Chapter 3.2), though care must be taken not to include too much data at a time. There is an increasing variety of ways of obtaining and analysing data for secondary schools. Almost all LEAs in England and Wales subscribe to the National Consortium for Examination Results (NCER), which provides information about the performance of pupils at GCSE level for each school within the LEA. The information identifies residuals, that is an index in terms of fractions of a grade, e.g. a –0.5 residual indicate a performance of half a grade below another subject. Subject performance can be compared with national data but also in comparison with each other within the school. The relative difficulty of different subjects is taken into account. Residuals are given for all pupils and also separately for boys and girls. Residuals are usually sent to headteachers to assist them with the management of the school. How the information is shared is at the discretion of the headteacher as the information could potentially be rather threatening to individual departments or staff. Similar data is made available to OFSTED inspectors as part of their background data for all secondary schools and for English, maths and science for primary schools. Before they set foot in a school inspectors are aware of the relative performance of the subject in that school.

Collection of data is a vital part of the target setting. Targets for particular key stages must be realistic and based upon information about the particular cohort. Evidence from any generic testing undertaken by the school can be used to supplement subject data. Historical trends may give a false picture on occasion, but effective record keeping and comparison with previous year groups enable attainable targets to be set.

Checking Other Aspects of Provision

Indicators of other achievements may be less easy to evaluate. How well science education is meeting the success criteria set out in the subject development plan and action plan from the previous inspection is part of the scheduled review process. Though the timing of an inspection may result in some aspects of review being brought forward, schools should not feel that they must be deflected from their own review priorities. Part of inspection is to evaluate the effectiveness of the school's systems and processes and as schools will only have 10 to 13 weeks notice of an inspection, any pre-inspection check will rely heavily on the review cycle already in place. Any progress check the science co-ordinator may wish to make on classroom practice should supplement the routine monitoring that is taking place. The monitor/evaluate/review cycle is a way of managing improvement through self-evaluation of effectiveness. The basic principle of monitoring and evaluation is to be clear about the purpose. In order to make the process manageable within the extensive repertoire of a department it must be realistic in the demands made on teachers' time. An OFSTED inspection, thorough and rigorous though it may be, still only provides a snapshot. The true picture unfolds on a daily basis. Monitoring can be 'soft' and informal including occasional visits to a colleague's classroom or informal conversations about how 'things are going'. It is difficult to use such evidence as part of a structured approach and informality may lead to individuals feeling threatened if attempts are made to use observations of these sorts.

Formal monitoring needs to be part of a planned and agreed process, which involves as many colleagues as possible in achieving the desired aims.

The sequence is to:

- Identify the subject of the monitoring as part of the development plan cycle or action planning in response to an inspection or other external review.
- List the criteria for the monitoring.
- Decide upon the strategy to be adopted.
- Decide who will be involved and the time scale.
- Decide on how and to whom the findings are to be reported.

The subject of monitoring will depend upon development priorities and where the school is in the OFSTED cycle or other review cycle. Unforeseen national directives may require action planning. Monitoring of policies should be done routinely on a fairly long cycle over several years, though some such as assessment may need more frequent checking. It is very important that policies are dated and the next review is also identified.

Approaches to monitoring can involve:

- Lesson observations.
- Sampling of pupils exercise books or other work.

- Questionnaires.
- Self-monitoring.

Essential to each of these is a checklist, taken off the OFSTED shelf or devised by the team or an individual. Criteria for classroom observation would probably be best based on the OFSTED criteria but could be focused on differentiation or assessment. In practice few schools have the luxury of time to carry out this exercise. In the schools where it does happen, it is usually part of senior management's monitoring role.

The sampling of pupils' work is probably the easiest way into monitoring. Small numbers of pupils' books across a year group can provide a representative range of evidence quickly and the task can be shared so that everyone is both monitor and 'monitee'!

For example, adherence to the marking and assessment policy can be checked:

- Is assessment used formatively to improve pupils' learning?
- Are the specified grades for effort and attainment actually used?
- Is marking correct, accurate and consistent?
- Does the marking of homework reflect the effort that pupils have put into it?
- Are there positive comments?
- Are comments to complete missing work followed up?
- Is the balance of comments about understanding to those about presentation appropriate?

Monitoring of marking is probably the most important routine monitoring activity and should result in improved feedback to pupils about their progress. Examples of good marking, which helps pupils to know how to improve should be photocopied as part of the science marking policy in order to share good practice.

The second most important routine monitoring activity is the checking of the delivery of the scheme of work. It is probably best to separate the two activities, but both could be covered as part of the same exercise. The following questions might be useful:

- Is the scheme being properly covered in terms of content and level specified?
- Is the variety of teaching and learning approaches specified by the scheme being delivered?
- Are the recommended worksheets being selected?
- Is work being matched to the abilities of pupils in the class, with different work set?
- Is the work sufficiently challenging?
- Is the scheme itself sufficiently detailed?
- Would aspects benefit from review?
- Does the response of pupils indicate that they are interested in their work and motivated by it?
- Are pupils making appropriate progress through the topic and longer term?

Feedback can be generic and minuted as part of subject meetings. For example:

- 'Most of us are not using the extension suggestions in the two-lesson block on magnetism.'
- 'Most of us did not give the pupils an opportunity to investigate their own ideas in this topic.'
- 'Few of the special needs worksheets we bought for the scheme are being used.'

Improvement of the effectiveness of the scheme of work is a tangible outcome of monitoring and evaluation. Schemes of work are probably always going to be under review. Another way of monitoring the performance of the scheme of work is to analyse the results of any testing of pupils that takes place. It may be that pupils are consistently performing badly in one topic, not because of the intrinsic difficulty of the topic but because of the way in which it is being taught and a revision of the scheme might be in order.

If monitoring is not part of established practice, a pupils' work scrutiny is the quickest way of checking how policies and the scheme of work are being implemented. A sample from each class to include two high-attaining, two average-attaining and two low-attaining pupils' work can provide information on how effectively science teaching matches up with documented intentions. The response to the findings should be the subject of an action plan designed to improve any shortcomings by identifying, for example, in-service training, policy reviews or resource requirements.

Evaluation

Once data and other information have been organised strategic planning is the next stage. Many schools churn out data without much in the way of analysis, particularly of successful strategies. Why were the results so good that year? What did we do that we can replicate to repeat that success? The same is true of the findings of monitoring. It is the evaluation stage that is crucial in identifying strategies needed, or those existing as successful. The relative performance of boys and girls is a case in point. To simply produce an analysis which says that boys outperform girls at GCSE and by how much is seldom accompanied by a list of strategies designed to raise the attainment of girls and subsequent evaluation of these strategies.

Analysis of the success of strategies should be based on both measurable indicators of success, such as test results, and intuitive evaluations. 'Gut reactions' can be just as important as statistics for something as personal as interaction with pupils. Professional experience is often underrated in the current vogue for quantification. What are the elements in improving attainment in science? The most important is the will to improve. Strategies need to be seen as positive rather than defensive. The ambition for perceptible, specific improvements needs to be realistic, based on a sound knowledge about what is and what is not currently being achieved. Promotion of self-esteem should not just be an aim for pupils' development, but also for the effective functioning of staff. Strategies should be reinforced by the sharing of vision and goals. Success should be celebrated with colleagues, pupils, senior managers, parents and governors. Rigour and pace are vital aspects of the process. The key to realistic pacing of raising standards initiatives is the subject development plan.

The Inspection

The subject teaching during the inspection week needs to be planned well ahead so that the variety of work going on represents the full repertoire of the school. During the inspection week exemplify the good practice you seek to demonstrate throughout the year.

Good practice means:

- Act and teach as you do on a good day!
- Make sure that you have planned the whole week thoroughly and that you share the purpose and aims of each lesson with pupils.
- Allow time for end-of-lesson review with pupils.
- Ensure that all the resources that you need are to hand.
- Make sure that any classroom support staff know what is expected of them.
- Leave your planning out for inspectors to read, include background information about pupils on the special needs register.
- Have somewhere available for the inspector to sit.
- Check the learning environment for tidiness, range of resources, range of pupils' work on display.
- Make sure that work is marked up-to-date.
- Keep as far as possible to your prepared timetable and make sure that sessions start and end on time.

Post-Inspection – Action Planning

Post-inspection an action plan needs to be devised to deal with issues raised by the inspection. There may well be an overlap with the subject development plan, but the issues in an action plan are specific to an inspection report or identified as a priority by the school. An action plan is normally devised when there is a need to bring about fairly rapid changes. It needs to include:

- The issue to be addressed.
- Actions planned.
- Time scales.
- Responsibilities for leading.
- Responsibilities for monitoring.
- Training required.
- Resource implications and costing (including time).
- Success indicators.
- Date of review.

The cycle of monitoring and evaluation begins again, with the progress of the action plan being the focus. Action plan issues usually become incorporated into subject development plans. It is important for the purpose of reporting on progress during future inspections that the action plan retains a life of its own, running alongside the development plan.

Future Directions

The current OFSTED guidance is already well honed and the subject of major revision. Fundamental changes in the near future are unlikely. HMCI Chris Woodhead has acknowledged that schools are moving towards self-evaluation, but still considers that the external check is an essential part of the process of school evaluation and improvement. More radical models for inspection still involve external evaluation/accreditation of schools' own work. In September 1997 re-inspection of secondary schools began, primary and special re-inspection followed in September 1998. The focus in the second, six-year phase is on how the school in general has improved or maintained high standards and how subjects, particularly core subjects, have moved on. The first report and the school's response to it through the action plan will be the starting point. External monitoring by the LEA required by the 1998 Education Act will also be considered, as will the results of the school's own monitoring. The re-inspection phase presents schools with an opportunity to show how they have tackled the subject issues raised by their first inspection in the intervening period and what systems they have in place to support improvement. The systems in place for science within the school must constantly be stimulated by reference to national initiatives. Keeping up with what is new in science needs to complement introspection. Networking is vital. Schools need new ideas. Awareness of new commercial schemes, research evidence, projects aimed at raising standards, new equipment, the latest revision guides, software, ideas for science clubs and visits, is part of creating an ethos of excitement, enjoyment and improvement.

About the Author

David Oakley taught science for 20 years in grammar and comprehensive schools and a tertiary college before becoming an advisory teacher then inspector for science in Dudley LEA. A past chair of the National Science Advisers and Inspection Group, he has been an OFSTED Registered Inspector since OFSTED inspections began in 1993.

References and Further Reading

Barber, M., Stoll, L., Mortimore, P. and Hillman, J. (1995) *Governing Bodies and Effective Schools,* London, DFE.

OFSTED (1994) *Improving Schools*, London, OFSTED.

OFSTED (1995) *The OFSTED Handbook, Guidance on the Inspection of Schools,* London, HMSO.

OFSTED (1995) *Planning Improvement: Schools' Post-inspection Action Plans,* London, HMSO.

White, P. and Poster, C. (Eds) (1997) *The Self-monitoring Primary School,* London and New York, Routledge.

4.3 The Role of Technicians

David Billings

Technicians are essential in assisting good science education. This chapter explores the roles of technicians and the need for professional qualifications and career structure.

Background

A recent survey carried out by ASE as a forerunner to work being developed on establishing a recognised technician qualification, asked the question of technicians, 'What do you do in your job ?' Over 1300 questionnaires were distributed with over 90% responding. On analysis, a listing of some 90 job functions were identified. This points to the fact that the role of the technician has moved on apace from those very, very early days when I was a technician in further education and found myself, really, only putting out equipment for practicals and clearing it away afterwards.

With the vast changes that have taken place in the curriculum and more so with the changes in delivery methods and styles, we have seen the role of the laboratory technician become more and more diverse. Consequently, it has become more and more important to the efficient and effective operation of the science department and of the curriculum that it offers. One question, however, still stands out. How far is this importance of science technicians recognised by the teaching staff and management of the school and college? Are they seen as key members of the department?

It is fair to say that until now technicians have been very much 'ignored' but the wheel is at last turning and as this chapter points out, science technicians do have representation and they do have specific qualifications in place to further their training.

The one item missing at the moment, but which will only come with the development of the above two items, is a clear career structure. Why should a young technician feel the need to move in order to further his/her career. Technicians in other fields do not. They have an opportunity to rise up to the higher plains within their field. The door of opportunity for science technicians in education needs to be pushed wide open and not just left ajar.

The Developing Role of Technicians

It is no accident that this chapter, on the role of the science technician, has been placed within the section on the management of science education. The science technician should, quite properly be included in the proper management of both the science curriculum and the management of the science department. However, technicians have an empathy with most areas of science education. They have an important role to play in ensuring the rightful place of science in the curriculum. They have an important role to play in the development of how science is learnt, particularly, but not wholly, in the skills and processes of developing investigative science. They most certainly have an important role to play in the planning and implementation stages of delivering the curriculum. All in all science technicians are important people in the every day running of a successful science department.

So, how has the role of the science technician developed over the years and is this reflected in a recognition of the work by employers? To answer these question we can look at the last few years to see the extent of this developing role. In April of 1994 the then Laboratory Technician Task Group of the ASE undertook a survey of technicians and their work. The summary report concludes that technicians undertook some 41 different job roles (ASE, 1994). In the survey that ASE has recently undertaken the response showed a listing of some 90 job functions. How do these two sets of job roles compare?

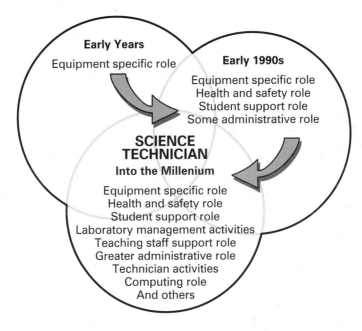

Fig 4.3A The developing role of the science technician

Fig 4.3A shows a comparison between the science technician roles in three stages of development. In the early days the science technician was primarily concerned with the equipment specific jobs – setting the equipment out in the laboratory, clearing away at the end of the practical session and generally looking after the equipment in terms of its repair and maintenance. Looking at the tasks performed by technicians in the 1994 survey, these now develop beyond the 'equipment' level. Fig 4.3A shows how tasks now extend into those concerned with administration, such as stock control, ordering etc., and those concerned with actual support in the classroom, in demonstrations and on trips. In the more recent analysis the job roles have widened still further. Not only are technicians still undertaking the tasks of a few years ago but can also find themselves in a more managerial role.

One can clearly see why it has been necessary for the science technician to develop into these other roles. Over the last few years there has been a tremendous amount of change taking place in education. Changes to the curriculum, new methods of teaching and delivery, a new emphasis on health and safety matters resulting in an importance being attached to such activities as risk assessments. Add to these the whole gambit of inspections and the move towards a total quality of operation and delivery and it is easy to see why any job in education has needed to show development. Fig 4.3A shows that technicians are clearly involved in these changes and rightly so. This wide range of duties which science technicians now have to undertake requires them to have a sound knowledge of, and experience in, a range of skills and safety procedures. Because of this technicians have an ever increasingly important role to play in the successful organisation and running of a science department. It is, therefore, important that managers and teachers recognise this fact. Technicians have at their fingertips the knowledge and experience of health and safety matters and they probably carry out the risk assessments within the department (see Chapter 3.7). Technicians can have the knowledge and experience of administrative matters such as efficient stock control techniques and computer spreadsheet usage. The science department must recognise the importance of its technicians. Technicians should be represented at department meetings, involved in all aspects of organisation and use of laboratories (see Chapter 4.1). Technicians are important resources and should be seen and recognised as such. The ASE, in its policy statement on technicians,

> *... is strongly convinced that the demands of the science curricula can only be delivered in an appropriate manner when an adequate level of trained technical support is available. Well-trained science technicians have an important contribution to make to the quality of learning. Further to this ... the ASE believes that technicians should be considered full and valued members of a science department.* (ASE, 1997a)

ASE Support for Technicians

In the light of the recognition by ASE of the importance of science technicians to the curricula, ASE has formulated a Science Technicians Policy Statement (ASE, 1997a). The main thrust of this policy statement is that it is essential for educational establishments to realise that the availability of well-trained science technicians will, have a big influence on the effective delivery of the curriculum. The policy also, rightly, informs that an absence of trained support will militate against effective delivery.

The policy also spells out that an appropriate training and career structure for technicians is paramount and that this would go a substantial way to creating a more valued and enhanced work model for science technicians.

To assist implementation of the policy, ASE has also provided a set of recommendations. These can be categorised generally into two groups – those to be implemented at a national level and those that are achievable within the establishment itself provided there is the necessary support from the management team.

At the national level the ASE seeks developments in two areas:

- the provision of a properly validated training programme for technicians with recognised end qualifications
- a proper career structure and professional development for technicians.

At the establishment level, the recommendations suggest a number of ideas that would establish technicians as a valued part of the science department. These are:

- clearly defined job specifications
- sufficient numbers of trained technicians to provide adequate support
- an entitlement to initial training programmes
- adequate in-service provision to allow technicians to develop training programmes
- appropriate working areas for technicians to carry out their work safely and effectively.

These are a good set of recommendations if only they could just be implemented! Now wait a minute. I can hear the comments. They appear every time. I have been a technician myself and recognise the signs. When anything new comes about initial comments are to the effect, 'That is all very well but it will never be achieved.'

Let us think positively here. The recommendations will not all happen overnight. A lot of hard work has been and will continue to be done. Recent developments are making a start towards the implementation of the ASE policy. The ASE Laboratory Technicians Task Group was set up with a two fold remit of providing the necessary support required for the technician membership of the ASE whilst at the same time seeking to implement a training structure for technicians.

The Task Group has implemented a number of ideas to provide support. These are:

- a dedicated information page, 'The Prep Room' within *Education in Science*, the publication which all technician members receive. This page provides up to date information and ideas for and from technicians.
- a dedicated technician strand of talks, discussions and workshops at the ASE Annual Meeting.
- an annual National Technicians Conference at which technicians have the opportunity to meet with each other and share ideas alongside a programme of talks on topics of national importance.
- production of *The Prep Room Organiser* (ASE, 1998). This is provided as a guide for technicians bringing much of the information acquired during their work and also required by them in the job, into one source. It provides the opportunity for technicians to add their own relevant information and to update the information as necessary.

- the production of sets of reprints, useful to technicians, from ASE journals.

Regarding technician training, technicians are very close to having a set of specific qualifications in place (ASE, 1997b). The project development has been co-ordinated by ASE and has involved many technicians both directly in the development work and also in the consultation stages. The result is a unit based qualification for a set of awards at progressive levels within the national S/NVQ framework. The units have been developed following a comprehensive analysis of technician job roles and will therefore focus on those roles. Technicians will be assessed by qualified assessors on the job and will be able to show competence in their job. The qualification will enable technicians to move up to higher levels of competence. The standards are at present being approved and will be available in schools and colleges.

A Career Structure?

All that has been written so far is happening. So what price a career structure, given the belief that laboratory technicians need and deserve such a structure. They need to be able to have the chance to remain within the job and to move up to a higher level of responsibility and to get the recognition for it. Many technicians choose this role and very much enjoy the work. They enjoy the challenge of supporting and helping pupils and students to achieve their ambitions. However, in many instances technicians are forced to move to other jobs in order to receive the recognition and rewards which their expertise deserves. But why should this be necessary when the job is clearly enjoyable to them? If a career structure was in place then school and college laboratory technicians would be able to develop their skills and expertise and to move up a suitable scale while still providing the increased support and help to the schools and colleges.

Two things need to happen before a career structure can even be considered as workable. First of all there must be a suitable set of available qualifications which enable them to increase their skills and knowledge base. This, as explained, is now very close to becoming a reality. The second will be more difficult to achieve: a national set of guidelines to enable technicians to be promoted as they achieve the different levels of qualification and increase the responsibility within their job. The sticking point may well be a reluctance on the part of management to recognise that a career structure is necessary.

I see a move in this direction as essential in the development of the technician role and I hope managers can see it as well. A career structure becomes more and more essential as the technician role develops with more sophisticated techniques and methods in the teaching and delivery of the curriculum. ASE has recognised technicians as important members of the science education community through representation on ASE Council. School and college management need to be aware that for the efficient and effective operation of the science department a professional technician structure is imperative.

About the Author

David Billings retired as Head of Mathematics and Science at Peterborough Regional College in 1995. Since then he has been working on projects in vocational education. He is currently Chair of the ASE Laboratory Technicians Task Group working to support the technician membership of ASE.

References and Further Reading

ASE (1994) *School Technicians – An Invaluable Asset*, Hatfield, ASE.

ASE (1997a) *Science Technicians: Policy Statement*, Hatfield, ASE.

ASE (1997b) National Vocational Qualifications for School and College Technicians, *PSSI Forum*, October 1997.

ASE (1998) *The Prep Room Organiser*, Hatfield, ASE.

4.4 Choosing and Using Published Science Schemes

James Williams

Now, what I want is, Facts. Teach these boys and girls nothing but Facts. Facts alone are wanted in life. Plant nothing else and root out everything else. You can only form the minds of reasoning animals upon facts: nothing else will ever be of service to them. (Charles Dickens, Hard Times)

Textbooks are full of facts. A common misconception among pupils is that science is about facts. The acquisition of facts, usually contained within the knowledge dimension of schemes and syllabuses, is only one aim of a rounded science curriculum. Others include understanding and skills associated with practical science and problem solving; appreciating the social, cultural and historical context of science. The effectiveness of an introduced published scheme will vary. Often the latest 'off-the-shelf' scheme does not live up to expectations. This may be more the fault of the user than the producer. Choosing and using published schemes requires careful thinking and planning. A mistake could be costly in financial terms and in pupil learning and motivation.

When using published schemes there are a number of factors to consider, not least how it may be used to best effect in lessons. Science is not renowned for presenting the human face of discovery. Traditional textbooks tend to present a body of knowledge as a series of facts. Leaving pupils with an impression that science is not a human endeavour is leaving them with a less than satisfactory view of a subject that is just as human as English or history. Recently there have been moves to rediscover the human voice in science.

This chapter explores a strategy for choosing a published scheme and looks at ways in which texts and worksheets can be used to best effect.

Assessing Schemes and the Problem of Using Schemes

SCAA's analysis of KS3 science schemes (SCAA, 1997) concluded that published schemes were well presented, had high quality resources, were well written, accurate and provided for progression in science concepts. Criticisms were minor and high-lighted the need to provide for extended reading and writing. They also identified a lack of progression in the approach and complexity of material presented. Choosing and using a published scheme is not an easy task, neither is its adoption cheap. When a science department invests in a new scheme, that investment must be an informed one.

If we accept that current texts are fit for their purpose, the methods of use becomes important in pupils' learning. Research into textbook and worksheet use highlights the distinct character that science textbooks have (Carré, 1981; Davies and Greene, 1984). Science texts provide pupils with a number of problems, particularly readability and comprehension. The technical language means that even with careful writing and editing it is difficult to lower the reading age without losing some of the precision. In the past few years authors have taken up the challenge of producing material suited to the age of its readership. They have been mindful of readability and accessibility. However, the drive to shorten sentence length and oversimplify the technical language can have the effect of losing the narrative of the text. Oversimplification of prose commonly leads to a total lack of human interest for the reader, making comprehension more difficult.

There is also a difference in how a reader interprets a text in science and one in English. Novels have the advantages of a story line and characters with whom the reader can identify. Readers are led through the text and there is a familiarity that allows them to understand the narrative. Such texts also allow pupils to use their imagination and free them to be creative. In science there is less involvement. The technical language and unfamiliar words needing precise definition require the pupil to break from the flow of text and re-read sections in search of information. This is exacerbated by the small percentage of reading that is encouraged by science teachers.

Worksheets present other problems – even those produced to match a scheme. They have short bursts of simple, technical language that has to be addressed in order to progress. If unfamiliar, non-engaging narrative is accompanied by technical diagrams or abstract theory then pupils have problems. They may not understand what the science is about or know what they are supposed to do.

Lunzer and Gardner (1979) showed that the pattern of reading in science was sporadic, described by them as 'short burst'. The purpose of the reading varied, but the activities were principally: to read questions from the text before writing answers in exercise books; copying key words or short sections of text. What was not happening was any period of continuous reading allowing pupils to develop skills needed to critically analyse or reflect on the text.

The Bullock report (DES, 1975) made recommendations on use of language. In the case of reading and readability it was not specific. It did talk of the need for science teachers to understand the role of language in learning (see Chapter 3.3):

In the secondary school, all subject teachers need to be aware of:

(a)   the linguistic processes by which their pupils acquire information and understanding, and the implications for the teacher's own use of language;

(b)   the reading demands of their own subjects, and ways in which pupils can be helped to meet them.

(DES, 1975)

Choosing A Published Scheme

SCAA's (1997) report on KS3 teaching schemes was part of a pilot analysis of educational resources. The main purpose was to help publishers enhance the quality of their educational resources.

The ASE recognises that high quality teaching is dependent on *'the availability of high quality and appropriate resources'* (ASE, 1997a). They also encourage learners to *'evaluate the nature of evidence from science and elsewhere in making judgements about the use of science'* (ASE, 1997b). In accomplishing this the use of controversial issues in science is advocated. ASE suggest that appropriate support materials should be made available. These materials will often be incorporated within science texts and published courses, though there is plenty available from the media.

The Process of Choosing a Published Scheme

Choosing the 'right' published scheme is important. There are many that allow you to simply photocopy and teach – providing teacher/technician notes, using worksheets that are differentiated, and having links to the latest curriculum orders. The resources themselves, however, will not guarantee success in securing high standards of teaching and learning.

The best scheme is written to the style of the individual teacher and caters for the specific needs of each and every child in your school. Only a tailor-written scheme can achieve this. Some schools do this, but in a large proportion of schools it will not happen for a number of reasons, e.g.:

- time
- resources
- the changing profile of year groups each academic year
- staffing changes.

Thus, the attraction of buying a scheme can prove irresistible. A systematic approach to choosing a published scheme is essential. Williams (1997, 1998) describes an outline procedure and this forms the basis of the following approach.

Stage One

Look carefully at the range of expertise in your department. Look at how you deliver your science curriculum. What you need is a clear idea of your department's strengths and weaknesses. Consider how you would like to structure the teaching and learning of science across all age ranges. For lower secondary, one teacher teaching all sciences is common but good use of specialist expertise is crucial, particularly beyond 14. An important consideration is progression and continuity between key stages. If the curriculum styles at different ages are different then the transition will not be smooth. Simply following the national curriculum will ensure neither continuity nor progression (see Chapter 3.6).

Consideration must be given to pupils' experiences at primary school. It helps if there is good two-way liaison with feeder schools over schemes of work and texts being used. Another factor is pupil attainment. Legislation requires the results of the end of KS2 tests to be forwarded on transfer. This information should form part of the evidence base for deciding the curriculum approach. Many published schemes have introductory units or modules that are a 'clean slate' approach. The pupils are not clean slates and will have many and varied experiences of science and the language of science.

Stage Two

Request inspection copies and/or packs from publishers. Draw up a checklist to help analyse the scheme. Fig 4.4A gives a specimen checklist. It is important that the initial evaluation is done by all science staff. One method is to ask staff to assess each element of the checklist and give a short presentation at a future department meeting. A key element to managing a major change is that the staff are involved and have ownership of the new curriculum. If they feel that any change is a *fait accompli* it will lead to resentment and loss of goodwill. By using a checklist, a fair comparison of schemes will be made. Attention to issues such as the management of the day to day running of the scheme are important (e.g. what are the resource and apparatus demands). An excellent scheme may not be adopted because of the logistics of providing the necessary resources or because of substantial capital investment in addition to the cost of buying the scheme.

Stage Three

After evaluating all schemes, you can narrow the choice down to one or two. It is important to look at the impact of your choice on the curriculum. Discuss your intentions widely with those responsible for other core areas, e.g. English and Maths and Special Educational Needs (SEN). Think about the impact on the timetable. Would adopting a new scheme mean that the current lesson length and organisation would no longer be suitable? Timetable changes cannot happen overnight. At this stage the advice of technicians is invaluable (see Chapter 4.3). They need to know what the resource implications are and if any capital purchases or changes in chemical and equipment stores are needed. They may also be able to advise on a strategy for the delivery of the practical work.

Plan the implementation of the new scheme carefully. It may take up to three years to implement fully. You should have an implementation, review and evaluation cycle for assessing how well the new scheme fits the curriculum (see Chapter 4.2). No published scheme can be taken off the shelf, dumped into the classroom and be 100% successful.

Using Schemes in Teaching Situations

There are difficulties associated with learning from science textbooks and worksheets. The purpose of reading the book or sheet is the over-riding factor. If interest in a subject is high, pupils tend to question their own knowledge and the concepts that are being put forward in the text. Pupils also put more effort into trying to understand. Pupils are more likely to make connections between their own knowledge and that presented to them if they are instructed to make comparisons or to contrast things when they are presented with what is new knowledge. In everyday science teaching the purpose of the text is usually to provide information, and the

---

Part 1 The Nature of the Published Scheme
- What are the stated aims of the scheme?
- What types of material are included?
- What do the main pupil books contain?
- Is there evidence of continuity and progression from primary through to 16?
- What do the teacher/technician guidance notes contain?

Part 2 Match to the Curriculum/Syllabus
- Does the scheme adequately cover the details of the curriculum orders/syllabus?
- Does the scheme cover the nature of science and experimental and investigative science adequately?
- What advice is given about the assessment?
- Is the assessment advice up to date?

Part 3 Fitness for Purpose
- Is the material scientifically accurate?
- Is the language level appropriate?
- Is there recognition of the contributions made by different cultures to the development of science?
- Does the material avoid stereotypes?
- Do the materials give appropriate health and safety advice?
- Is there use of varied presentation in the materials?
- Does the presentation attract teachers and, more importantly, pupils?
- Are the contexts used appropriate?
- Is there evidence of progression in the language, illustrations and activities used?

Part 4 Use of The Materials in The Classroom
- Do the materials adopt a particular philosophy for teaching and does it match with your philosophy?
- Do the materials promote a particular teaching style and how does this match with your current style?
- Is there differentiated material available for use in the classroom and for homework?
- Are unit tests and mark schemes available?
- How will the material be managed in the classroom (i.e. worksheet based, textbook only, combination of worksheets and textbooks)?

N.B. This is based on a more detailed version which can be found in the SCAA (1997) report.

Fig 4.4A Analysis checklist

reading of texts in science tends to be about searching for information in response to questions set out at the end of a chapter or section. This strategy has the effect of preventing pupils from making connections with any pre-existing knowledge. Methods should be encouraged which allow pupils to be active rather than passive learners in considering text.

Using Textbooks and Worksheets in an Interactive Way: DARTS

DARTS (Directed Activities Related to Texts) are a commonly used set of activities to encourage active use of text (Davies and Greene, 1984). The directed activities broadly fall into two categories:

1) Analysis of text.
2) Reconstruction of text.

Analysis of Text

In the analysis activities the reader is required to focus on what the writer is saying. Analysis of text can be achieved by asking the reader to perform the following:

- underlining (e.g. parts of the digestive system on a worksheet)
- segmenting (e.g. putting or grouping parts of the text that belong together)
- labelling (e.g. parts of a flower or representation of an atom).

Another way of analysing is to ask the reader to give an alternative representation of the information:

- turning prose into a table
- turning prose into a diagram
- turning prose into a flow chart
- extrapolation (i.e. going beyond what the text is saying)
- listing underlined words in order of importance
- diagrammatic representation
- flow chart
- making a poster
- concept map (see Chapter 2.3).

Extrapolation can generate useful material during the analysis of text:

- pupil generated questions
- imaginative extension work (e.g. asking the pupil to produce a creative piece of writing following on from the author's views).

Reconstruction of Text

This involves the deletion of selected text, the rearrangement of text and partial concealment of text by the teacher. Reconstruction activities are sometimes referred to as completion activities:

- *deletion* – the teacher removes words and/or phrases and leaves gaps – Cloze techniques
- *rearrangement or sequencing* – this can be achieved at a number of levels from a few short, simple sentences to paragraphs to whole pages of text (see example in Chapter 2.6)
- *predicting* – pupils can predict the next event or step in a sequence, e.g. the method section of a practical activity or pupils could be asked to write the next paragraph/line of a partially completed conclusion to an experiment
- *table completion* – pupils fill in the missing cells of a table

- *diagram completion* – pupils complete the labelling of a diagram or complete the drawing of a diagram.

DARTS can be used with textbooks and worksheets and are a way of encouraging reflective reading. The key to using effective DARTS in lessons is to ensure that the pupils are clear on the nature of the activity in relation to the text in front of them. One of the most common misuses of texts in classes is blind copying of work from the book or worksheet into the pupils' exercise book. At no point does this involve reflective reading and should be discouraged. When using published schemes, teachers must be just as particular about the instructions given and how the pupil should use the worksheets and texts. Exactly why a seemingly successful published scheme fails to work can be hard to pin down. A common failure is that teachers rely too heavily on the published materials and do not give enough thought about how the materials are best used with their pupils. They see the scheme as replacing planning. Nothing can replace good planning for effective teaching.

About the Author

James Williams lectures in Science Education at Brunel University. He was on the SCAA Ad Hoc Committee advising on the analysis of Key Stage 3 schemes and is a regular contributor to the TES.

References and Further Reading

ASE (1997a) *Quality in Science Education: A Policy Statement,* Hatfield, ASE.

ASE (1997b) *Values and Science Education: A Policy Statement,* Hatfield, ASE.

Bentley, D. and Watts, M. (1992) *Communicating in School Science,* London, Falmer Press.

Carré, C. (1981) *Language Teaching and Learning. 4: Science*, Ward Lock Educational.

Davies, F. and Greene, T. (1984) *Reading for Learning in the Sciences,* Oliver and Boyd.

DES (1975) *A Language for Life: The Bullock Report,* HMSO.

Lunzer, E. A. and Gardner, K. (1979) *The Effective Use of Reading*, London, Heinemann.

Osborne, R. and Freyberg, P. (1985) *Learning in Science: The Implications of Children's Science*, London, Heinemann.

SCAA (1997) *Analysis of Educational resources in 1996/7: Key Stage Three Science schemes,* SCAA Publications.

Sutton, C. (1992) *Words, Science and Learning,* London, Open University Press.

Williams, J. (1997) Choosing a Scheme of Work. *Education in Science,* September 1997, No 174.

Williams, J. (1998) Plotting a Change of Course. *Times Educational Supplement* Friday, 9 January 1998, p 33.

4.5 Industrial Links: Purposes and Practice

Bill Harrison

It is crucial for schools to make science mean something; to build up links with the outside world, the world of work, and specifically the world of real science. Young people need to know that science is not a dry academic subject, that it is real and exciting, and that it can be a fulfilling career. Only real partnerships between schools, industry and research establishments can do this...

That statement was made by William Waldegrave, then Chancellor of the Duchy of Lancaster, opening the 'Pupils as Scientists' conference for teachers and scientists (organised by Clifton Scientific Trust with the Wellcome Trust) in London in 1993. It highlights why it is important for school and college science departments to forge industry–education partnerships.

This chapter considers principles and practice of good education–industry partnerships.

Background

For the purpose of this chapter 'industry' or 'company' are used to include all sectors of the manufacturing and service industries; research and development organisations and activities in industry and the public sector, including higher education. It covers the multi-national company as well as the small garage and corner shop.

Science and industry go hand in hand. The products and applications of science, produced and used by industry, are essential to our well being, our life styles and the economy. Surely therefore, learning about the applications and processes of science in industry and their importance, and having direct contact with practising scientists and engineers, should be essential experiences in everyone's science education. Although this has long been recognised, it has not been given priority in practice. Too often these valuable learning experiences have been marginalised or even eliminated in the drive to cover the 'facts and principles' in a content-laden curriculum.

Industrial Links – Everyone Benefits

There are many undoubted benefits from developing industrial links and partnerships, and bringing an 'industrial' dimension into the science curriculum. These have been well documented in, for example Harrison (1994), Pain *et al* (1997) and in ASE's policy statement on Education–Industry links (ASE, 1997a). Benefits include:

- heightening the awareness of pupils and teachers of the world of industry
- providing realistic and relevant contexts for science education
- enabling teachers and pupils to develop their own personal and professional skills through working in an industrial environment
- mobilising practising scientists and engineers to support and enrich the school curriculum
- enabling industrialists to gain greater awareness of schools
- enabling industrialists to develop their own personal and professional skills through working in an educational environment.

So, it is clear that everyone benefits from education–industry links, and it is not just pupils, teachers and schools, but the scientists, engineers and their organisations.

The Development of Industry–Education Partnerships

Curriculum Initiatives

Industry–education partnerships go back over forty years and cover such activities as site visits, industrial scientists and engineers giving talks in schools, careers support, sponsorship and resources for schools. Until the last 10 years or so, the majority of company resources focused on the organisations' products and processes and it was largely left to the teacher to adapt and extract the content relevant to the curriculum. Although many excellent individual, often localised initiatives took place prior to the 80s, industrial contexts and activities impacted on the school curriculum mainly from the mid 80s largely as a result of initiatives such as TVEI (Technical and Vocational Education Initiative). The introduction of a social, economic and industrial dimension within GCSE Science syllabuses and a strong government push on vocational education provided a helpful welcome boost. During the late 80s and early 90s several major curriculum initiatives involving industrial collaboration were undertaken which helped to bring industrial applications of science into the classroom.

These initiatives included:

- Problem Solving with Industry (1991) developed by the Centre for Science Education at Sheffield Hallam University. It involved some 20 science teachers each linked with a company to produce science problem solving investigations for secondary science and GNVQ science.
- Exciting Science and Engineering (1991) developed by the Chemical Industry Education Centre at the University of York, in collaboration with BP. Problem Solving materials were produced for the 7–14 age range.
- The Salters projects at York, which have done much to enrich the science curriculum through their 'applications' approach. For example, the new Salters A-level physics course involves close collaboration with scientists and engineers.

All of these initiatives have had significant uptake and were able to demonstrate that industrial contexts could provide realistic and highly motivating activities relevant to the science curriculum.

School–Industry Placements

Besides the development of curriculum resources, there are many other types of activity to support the teaching and learning of school science. They involve a wide range of approaches and activities.

There are several schemes available to place teachers into industry or research environments for short periods ranging from several days to several weeks in order to increase their awareness of industrial/research activities, update their science knowledge and skills, gain ideas and information for curriculum resources, etc.

Some current examples are:

- British Telecom/ASE Teacher Fellowship Scheme.
- Pupil Researcher Initiative Teacher Bursary Scheme.
- Nuffield Teacher Bursary Scheme piloted by the Nuffield Foundation.
- Royal Society of Chemistry Industry Study Tours.

Teachers fortunate enough to experience these schemes enthusiastically expound the benefits to themselves and ultimately their pupils.

Conversely, there are also several initiatives currently operating that bring industrial and research establishment scientists and engineers into the classroom, and/or involve them in educational support activities out of the classroom. Most notable of these is the EPSRC/PPARC funded Pupil Researcher Initiative's Researchers in Residence Scheme. This places young science and engineering research students into science departments for up to six to eight visits.

Other schemes include:

- School placements for biology/environmental PhD students, run by ASE and funded by BBSRC, NERC and the Wellcome Trust.
- Norfolk Teacher–Scientist Network based at the John Innes Centre, Norwich.
- Clifton Scientific Trust 'Science for Real' initiative based in Bristol.
- The Science and Engineering Alliance operating in 10 primary schools in Sheffield. It is funded by British Telecom and managed by staff at the Centre for Science Education at Sheffield Hallam University.

These all provide excellent opportunities to bring real science and scientists from industry and higher education into the classroom.

These schemes not only help to enrich and support science teaching and learning but also provide challenging and stimulating environments to help develop the personal and professional skills of the staff involved.

There are also schemes to place GNVQ/GSVQ and 'A'/Higher/SYS students into industry.

The very successful Nuffield Science Bursaries Scheme (1998), funded and developed by the Nuffield Foundation and operated mainly by the SATRO Network, places students into industrial/research laboratories for up to four weeks to carry out their own practical and experimental work. This enables students to gain insights into the world of work and the applications of science, and to further develop their scientific skills.

The national CREST Awards Scheme (1997) has done much to encourage close links between schools and the science and engineering communities. CREST projects promote industrial applications/contexts and links, and at the gold and platinum levels require an industrial or research scientist/engineer to help with supervision.

The Engineering Council/Association of School Science, Engineering and Technology (ASSET) Neighbourhood Engineer Scheme, Young Engineer for Britain Competition and Young Engineer Clubs, foster links between industry and education and bring considerable benefits to the pupils, teachers and engineers involved. Many competitions, science fairs and student conferences are supported by industry and actively involve industry–education partnerships. Practising scientists and engineers are often involved at all stages including planning, running and participating in, and judging and making awards.

The ASE and the BA organise a number of competitions/activities for schools that are supported and sponsored by industry, for example ASE's Science Challenge, Health Matters and Spotlight Scientist schemes (McGrath, 1997), and the BA's British Youth Science Fair (1997). Several companies are interested in these types of educational activity that involve the development of skills relevant to industry such as problem solving, communication, and teamworking.

There are a number of club schemes for young people such as Young Engineers Clubs (1998) and Salters Chemistry Clubs (1998) that involve the active support and participation of industry/ H.E. scientists and engineers. The youngsters are highly motivated, produce very high standards of work and gain a greater appreciation of the applications of science and engineering.

One of the major networks for promoting and operating industry–education partnerships in school science is the Science and Technology Regional Organisation (SATRO) co-ordinated by (ASSET), formerly the Standing Conference on School Science and Technology (SCSST). SATROs are providing an impressive network of regional activities. In many cases the SATRO director is also the British Association Field Officer, enabling close collaboration to occur between the activities of the two organisations. Thirteen SATROs are also responsible for overseeing CREST activities in their regions, and all SATROs manage a large portfolio of education–industry activities for schools, including Neighbourhood Engineers, Young Engineers, Nuffield Science Bursaries Scheme, Ciba Bicycle Pack training, SET weeks, etc.

Partnership in Action

It seems that the key areas of partnership activity essentially fall into four categories:

- Development of industry based resources as contexts for learning school science.
- Scientists in schools.
- Teachers and pupils in industry, i.e. placements or visits.
- Industry support and contexts for science activities, loan of equipment, provision of expert advice and services.

One school science initiative utilising all four of these categories is the Pupil Researcher Initiative (1998). A major aim of PRI is to mobilise on a large scale the science and engineering research communities to work with schools in supporting the teaching and learning of investigative science at Key Stage 4. Research scientists and engineers have been actively involved in helping with the development of Pupil Research Briefs, suggesting real contexts for the activities; providing insights into the work of researchers; supplying information and data, and checking accuracy and realism. Almost 1000 PhD researchers have visited schools helping with pupil investigations, science clubs, field trips, science fairs, giving talks and acting as good role models for young people. They have often helped to forge new links between the schools and their research departments, provided special equipment for lessons, and arranged school visits into the university or laboratory.

The PRI Teacher Bursary Scheme has enabled around 80 science teachers to spend up to 2 weeks on placement in a research laboratory, working alongside researchers in industry and universities. This has helped teachers to: get up to date with the latest techniques and developments; develop greater awareness of the research enterprise; gain ideas for curriculum development and forge strong school–industry links.

In developing these activities, PRI has capitalised on the many benefits of involving practising scientists from industry and research departments in the teaching and learning of school science. Teachers and researchers on industry or school placements comment positively on the experiences for themselves and for the pupils (Walker, 1996).

If It's a Good Thing Should We be Doing More?

There is now a significant body of qualitative evaluation evidence available to support the considerable benefits of industry-related curriculum activities. Whilst it is not easy to gain evidence of any long term impact on pupils' learning, motivation or career interests as a result of these types of interventions, largely because of the many other influences on the learning experience, there is little doubt that such activities generally have a very positive immediate impact (Walker,1998). There is very persuasive evidence from schemes such as CREST, the PRI, Nuffield Science Bursaries, Science Challenge and many others, that pupil achievement within these activities is often significantly greater than would normally be expected.

There is also a solid body of research which points to the increased motivation, positive attitudes and achievement of students experiencing realistic and relevant learning contexts and activities (Woolnough, 1995).

Positive feedback from teachers and pupils (Hollis, 1997) strongly suggests that much more partnership work should be taking place. It is particularly encouraging that there seems to be an increased interest in recent years from industry/higher education to link their scientists and engineers with schools.

This would suggest that there should be little difficulty for a teacher or department to make links with their local industry or HE scientists. Certainly schemes described above are able to offer direct support to teachers wishing to make such links. Other networks such as SATROs and the Education Business Partnerships can help schools to make links with industry, as can the ASE and the BA Field Officer networks. Another useful source of information can be obtained from SETNET (Science, Engineering and Technology Network) and its regional

SETPOINTS, either by direct contact or through available web sites. Indeed, many companies, universities and other organisations provide valuable information for working with schools on their web sites.

As to the future, it would be of great benefit, for example, if the vision of eminent scientist Professor Susan Greenfield of Oxford University, to connect every school with a practising scientist, could be realised. This vision may soon become reality, if the project CONNECT gets underway (Greenfield, 1997).

About the Author

Bill Harrison is Professor of Science Education and Head of the Centre for Science Education at Sheffield Hallam University. He is currently directing the Pupil Researcher Initiative. He was a member of the SATIS project central team and directed the Problem Solving with Industry project. He is active in promoting the Public Understanding of Science and supporting science teachers and pupils in classrooms.

References and Further Reading

Bristol Teacher–Scientist Network (1998) (http://www.Clifton-Scientific.org/)

CREST Award Scheme (1997) Realising Potential Information Brochure, CREST National Centre, 1 Gilspur St., London EC1A 9DD.

Exciting Science and Engineering Project (1991), Chemical Industry Education Centre, University of York.

GCSE Salters Chemistry, GCSE Salters Science Courses and *A-level Salters Chemistry* (1987 on), Science Education Group, University of York.

Greenfield, S. (1997) Under the Microscope, Joining Schools and Scientists: a Win–Win Case. *Independent on Sunday, Sunday Review Magazine*, December 14.

Harrison, B. (1994). *Problem Solving in Science and Technology*. Chapter 4: Problem Solving – the Industrial Context, David Fulton Publishers.

Harrison, B. and Ramsden, P. (1992). *Open Chemistry*. Chapter 2: Where Do We Start from, Theory or Practice? Hodder and Stoughton.

Hollis, S. (1997) Can Contact with Industry Really be of Value to Your School? *Education in Science*, No 173.

Industry–Education Readings for Science Teacher Education (1991) The Bassett Press, 61 Glen Eyre Road, Southampton SO2 3NP.

McGrath, C. (1997) Nurturing Education–Industry Links. *Education in Science*, No 173.

Neighbourhood Engineers (1998). (http://www.engc.org.uk/)

Norfolk Teacher Scientist Network. TS News (1997) No 8, Autumn. (http://www.uea.ac.uk/~e490/tsn/tsn.htm).

Nuffield Science Bursaries (1998) Information Booklet. Nuffield Curriculum Projects, 28 Bedford Square, London WC1B 3EG.

Pavin, J., Key, M. and Mapletoft, M. (1997) *Science Education in the 21st Century*. Chapter 11: Industry as a Resource for Teaching Science, Arena, Ashgate Publishing Ltd.

Problem Solving with Industry Project (1991) Centre for Science Education, Sheffield City Polytechnic.

Pupil Researcher Initiative (1998). (http://www.shu.ac.uk/schools/sci/pri)

Salters Chemistry Clubs (1998). Salters' Hall, Fore Street, London EC2Y 5DE.

SETNET – What is SETNET? (1997). SETNET, Freepost LON12017, London NW1 1YU. Tel: 0171 380 0562.

SETPOINT – What are SETPOINTS? (1997). In *What is SETNET?* SETNET, Freepost LON 12017, London NW1 1YU. SETPOINT Help Line Tel: 0800 146415.

The British Youth Science Fair (1997) British Association. (http://www. britassoc.org.uk/)

Walker, D. (1996 and 1998). *Evaluation Reports to Steering Group – Pupil Researcher Initiative*, Centre for Science Education, Sheffield Hallam University.

Woolnough, B.E. (1995). *Effective Science Teaching*, Milton Keynes, Open University Press.

Young Engineers Clubs (1998). ASSET, 1 Giltspur Street, London EC1A 9DD.

Index

A-level courses *34*
Access to science education *44*
Action competence *122*
Action plan *226*
Active use of text *240*
Administrative work *195*
Air pressure *59, 62*
Alkali metals *188*
Analogy *160*
Analysis of text *240*
Assessment *139*
  instruments *141*
  issues *47*
  of practical work *141*
  policy *139, 224*
  schemes *235*
Audit of approaches *17*
Awareness of learning *179*

Background knowledge *177*
Balanced science *26*
Baseline data *143*
Benchmarking *143*
Benefits of using computers *194*
Bridging *70–71*
BTEC *34*

Career structure *233*
CD-ROM *192*
Charles Drew *46*
Children's thinking *67*
Chlorine *189*
Choosing a published scheme *237*
Choosing software resources *198*
Chunk information *76*
Citizen science *9*
Classroom talk *147*
Close matching *168*
Cognitive acceleration *72*
  development *68*
  maps *74*
Competitions *245*
Complexity of classroom talk *155*
Computer sensors *196*
Concept maps *74, 78*
Conceptual challenge *69–70*
Concepts of evidence *93*
Conjecture and refutation *105*
Consensus model *160*

Consequence mapping *113*
  maps *77*
Construction *70*
Continuing professional development *205*
Continuity *175*
  and progression *16*
  map *75*
Controversial issue *113*
Correlational studies *100*
Cost–benefit analysis *116*
Criteria for the selection of a model *163*
Critical incidents *149*
Cued elicitation *152*
Curricular continuity *179*
Curriculum *14*
  evolution *23*
  implementation *11*
  initiatives *243*
  models *25*

Data *193*
Data logging *196*
Dearing Review of 16–19 *36*
Definitions of environmental education *120*
Definitions of science *3*
Departmental meetings *216*
Departmental safety policies *187*
Development plan *218*
  process *212*
Dialogues *146*
Differentiated learning *168*
Differentiation, resources *172*
  strategies *86, 173*
Direction and purpose *180*
Discriminatory behaviours *47*
Doing science *102*

Educational objectives *122*
Effective leaders *210*
  teaching *38*
  teaching and learning *128*
Employer and HE tutor perspectives *40*
Employer's responsibility *184*
Employment in Science *94*
English *28*
Environment *55*
Environmental education aims *119*

Equality *43*
Essential concepts *10*
Ethanol *189*
Ethical applications of Science *109*
Ethics *110*
European perspective *52*
Evaluating the quality of teaching *15*
Evaluation *225*
  cycle *238*
  of learning outcomes *136*
Everyday knowledge *59*
Everyday thinking about air *60*
Evidence *104*
Existing conceptions *134*
Expectations *180*
Explaining *153*
Explaining about models *164*
Explanations of science *159*
Expressed model *160*
Expressive arts *31*
External inspection *19*
Extra-curricular activities *18*

Financial planning *217*
Fireworks *189*
Fitness for purpose *18*
Flexible curriculum model *26*
Flow charts *74*
Focusing in interactions *154*
Formative assessment *60–61, 139, 142*
Frameworks of understanding *178*

General skills *40*
Generalisability of scientific explanations *65*
GNVQs *33*
Goals, rights and duties *115*
Good lessons *135*
Good teaching *14, 129*
Graphs *90*

Hazard *184*
Health and safety *183, 231*
High-voltage transmission line *189*
Historical model *160*
History and geography *30*
How children learn science *127*